HYTHE HAVEN

The Common Seal of the
Barons of Hythe and
of today's Town Council

HYTHE HAVEN

The Story of the Town and Cinque Port of Hythe

by

DUNCAN FORBES

Illustrated and with maps

SHEARWATER PRESS, HYTHE

First published in Great Britain 1982
by
Shearwater Press, 25, Fisher Close, Hythe

ISBN 0 946128 00 6

Printed in Great Britain
by Whitstable Litho Ltd., Whitstable, Kent

CONTENTS

Dedicated to the memory
of
Alfred Bull
and the
Hythe Institute

The Hythe Institute about 1900

ILLUSTRATIONS

Acknowledgements

MY thanks are due to the Trustees of the Hospitals of St. Bartholomew and St. John for permission to reproduce the Hospital Map on page 83 and to Mr. Lionel Osborne for the reproduction of the Hospital Seal of Hamo of Hythe on page 73, and also to the Hythe Town Council for allowing me to reproduce the Town Seal on page 1, the Mayor's Seal on page 49, and the old photograph on page 116.

I wish to thank Miss Muriel Sharp for the old photographs shown on pages 143 and 155 Mr. Jack Adams for those on pages 37, 150 and 217 and Miss Anne Roper and the Folkestone Reference Library for the one on page 153. Amongst the modern photographs, the Editor of the Folkestone, Hythe and District Herald has kindly allowed me to use those on pages 67, 184 and 191. All the other recent photographs are my own, and I thank the Vicar of Hythe, the Rev. Norman Woods, for allowing me to use the one on page 67, taken in the crypt of St. Leonard's Church, and Councillor and Mrs. Harry Margary for letting me photograph Lympne Castle from their private land.

I am also indebted to Curtis Brown Ltd., London, literary executors of the Estate of Elizabeth Bowen for permission to quote from her book entitled *Pictures and Conversations,* and to Jonathan Cape Ltd. and the Estate of Elizabeth Bowen for the quotations from her novels *The House in Paris* and *The Death of the Heart.*

The three maps on pages 29, 180 and 224/5 are by Major I. C. Austin.

1

The Story Begins

IN being persuaded to write the story of Hythe, I was very conscious of it never having been fully done before, in spite of the fascinating and intriguing nature of the subject. Fifty years ago, the Rev. H. D. Dale, formerly Vicar of St. Leonard's, having sorted out the archives together with Dr. C. Chidell, wrote a most interesting account of the medieval history of our ancient Cinque Port, but included little that happened after Elizabethan times. I, myself, found much in more recent years that was just as absorbing as the events that occurred when Hythe still had a harbour.

There were the alarms and excursions of the Napoleonic era, with its Martello towers and Military Canal; the soldiers and smugglers of Regency times ; the politicians and developers of the Victorian age; the railways that appeared and disappeared, and the one that remained unique in the world: the First World War on the home front and the second one in the front line; and in our own day, the refurbished castles of our ancient heritage, the wild-life park, and the new community of retired folk and holidaymakers mixing with the long established families of the Men of Kent.

Inevitably, some of my sources have been the same as those of my predecessor. The scanty references to the locality of Hythe in Roman and Saxon times must be sought outside the town, or in the volumes of *Archaeologia Cantiana*. But there is a wealth of material, referring to medieval times and later, now carefully stored in the town's own archives room, to which Miss Anne Roper, Hythe's archivist, kindly gave me access.

A lot of the material from early times is presented in an easily digestible form in those pages of the *Fourth Report of the Royal Commission on Historical Manuscripts, 1874,* which refer to Hythe. I have also made use of the Rev. T. S. Frampton's

manuscript transcription and translation of the jurats' account
books for the years 1412, 1413 and 1419, which give a vivid
picture of life in the Cinque Port in those days, and of his
printed account of the vicars of St. Mary's, West Hythe.
Then, in 1892, the Town Clerk, Mr. G. Wilks, published
The Barons of the Cinque Ports, which traced the town's parliamentary representation up to that time through copious
extracts from the Assembly books and other documents in the
archives.

Apart from these key sources, I am indebted to a wealth of
material, some published and some not, which has given me a
living picture of the development of our town. The published
sources include the existing pamphlets on the lovely parish
church, on the neighbouring historic castles at Saltwood and
Lympne and on the Small Arms School, books on the Military
Canal, the Martello towers and the Light Railway, past issues
of the Folkestone and Hythe Herald and the Hythe Reporter,
which can be seen in the Folkestone reference library, and, for
the recent past, the writings of the novelist, Elizabeth Bowen.

Unpublished sources have been so numerous and varied
that it is impossible to mention them all. But I would like to
refer particularly to Miss Muriel Sharp, whose files of carefully recorded information first spurred me on to undertake
the work, and to the other members of the Hythe Civic
Society, whose encouragement has kept me going, especially
their President, Lt.-Col. R. F. H. Drake-Brockman, Mr. Ron
Collins, a former chairman, Mr. Alan Stirk, Chairman, Mr.
John Sutton, Vice-Chairman, and Mr. Tim Lawrence, in
charge of the Historical Section of the Society.

Furthermore, the trustees of the Hythe Institute Trust have
given me invaluable assistance in getting this work published.
In addition, the support of the Town Clerk, Mr. L. Thomas,
with his intimate knowledge of the government of our town,
has been greatly appreciated and also the interest of the Vicar,
the Rev. Norman Woods, whose church, itself, is the reposit-
ory of much of its history. My book is, by no means, an
exhaustive and all-embracing work of historiography. But it
does aim at presenting a comprehensive picture of the progress
of a town that was once an important port, declined into
insignificance, then rose again as an army stronghold, and

developed yet again as a favoured place of residence for people who are in a position to choose where they live.

Elizabeth Bowen wrote in *Pictures and Conversations:*

> The part of Kent I am living in has wide views, though also mysterious interstices. It can be considered to have two coast-lines: a past, a present—the former looks from below like a ridge of hills, but in fact is the edge of an upland plateau: originally the sea reached to the foot of this. Afterwards the withdrawal of the sea laid bare salty stretches, formerly its bed; two of the Cinque Ports, Hythe, New Romney, consequently found themselves high-and-dry, as did what was left of the Roman harbour under the heights of Lympne . . . The existing coastline, a long shallow inward curve westward from Folkestone to the far-out shingly projection of Dungeness, is fortified for the greater part of its way by a massive wall, lest the sea change its mind again. Inside the sea-wall, the protected lands keep an illusory look of marine emptiness—widening, west of Hythe, into the spaces of Romney Marsh, known for its sheep, its dykes, its sunsets and its solitary churches. On a clear day, the whole of this area meets the eye: there are no secrets.
>
> Not so uphill, inland. The plateau, exposed to gales on its Channel front, has a clement hinterland, undulating and wooded. It is cleft by valleys, down which streams make their ways to the sea . . .

And again, recalling the time when she was a little girl and became fascinated by history:

> . . . Here it burst from under the contemporary surface at every point, arousing enthusiasm. A success story—or in these days one might say, a gigantic musical. Everyone figured, including the Ancient Romans. Nor had any of the stage-sets for the performance—or indeed, any of those rigged up for perfor-mances which had not, after all, taken place, such as a Napoleonic invasion—been cleared away: east of me Dover Castle, shored up on tier-upon-tier of fortification, flew its triumphant flag; west of me Martello towers diminished into the distance, more than one of them pounded down into massive jumbles of broken masonry, not, after all, by enemy cannon-fire but by the sea, which had also breached the sea-wall, for the elements had also taken a hand. Our Military Canal was not the less seductive for boating-picnics for having as yet no military purpose. Foundations of circumspect-looking buildings were (I heard) riddled with secret passages. The

Cinque Ports navy had torn up and down the Channel harassing any marauding French; smugglers had cat-and-moused with revenue men over the marshes, into the woods. To crown all, there had been terrific marine pageantry, spectacular arrivals and departures, monarchs, brides, envoys and so on—a constant, glittering, affable come-and-go between here and France. Not a dull moment.

I trust the reader of this work will not have a dull moment either.

2

The Last of the Romans

WHEN I went to see Mr. Norman Tournay at home in Sandgate, the seaside place which lies between Hythe and Folkestone, I found a sprightly, elderly gentleman of eighty-seven. Comfortably installed in his room in St. Michael's Rest, he had the souvenirs of his life and family around him.

They included the arms of the Tournay family of Brockhill Park—argent a chevron between three bulls statant sable—painted on a white replica of a mortar of the time of Cromwell, which had been discovered in Hythe, and a photograph of the grave of his cousin, William, buried on an island in the lake on the estate, together with his faithful dog, Daisy. The story was that, since the dog could not be buried in the churchyard, the last Tournay of Brockhill would not be buried there either.

Brockhill Park is next to Saltwood on the hills behind Hythe, and now accommodates the secondary school for the area. But I knew that the Mr. Tournay I was talking to, was the last of a long line of prominent citizens of our town. They trace their ancestry back to the birth of Sir Warren de Brockhill in 1239, in the time of Henry III.

It is sad to say, the last of a line. But such is life. The Tournays had fifty-four daughters in nine generations, and few sons to carry on the name. When I looked in the Canterbury area telephone directory, which covers the greater part of Kent, I found the name occurring only three times, none of them in Hythe.

John Tournay, or Torney as the name was often spelt, was a wool merchant of the Staple in Calais, who came south to Kent from Lincolnshire and married Joanne, daughter of John Sellinge of Brockhill and heiress of the estate, in 1498. Nineteen times mayors of Hythe, the Tournays' names are recorded for all to see on the carved oak panels on the eastern wall of the council chamber of the Town Hall. The date of the first is 1712 and of the last 1815.

Naturally, families that proudly trace their ancestry back to the Norman conquest in 1066, will not think much of 1498, or even 1239, as a starting point. Tournay, the wool merchant, immediately brings to mind Tournai, Belgium's oldest city and a long established centre for the manufacture of woollen cloth. But the link with Tournai, in fact, goes back nearly twice as far, since it is one of the few names that can be traced back to the distant days of Roman Britain.

It was the practice of the Romans, in the heyday of their empire, as it was of the British in India, to enlist men in one region for garrison duties in another. To expect them to serve in their own homelands and possibly be called upon to put down civil disorders and insurrections amongst their own people, would be straining their loyalty to the *Imperium Romanum* to breaking point.

Thus it came about that, in the latter days of Roman *Britannia,* a company of Turnacenses was stationed at Lympne. They were auxiliary troops, recruited for the Roman army from the district round *Turnacum,* the old Tournai. It was the chief town of the Nervii, whom Julius Caesar vanquished amidst great slaughter in his Gallic wars, and a staging–post on the road from Cologne to Boulogne, which was then the principal port of embarkation for Britain.

So we can, in a sense, trace the Tournay connection with our region right back to the fourth century of our era. At that time, our present–day town of Hythe did not exist. Its origins are to be found at Lympne, three miles to the west of the modern town, and the visible remains of that older haven are to be seen on the hillside below Lympne Castle.

They are the stone walls of Stutfall Castle, lying at crazy angles amongst the sheep grazing in the meadows between the modern castle and the Military Canal. As H. G. Wells wrote in *Kipps,* published in 1905, ". . . you look down the sheep-dotted slopes to where beside the canal and under the trees, the crumbled memories of Rome sleep for ever".

The slopes are, in fact, the broken remains of the seashore cliff, on which the old castle once stood proud, with a panoramic view of the shoreline and the English Channel, or

Stutfall Castle

The eastern gateway, excavated by Roach Smith in 1850

The ruins asleep today

Fretum Gallicum, as the Romans called it. Behind, lay the prosperous county of *Cantium,* which we know as Kent.

And the ruins do, indeed sleep. But in the middle of the nineteenth century, a Fellow of the Society of Antiquarians, C. Roach Smith, woke them up for a while. He got up a subscription from a hundred and nine interested people, and out of the £138, which he obtained thereby, he paid labourers to dig out the ruins during the summer season of 1850. His colleague, James Elliott, was in charge of repairs and modifications to the Dymchurch Wall, and lived locally. He, himself, lived in London. But he had been given a free pass from London to Westenhanger on the recently opened railway, and was able to make frequent visits. Thus, as a result of his excavations, he was in a position to make a reasoned plan of the *castrum,* or fort.

Smith was able to trace an outer wall which, although much distorted by the slippage of the land, appeared to be apsoidal in shape, with the flat end facing the sea. He also found the remains of some semi-circular towers and gateways. The main entrance appears to have been on the eastern side. It would be logical to assume that it faced the road down to the port itself—the break in the cliffs known to many generations as the Shipway, which now carries the road down the steep hill from Lympne to West Hythe.

In 1894 a well-known surgeon, Professor V. Horsley, returned to the attack, and uncovered the southern line of the fort. In recent years the ruins have been partially woken up again by Barry Cunliffe, Professor of Archaeology at Oxford University, who suggests some modifications to the conclusions of his predecessors.

The massive stones of which the *castrum* was built are typically Roman. It is all the more surprising, therefore, that they appear to have been flung about the hillside like pebbles on a beach. No sensible person could accept the legend that the Saxons tossed them about like that in their ultimate victory. Indeed, if the fort's subsequent name, Stutfall or Studfall, is anything to go by, they would have preferred to keep the walls intact, since it designates a *stud fold*—a corral or enclosure for horses.

Our ancestors did not think that a landslide was sufficient to account for the confusion either, and retained a long tradition of an earthquake. Was this impossible on our safe little island? Perhaps. But in the year 1580 there was a tremor in the locality strong enough to shake the church tower in Hythe and make the bells ring. Who knows whether there was not a stronger, unrecorded tremor in earlier times?

Go up to Lympne Castle today, ascend the tower, and you will find a magnificent panoramic view across Romney Marsh. To the right is the long line of crumbled cliffs reaching past Port Lympne and Aldington Knoll. Below the cliffs runs the Military Canal, and in front of you, between the canal and the sea, lie the flat lands of the marsh, protected by the shingle banks of Dungeness and the Hythe ranges, with Dymchurch Wall between them.

The fertile pastures of the marsh, covering over 50,000 acres, which now support half a million sheep, stretch as far as the distant hills of Winchelsea and Fairlight, seen blue on the horizon on a clear day. But when the Romans came to Britain, the view was very different. Between the shingle banks and the greensand cliffs, there was probably a lagoon of sheltered waters, an area of low islands with marshy saltings around them and tidal channels flowing in between.

The fact that the sea reached far inland in those days was well attested when the Military Canal was dug. It was found that, under five or six feet of mould and clay, there was sand. The part between Seabrook and Bonnington, which is the section going past Hythe, West Hythe and Lympne and another four miles westward, was very sandy, the sand being as pure as that on the seashore.

Into this lagoon flowed the main river of East Sussex, the Rother, which was earlier called the Limen. It seems to have had a broad outlet to the sea below the cliff on which the Romans subsequently built their fort, roughly along the present line of the canal. But whether this was still so in late Roman times is a point disputed by the experts.

As every boy at grammar school used to know, Julius Caesar wrote briefly and to the point in his report *On the Gallic Wars,* and his account of his expeditions to Britain does not specify his landing places. But it is generally agreed that they were probably closer to Sandwich than to Lympne.

Nevertheless, Lympne had similar natural features to Sandwich's Pegwell Bay—an expanse of water sheltered from the waves, with open country round about. So, like Richborough at the northern end of that bay, it rapidly became one of the principal ports for arrival in Britain. It was probably used from the Claudian invasion of 43 AD onwards, since the waters that became the marsh could shelter a whole fleet if necessary. The third port of disembarkation was, of course, Dover.

We are all too apt to think of ourselves as having been naked savages before the Romans took charge. But this is not so. Ancient Britain had some of the most impressive stone-age monuments in Europe, and Kent had only recently been colonised by a well-organised group of invaders from the Germanic people called the Belgae, when the Romans arrived on the scene. Before that, the Celts had been in occupation for some hundreds of years.

It is from the pre-Roman Celtic tongue that the River Limen is said to have taken its name, meaning the "place of elms". As it emerged from the deep forests of Anderida, which lay over most of Sussex and eastern Kent at that time, the description may have been apt.

But the name of the river has caused confusion. The Romans called Lympne, *Portus Lemanis* or *Portus Lemanae,* the gateway of the Limen. However, the word *limen,* carried over into the Roman world from the Greek language, itself means "harbour" or "haven". The harbourmaster was called the *Limenarcha,* and Ptolemy, the geographer of the second century AD, who wrote in Greek, called the place *Kainos Limen* meaning "New Haven".

The port of embarkation for either Richborough, Dover or Lympne was the same. It was Boulogne, the Roman *Gessoriacum.* This was certainly so from the second century onwards, because the Antonine Itinerary, which was a sort of guide-book for government officials on tour, tells us so. We are told the distance from Portus Lemanis to Canterbury—sixteen miles on Route IV. The three routes converged on Canterbury, and the remains of the Roman road from Lympne to Canterbury can still be traced along most of its length. In fact, known as Stone Street, it is still in use.

The acknowledged expert on Roman roads in Britain, I. D. Margary, who was a cousin of Harry Margary, the present owner of Lympne Castle, has traced this road in some detail, and he has also followed the coast road, which linked up the Roman ports. The latter, running along the cliff top, must have crossed the road from the port to Canterbury at the famous junction, which has been known since Saxon times as Shipway or Shepway Cross. It then turned inland to avoid the gullies between Hythe and Folkestone, and must have passed by Saltwood Castle, which has traces of Roman building in its foundations.

Margary thought that this route ran along North Road in Hythe and then crossed the Saltwood stream and climbed Blackhouse Hill to reach the heights behind Folkestone. Roman burials have, indeed, been discovered in the old ragstone quarry at the corner of Hillcrest Road and Castle Road, which is a few yards above North Road. Traces of a Roman villa have also been found north-west of Hythe in the Slaybrook valley.

However, I am inclined to the view that any road which existed here was a detour, since the Saltwood stream at the supposed crossing point would have been an inlet of the sea in Roman times. The traces which have been discovered, merely tell us that the area was inhabited.

But take the footpaths for yourself, and see what you can find. Nobody going from Lympne to Folkestone and on to Dover is going to lose height by going down to where Hythe is today. From Lympne you cross the open farm lands, skirting Folks Wood, to Pedlinge. Carry on eastwards and down the forty steps into the deep vale of the Slaybrook beside the lake in the Brockhill Estate, where William Tournay lay buried with his dog, and then up again immediately, skirting the school made out of the old house on your way to Saltwood.

Past the castle, you keep going on the signposted but miry footpath down into the upper waters of the Saltwood stream, and once again up, heading straight for ancient Newington, or else by Sene farm for the equally ancient church of Cheriton. Thence the old road goes round the back of Folkestone, past the iron-age motte and bailey of Castle Hill and onto Crete-way Down, avoiding the unnecessary plunge down into the town and up again by way of Folkestone Hill.

Some may disagree. But that is the way I would go, forgetting the modern roads and towns, and riding Shanks' pony. It is a pathway of unbeatable interest and variety, linking the ragstone ridge with the chalk downs, and giving a constant view of the sea in the dips of the hills. Still signposted along most of its length, I regard it as the most likely line of the old Saxon Shore Way.

The modern Saxon Shore Way does not stray far from the route that I have described. But, although it is marked on the Ordnance Survey map, it does not pretend to try to follow the original Roman coast road. Created by the Kent Rights of Way Council, with the enthusiastic support of the Kent County and District Councils, it is simply the most attractive long-distance pathway that could be found, and can be recognised by the red waymarks along its length, which depict a horned helmet of the legendary Saxon type.

As far as the evidence is concerned, we might wish that a Roman villa had been discovered at Lympne or Saltwood, like the one that was found in Folkestone in 1924. But the building that Smith found yielded little, and even the exact location of the actual Roman port is not quite certain. What he did discover in the fort was an altar stone, encrusted with barnacles, which had probably been rescued from lower down the hill. But the likelihood is that any port installations which existed, have been engulfed in the slippage of land.

They could have been considerable. Portus Lemanis was, from the beginning, an important place on the Roman line of communication. And it retained its importance when the ports on the south-eastern seaboard of England were organised and fortified to resist the increasing incursions of Saxon raiders.

These ports were placed under the command of the Count of the Saxon Shore, or *Litus Saxonicum,* as they called it, and extended from Porchester in Hampshire to Brancaster in Norfolk. The excavations at Stutfall Castle in 1850 produced several tiles inscribed with the initials CL BR, standing for *Classis Britannica,* the British fleet. They indicate that there was a separate fleet assigned to the defence of Britain from the pagan marauders or even, if the latest theories are to be believed, to defend Britain from the Romans themselves in a period of unilateral declaration of independence. But it was a fleet that, in the end, was unable to stem the tide of conquest.

We have some knowledge of the organisation of Lympne and the other strongholds of the Saxon Shore from the fourth century *Notitia Dignitatum,* which was a sort of Civil and Army List of the government and military appointments throughout the Roman Empire. The nine forts under the command of the Most Honourable, the Count of the Saxon Shore, included Lemanae, or Lympne, which, in turn, was under the Commander of the Turnacensian band.

Thus we can see that the later institution of the Cinque Ports, of which Hythe was one, followed the Roman precedent in many respects. Portus Lemanis can be matched with Hythe, Dubris with Dover, and Rutupiae, or Richborough, with Sandwich.

Roach Smith informs us in the report on his excavations, which has been reprinted by Harry Margary, that 260 brass coins had been found there, and we know from earlier writers that other Roman coins had been found there previously. Most of the coins from Smith's haul, which could be deciphered, were found to belong to the reigns of Constantine the Great and his progeny. He was the Emperor who, at the beginning of the fourth century, went from York to claim the imperial purple and make Christianity the state religion.

Thereafter, the Roman power began to wane in the West, and the outer regions of the empire could no longer be maintained. Inward-looking, unworldly Christianity was ill-suited to check the waves of barbarians descending on British shores, and those who had known the Roman peace for nearly four hundred years, were forced to come to terms with the new settlers. For, as Rudyard Kipling has written:

> There was no Count of the Saxon Shore
> To meet them hand to hand,
> As she took the beach with a surge and a roar,
> And the pirates rushed inland.

Some say that, by this time, the estuary of the River Limen had already been diverted from Lympne by the construction of the Rhee Wall across Romney Marsh from a point near Appledore to Romney and with it the formation of another exit to the sea of relatively deep water between Great Stone and Little Stone, and a new port at Old Romney, the "Roman river". To reclaim the low-lying marshland east of this wall, it would have been necessary to construct the Dymchurch Wall as well, and the discovery, in the last century, of some Roman pottery and other artifacts in the area of the wall lends credence to this theory. But it is not real proof.

Nevertheless, at some stage unrecorded in history, the harbour at Lympne became a mere arm of the sea, and it was an arm that was to become more and more withered as the centuries passed. Subsequently, the old Roman buildings were cannibalised in the time-honoured fashion to provide easily accessible building material for the Norman church on the hill top, and the fortified house, called the castle, which was, itself, built on the site of an old Roman watchtower. And there is still a watchtower there today, at the eastern end of the castle, which has been used whenever there has been an invasion scare, up to and including the time of Hitler's war.

Lympne is thus the father of Hythe, or if we take West Hythe into account as a separate place, the grandfather. Derived from the old Roman name, it has been variously spelt Liminum, Limene, Lymene, Lymen, Lymine, Limne, Lymne, Lime, Limme, Lyme, Lymme, Limpney and even Lymph and Limbe.

Clearly the second syllable of the name was originally pronounced. But it was reversed from *en* to *ne* in a change that has been noted in other examples in our language. After that, inserting a *p* between the two consonants *m* and *n* was an addition that is not uncommon, as for instance, in the name Thompson, and indeed in the nearby Sampton, which was derived from *Sandtun*. When the name was written *Limpney* in the survey of 1649, it must still have been pronounced with two syllables. But now, within living memory, it has always been pronounced *Lim*.

Thus Lympne survives, although the last limenarcha held his appointment there long ago. The original excavations have been filled in to protect the Roman site, and hopeful amateur investigators with metal detectors have to be discouraged, footpaths once public closed.

The Military Canal distorts the lie of the land as it must once have been. But judging from the number of groups of researchers who still visit the site with the permission of the owners, conduct controlled digs and make careful measurements, the last word on the Romans in this part of the world has definitely not been spoken.

3

The Saxon Shore

STAND at Shipway Cross, or Shepway Cross, as it is called today, half a mile to the east of Lympne Castle, and look southwards towards the English Channel. You will see land for nearly two miles before your eyes reach the fortifications of the Napoleonic age on the shingle bank of the shore. But time was when an arm of the sea came up between you and the shingle, fetching up at the foot of the hill.

There lay Old Hythe, or the Old Haven, where West Hythe is now marked on the map. For *Hythe* means "haven" just as Lympne does. We find it in other parts of Kent, joined with other words to form, for instance, Rotherhithe and Greenhithe. We find New Hythe on the Medway near Maidstone, and west of Hythe on an old branch of the Rother, we find Small Hythe.

The Shepway Cross, which stands at the crossroads today, is a modern one, set up by Earl Beauchamp in 1923, when he was Lord Warden and Admiral of the Cinque Ports. But Symonson's map of 1596 shows that there was some kind of a cross there previously. The four roads that meet there are as old as the ruins of the Roman castle, and I write "four" deliberately, since it is still possible to follow the line of the old road to Canterbury along a footpath, if it has not been ploughed up by the local farmer. It takes you as far as Newingreen, where Stone Street becomes a modern highway.

The modern name is Shepway, but in Symonson's day it was Shipway, and Leland, the famous antiquarian of King Henry VIII's time, certainly considered it to be the way of the ships. This is what he says, in 1540, in his *Itinerary:*

> Lymme Hill or Lyme was sumtyme a famose haven and good for shyppes that myght cum to the foote of the hille . . . The place ys yet cawled Shypway and Old Haven.

Shepway Cross

He adds, in modernised spelling, that:

> The Marsh of Romney increases daily in breadth. It is a marvell-
> ous rank (rich) ground for feeding of cattle, by reason that the
> grass grows so plentifully upon the oose (mud or silt) sometime
> cast up there by the sea.

The word "cattle" included sheep in those days, as well as
the horned variety. But Camden, writing the Kent section of
his well-known *Britannia* in Queen Elizabeth I's time, still
follows Leland with *Shipway*. However, many modern scho-
lars disagree. Mindful of the fame of the sheep down on the
marsh, they have derived the name from the Old English
sceapweg of Saxon times, meaning the way or path of the
sheep, though the great days of the sheep on the marsh were
not until the fifteenth century, when it became extremely
profitable to smuggle wool to the Continent in defiance of
Edward III's ban.

Sightings in the early records—Shepweye in 1227 and

Shypwey in 1254—do not resolve the argument. But the official documents certainly favour *ship*. When Henry II issued individual charters to the Cinque Ports in 1155 and 1156, addressing his men of "Heia" in Hythe's charter, he referred specifically to the place where they had to plead as *apud Sippeweiam*—at Shipway. And when Edward Guldeford, Constable of Dover Castle, summoned the Cinqueportsmen in 1526, it was *ad curiam Shipweya*—to the Court of Shipway.

Shepway was not just a path. It was a *lathe,* a territorial division peculiar to the County of Kent. In Saxon times, according to the evidence of Domesday book, our region was in the Lathe of Limowart, based on ancient Lyminge. But from medieval times, the Lathe of Shepway was one of the five into which the county was divided. It stretched from Capel-le-Ferne, east of Folkestone, and Elham on its eastern and northern borders, and embraced the whole of the marsh to the south-west.

When this ancient division was revived in the new administrative district created in 1974 to embrace both Hythe and Folkestone, the name was also restored. The intention to name it after its largest town, Folkestone, did not please the citizens of Hythe, and so it became Shepway once again, though covering a smaller area than the former lathe.

Be it Shepway or Shipway, the business of Shepway Cross, the meeting place of the lathe and of the men of the Cinque Ports, has always been concerned with ships, as the words on the modern monument indicate:

> To the glory of God and in memory of the heroic deeds of the Cinque Ports.

Today, the Old Haven of West Hythe consists of a ribbon of development reaching out towards Hythe between the old cliffs and the Military Canal, together with some larger properties in the dip in the cliffs and on the road to Botolph's Bridge. Of its condition in Saxon times we know next to nothing.

There is an account in the Anglo-Saxon Chronicle of a Danish raid. The Saxons, who had broken the Roman dominion, were being harried in their turn. In the year 892 a great army of Danes went "westward to Boulogne", crossed over in one voyage "with their horses and all" and "came up to the mouth of the Limen with two hundred and fifty ships". They "dragged their ships up the river as far as the forest, four miles from the river mouth, and there destroyed a fortress within the fen".

It is an interesting story. King Alfred the Great was resisting the invaders from his power base in Wessex, but the Danes were still coming, hungry for land and loot. However, it is not likely that this particular body of Danish Vikings called at Hythe, since the main estuary of the Limen or Rother was now further west.

There is evidence for this in the first written reference we have to our locality from the sparse records of Saxon times. In the year 732, not so very long after St. Augustine had converted the Kingdom of Kent to Christianity, King Ethelbert made a grant of land at a place called Sandtun to a convent for men and women, which had been established for Queen Ethelburga in the old royal palace at Lyminge in 633 by her brother, King Eadbald. That Sandtun was the place that later became known as Sampton, lying between Botolph's Bridge and the present line of the Military Canal, is clear from the description.

The holding of about 150 acres was bordered to the north and west by the Fleet of Huda, to the east by Crown land, and to the south by the River Limen. It, therefore, appears to have been a spit of land, since a *fleot,* or *fleet,* was a creek or inlet of the sea. In fact, *Hudan Fleot,* which probably means the "Inlet of the Haven", must have been just about where the old Roman port was. But notice that the river flows south of Sandtun, not north, thus finding its way to the sea somewhere east of Dymchurch, past the old Hythe Oaks, rather than where Hythe is today.

Go to West Hythe and see for yourself. The field between the Canal Cut, leading from the canal to the sea, and the slightly higher land of Sandtun, is still the lowest in the area, ill-drained, overgrown with vetches and unfit for cultivation—the old fleet, or creek, which was the harbour to the Romans and the Saxons.

Sandtun, itself, was still used as sand pits up to the Second World War, and after the war the pits became a dump for the broken-up reinforced concrete of Hythe's shore defences. This, together with the effluvia of the piggery, makes it an ugly spot today. But the lie of the land leads one to suspect that the Roman and Saxon ports had outlets to the sea more southward than the line of the Military Canal past Hythe.

The Sandtun land had, apparently, already been given to a priest and abbot, named Hymora, and was granted to Abbot Dun "not for any earthly money, but simply for the salvation of my soul, to thee and to the Church of the Blessed Mary which is in thy charge". It was for the establishment of a salt works to exploit the surrounding salt pans of the marsh.

In the year 833, King Egbert confirmed the original grant by bestowing 150 acres "at a place called Sandtun and in the same place a salt works near Limen" on the abbot "not for money but for welfare of my soul, and for the expiation of my sins". The owners were also allowed wood from the forest of Anderida for the fires needed to evaporate the brine from the salt.

Both these documents, separated by a century, are in the British Museum. About ten years after the second grant was made, the convent of Lyminge was over-run by the Danes.

Some authors say that Hythe, itself, is first mentioned in the year 889, when King Alfred the Great made a grant of land there to the Church at Canterbury, at a time when Plegmund was archbishop. But I have not been able to trace the documentary evidence, and we do not know exactly where this Hythe was. But we can be sure that the Old Haven continued in existence for some time after the Norman conquest, since the one antiquity in West Hythe is the shell of the Chapel of Our Lady, which was undoubtedly built in Norman times.

Camden says that the sea "withdrew itself from West Hythe" two centuries before his time, which would bring us down to the mid-fourteenth century, when Hythe itself was beginning to experience the troubles that led to its decline as a port. Indeed, it is probable that, in the two miles of sheep pasture on the broken cliffs between West Hythe and Hythe, there was at one time a string of habitations facing the inlet of the sea. As Leland says, again modernising the spelling:

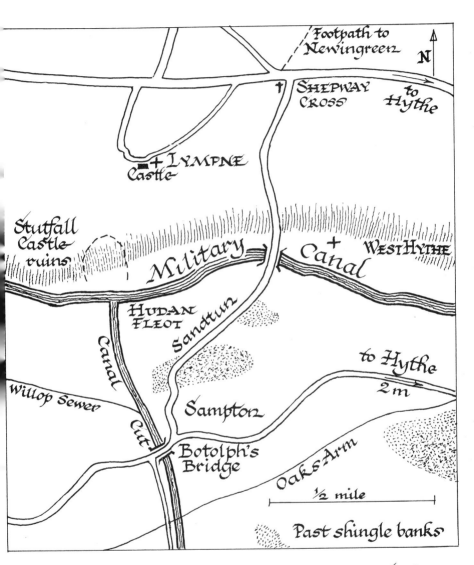

The Grandfather & Father of Hythe

Hithe has been a very great town in length, and contained four parishes that now be clean destroyed, that is to say St. Nicholas parish, Our Lady parish, St. Michael's parish, and Our Lady of West Hythe . . . And it may well be supposed that, after the haven of Lymme and the great old town there failed, that Hithe straight thereby increased and was in price (prosperous). Finally to count from West Hyve to the place where the substance of the town is now is two good miles in length, all along on the shore to the which the sea came full sometime, but now by banking of oose and great casting up of shingle the sea is sometimes a quarter, sometimes half a mile from the old shore.

The roofless walls of Our Lady of West Hythe can still be seen, and the debris of the foundations of St. Michael's can still be found in the sheep field, called St. Michael's Ash, between West Hythe and Hythe by those who diligently search. But the town has caught up again with St. Nicholas, which was near North Road at the western end of the town. It was already in ruins by 1425, though as we shall see, another chapel, dedicated to the patron saint of fishermen, sprang up at the seaside to the east of the town.

Not long after Leland's time, in 1563, West Hythe had dwindled to four households, containing twenty souls in all, fourteen of them being communicants and six "unable". In the following century, in 1620, the roof of the church was burnt out.

But before that, in the fourteenth century, West Hythe was still a big enough place for mass to be celebrated there. In 1374 the little port flashes across the stage of history because of a particularly shocking murder that was committed nearby. The victim was no less a being than the parochial chaplain, and the event is thus recorded:

Certain sons of perdition, intoxicated with wickedness and the spirit of rage, craftily contriving the death of Sir Robert Valent, priest at Westhethe, in our diocese, who celebrated Divine Service while he was alive, ensnaring the said priest, who was wholly unaware of their malice, on the King's highway between the villes of Lymene and Westhethe aforesaid with bows and arrows and divers other kinds of weapons, suddenly and hostilely rushed upon him, and at first wounded him again and again with arrows,

Church of Our Lady of West Hythe in ruins

mortally, and afterwards when on bended knees he tearfully
besought their mercy, they with the abovesaid other deadly
weapons, with malice aforethought, as it is said, inhumanly killed
him; thereupon culpably incurring the sentence of the Greater
Excommunication, directed in that case by the canon against such
sacrilegious men and malefactors.

We are not told whether the murderers were known or not,
though the report implies that the evil deed was witnessed.
But in any case, Archbishop Langham ordered the sentence of
excommunication to be announced in the Cathedral at Canterbury, in the Church of Saltwode and the "respective
chapels annexed to the same"—*singulesque Capellis eidem
annexis*—and in all the churches in the diocese, mentioning the
deaneries of Elham and Lymene in particular. Thus the ritual
was performed, with bells ringing, candles lighted, exting-
uished and then thrown to the ground, and the cross held erect
above them.

From this we can deduce that, by this time, there were several chapels under Saltwood. But as West Hythe dwindled, its needs were frequently ministered to by the Vicar of Lympne. In 1640 the Parish Register stated that "The Church is burnt downe, therefore noe Minister to subscribe" or, in other words, to sign the entry. And again, "In the parrishe of Westhith there is noe Church, onely the walles of the Church remayne, therefore noe Minister to certefye this bill".

However, there was still a living. It was held by Stephen Sackett, Vicar of Blean, from 1633 to 1679. He paid occasional visits to West Hythe, and reported on July 22nd, 1664:

> Burials in the parish we have none, nor noe place for burying, or Marrying: our church defaced: Lymph, the parish to which we should resort for religious exercises, having noe Minister is seldom supplied by any, and our Register should be kept at Limbe Church.

Even so, such was the inertia of the Church organisation that it was not until 1840 that West Hythe was actually united with Lympne and ceased to be a separate parish on its own. But of course, we are now anticipating the Norman conquest and many years after it. The other documentary evidence from the pre-conquest era concerns Saltwood Castle, which overlooked Hythe much as Stutfall Castle must have overlooked West Hythe.

It was in the year 488 that Aesc, son of Hengist, the first King of Kent, built a castle there, on a site that had probably been used by the Romans and was much closer to the sea than it is today. Then in the year 833, Saltwood again appears, bestowed, like Sandtun, on the Church at Lyminge by King Egbert. From that date onwards, the names of most of the tenants of the castle have been recorded in the old documents—sometimes noblemen, sometimes churchmen, and sometimes noble churchmen.

Indeed, it is in this castle, which lies on a hill three quarters of a mile inland from Hythe, that we find the strongest link between Roman and Norman times. If we place the final failure of the Roman power in Britain in the first decade of the fifth century, we find Aesc building his castle there scarcely three generations later.

In those days, an inlet of the sea came right up to the foot of the hill, on which the castle stands, following the dip where the millstream now runs through the meadows. In fact, early in the eighteenth century an anchor was ploughed up somewhere in that area.

This propinquity of the sea has led some to derive the name of Saltwood from the romantic idea of trees overhanging the briny and dipping their leaves in the salt water. But the truth is probably more prosaic. It is more likely to have been a wood, in which the salt manufacturers had the right to gather timber for the fires they needed to boil off the sea water. Less likely is the idea that the Latin word for a woodland vale, *saltus,* was bled on to the Saxon *wood.*

Next we come down to the year 1026. The Saxon nobility, under Ethelred the Unready, or more correctly, the *ill-advised,* have succumbed to the Danes, and King Canute is on the throne of England. A Saxon thane, named Halthigen Scearpa and also called Halfden, conveys the Manor of Saltwood and Hythe to the Church at Canterbury and the monks serving Christ there, or in other words the Benedictine Priory. King Cnut himself signs the document, together with his Queen Aelgifa, archbishops, bishops and noblemen, including Earl Godwin.

The conveyance is in the British Museum. In it Halfden explains to Canute that he wishes to give the lands of *Hith* and *Saltwood* for ever to the monks of Christ Church, together with all the things pertaining thereto, as for example fields, meadows, woods, bondmen, bondmaids, flocks etc, for the salvation of the soul of Halfden himself, and of the woman, Leoflad, who had previously granted the same lands to Christ Church.

Saltwood was nobility and church. But what of the townsfolk down below? Whether their lives were exciting or not, they were certainly rough and hard. Hythe was already a borough, and when Edward the Confessor succeeded the warlike Dane, Canute, the town was brought into a new system of coastal defence, modelled to some extent on the old Roman one. This was the origin of the Cinque Ports, that were to provide ships for communication with the Continent and to repel invaders.

It was King Canute who first co-opted them for these duties. If he could not stop the tide, as his courtiers suggested, he could at least deter an enemy. Edward formed them into a confederation. But in his time they performed their communication duties rather than their defence commitments. His court filled up with Norman nobles, churchmen and clerks from across the water, and other continental advisers.

Godwin, the powerful Earl of Wessex, whose daughter he had married, did not like it. After a quarrel in defence of his Men of Kent, he went into exile and decided to make a bid, with his son, Harold, for the throne. He held the Manor of Saltwood and Hythe in knight's service under the archbishop, and ordered the men of Hythe to join the fleet that sailed up the Thames to invest London. There, the Kentish seamen found themselves in superior numbers to the men of the King's fleet, which they surrounded. This is probably why the saintly Edward received Godwin and Harold back into his favour.

Many of the Normans were sent packing. So, when Edward died, Harold was declared King and crowned the very next day in proper fashion in Westminster Abbey. But he was betrayed by his brother, Tostig, who also got hold of some of the men of the Kent ports and sailed north to meet Harold of Norway.

The main fleet of the Cinque Ports then sailed north to Northumbria to assist Harold of England in defeating Harold of Norway at Stamford Bridge. It is for this reason that few of them were left to stand against Duke William's invasion force, which landed in Pevensey Bay. Those that went out from Romney to do so had reason to regret it later, since the town was singled out after the Conquest for particular vengeance.

This was the end of the Saxon period, which has not left any visible marks on Hythe. But there is just one legend of the Saxon days that should also be recorded. It concerns St. Botolph.

This monkish English saint lived in the seventh century, and many popular tales have been told about him, since there is very little known historical fact. His monastery is thought to have been at Boston, Lincolnshire, which has derived its name from *Botolph's town*. But our legend about the saint concerns his dead body and Botolph's Bridge.

Go to the bridge across the Canal Cut at West Hythe, which is not the same as the original bridge before the canal was constructed, and look at the inn sign there, which illustrates the story. There is a boat, with a coffin, like an ark, being carried on to it by two tonsured monks. Two more monks are following them from the bank, and a shaft of light is seen shining down on them all out of a dark sky.

The legend is that the body of St. Botolph was being borne to some place where it would be kept safe from desecration by the heathen Danes. There was water to cross, and the night was pitch dark. Then suddenly a shaft of light, which was not the moon, shone down from heaven to guide the escort as they went aboard. But where the body now lies, no one knows.

The bridge by the inn spans a stretch of water that is now a branch of the Military Canal, draining into the sea through the sluice beside the Grand Redoubt built during the Napoleonic wars. But in the past it carried travellers to the shore across one of the many creeks of the marsh. It was called Boter's, Butter's or Butler's Bridge on the old maps, and whether Butler is derived from Botolph, or whether there really was a man in charge of the drinks there, as there is today, or whether, as is more likely, the name came from that of a well-known local family, I do not know.

What I do know is that, with the sheep meadows around you, the placid water nearby, the Roman ruins, looking like old, decayed teeth sprouting out of the hillside, and the more modern castle with its Second World War reinforced concrete watchtower on the skyline, there in no pleasanter place to stop and take a glass.

4

Barons and Churchmen

IN describing the history of our English towns and villages, it is natural to use the main turning points in our island story to mark the chapters in the tale. So we come to 1066, known to every schoolboy as the date of the Norman conquest. It was a particularly significant date for Hythe, since the centuries that followed it—our Middle Ages—were a peak period of the town's importance and prosperity. From now onwards the documentary evidence increases considerably, and more remains of the past can be seen, to add to the massive walls at Lympne and the fragments of walls at Saltwood, which the Romans left behind them.

It may well be that the Norman invasion did little to disturb the day-to-day business of English country life. It may indeed have been a check on change, bringing strong government and security to wider areas. But it certainly made sweeping changes at the top. In return for the boon of legitimacy in their conquests, these converted Vikings from Normandy, absorbed into the orbit of Franco-Roman civilisation, promoted the interests of the Church alongside their own.

England was carved up by the Norman king, who was still considered in Kent to be no better than a duke. The land was meticulously surveyed by his clerks and given in fief to his barons and churchmen. The Saxon lords found themselves everywhere pushed down the social scale in a hierarchy that was to be crystallised in the feudal system.

Thus class and caste were confirmed by both the secular and the religious arm. It was a situation that, with many ups and downs, still lingered on in recent times, as described in the satirical prayer: "God bless the squire and his relations and keep us in our proper stations". Again it is the two castles, Saltwood and Lympne, both facing the sea two and a half miles apart, that provide the evidence.

Saltwood Castle

In 1829 before restoration (Shepherd engraving)

In modern times, seen from the lost railway line

The top station in Hythe was held by the tenant of Saltwood Castle. The Domesday survey of 1086 refers to the Manor of Saltwode and Hede as being held by a knight. It was still Church property, since it was leased from the Archbishop of Canterbury, and the knight was a Norman baron, Hugo de Montfort, who had fought with Duke William at Hastings, placed there by the new Norman archbishop, Lanfranc. He held it as *terra militum archiepi,* by knight's service, along with other manors in the strategic south-east.

Of the two places embraced within the manor, Saltwood was the senior one, having a rector and a church, whereas Hythe only had a vicar and a chapel, although it was more populous. The details in the Domesday book are as follows:

> It was taxed at 7 sulings in the time of Edward the Confessor, and now for 3 sulings; the arable land is 15 carucates. In the demesne there are 2 carucates and 32 villeins, with 12 borderers having 3½ carucates. There is a church and 2 servants, and 9 mills of 20 shillings, and 33 acres of meadow, wood sufficient for the pannage of 20 hogs. In this manor belong 225 burgesses in the borough of Hede, between the borough and the manor. In the time of Edward the Confessor it was worth £16, when he received it £8, now in the whole £29 6s 4d.

A suling covered about 160 acres, so that the holding seems to have shrunk from about 1,120 acres, or two square miles, to less than half that. It was, therefore, only one tenth the size of the neighbouring barony of Fulchestan (Folkestone). On the other hand, there seems to have been a startling increase in taxation, although the land area has been reduced to less than one square mile.

The Domesday book also mentions Sandtun, and states that there are six burgesses of "Hede", who are tenants of the land in that place, and therefore belong to the Manor of Lyminge.

The *carucates* were the strips of ploughland worked by the villeins and borderers, the latter being bondmen. One carucate was the amount one man could be expected to cultivate with the plough. It is notable that no mention is made of a church in Hythe, although there were 225 families in the borough. We must conclude that one of the two "servants" of the church at Saltwood was responsible for the chapel down the hill.

Indeed, the development of Saltwood Castle matched the growing importance of Hythe at this time. The large stone blocks, that are thought to be the remains of a Roman watch-tower, were built over with new walls and towers. Two large walled areas, the inner and outer baileys, were created. The inner bailey was specially fortified by Henry d'Essex, who was the king's standard-bearer during the troubled reign of Stephen. The outer bailey was constructed much later, but its walls were severely damaged by the earth tremors of 1580 and are now in a poor condition.

Clearly, King Stephen, a grandson of William the Conqueror through the female line, considered Saltwood Castle to be a key point in his coastal defences. For Henry of Essex was not only standard-bearer, he was also Constable and Warden of the Cinque Ports. Since the former appointment was hereditary, he was still the royal standard-bearer when he came to grief during the reign of Stephen's successor, King Henry II,

It was during a campaign in the Welsh marches. Essex was ambushed, threw away his standard, and ran for it. Or so said Robert de Montfort, who was a descendant of the first Norman lord of Saltwood. Robert publicly accused him of treason on account of his cowardly conduct in failing to defend his monarch, and fought him in a duel.

It was the year 1163. Henry of Essex was left for dead. But he was succoured by some monks, who saved his life and received him into their order. As Lambarde, who published his great work on Kent in 1576, neatly put it, he thus exchanged a natural death for a civil one.

Lambarde says that it was for this reason that Henry II seized Saltwood and held it during his lifetime. But the fact is that, being still the property of the Archbishop of Canterbury, it was not his to seize. Only a year had passed since he had appointed his trusted friend, Thomas Becket, to the highest office of the Church in England.

A year later Henry produced the Constitutions of Claren-don, which were intended to cut down the power of the Church, that had grown by leaps and bounds during the

uncertain, warring times of Stephen. Becket angered the king
so much by his resistance to the Constitutions that he felt it
prudent to take refuge on the Continent.

But their quarrel appeared to be patched up, when King and
High Priest met at Chaumont in 1170. Henry wrote to his son
in England that Thomas Becket was to have restored to him all
the goods, lands and fees that had been taken from him during
the king's displeasure. Saltwood was specifically included:

> . . . faciatisque venire coram vobis, de melioribus antiquioribus militibus,
> de honore de Saltwood . . .

Probably the Honour of Saltwood was mentioned by name
because Becket had particularly requested it, referring to it as
manerium praedelictum, most select of manors. There was one
difficulty, however, which was to prove fatal. After Henry
d'Essex's near death and departure from the world of affairs,
King Henry had given Saltwood to a most unruly knight,
named Sir Ranulf de Broc.

De Broc, the "badger", was a local man, lord of the nearby
Brockhill estate, which came to the Tournays in more recent
times. He had such a bad reputation in the neighbourhood,
that people said he and his henchmen had turned Saltwood
into a den of thieves.

It was hardly likely that such a man would give up his castle
without a struggle. And so it proved. After meeting the old
king in France, Becket returned to England, made his peace
with the young king, his son, whom Henry had had crowned
in his absence, and went back to Canterbury in triumph. But
Broc, the badger, was determined to worry him.

Ranulf de Broc seized a cargo of wine consigned to the
archbishop from France by the old king. He went hunting the
archbishop's deer in the archbishop's woods. A young cousin,
Robert de Broc, went out on Christmas Eve and docked the
tails of a sumpter mule and a horse belonging to the archbishop.

Becket reacted vigorously. A jesting gesture of defiance
against the all-powerful Church in Kent was construed as a
mortal insult. In a famous Christmas Day sermon, he made it
clear to the congregation that the text *Pax hominibus bonae
voluntatis* means, "Peace to men of good will" and not, "Peace

and good will towards men", as more sentimental clerics would have us believe. He thundered out the excommunication of Ranulf and Robert de Broc, and with them, for good measure, three bishops who had crowned the young king during his exile. Then he dashed the symbolic candle to the floor of the cathedral.

A few days later, the three excommunicated bishops reached the King at Bur Castle near Bayeux in Normandy, provoking his famous outburst against the "low-born" or "turbulent" priest, who had come to court "on a lame sumpter mule" and now "sits without hindrance on the throne itself".

The four knights, gentlemen of the bedchamber, who heard it, left him on the spot. They dashed across the Channel and were welcomed by the badger at Saltwood Castle. Thereupon he deputed young Robert de Broc and an escort of cavalry to go with them along Stone Street to Canterbury, where the fatal murder in the cathedral was committed on December 29th. The murderers were then led by Robert to the archbishop's palace, where they took possession of papal bulls and charters, which they later sent to the king, and also went in for some ordinary looting.

As is well known, the emotional shock of the murder, not of a haughty man in his arrogance, but of the chief priest of God in his cathedral, was so deep that the old king, himself, came to Canterbury in penance and restored to the Church the privileges and properties that he had sought to wrest from it.

Even so, the Church had to wait twenty years to get back Saltwood Castle, itself, at the beginning of King John's reign. It then became as favourite a place of residence for later archbishops as it had been for Becket.

But it must not be imagined that the prelates lived there permanently. Like kings, they moved from palace to castle and from castle to palace, as they progressed round their see. There would always be a bailiff in permanent residence, looking after the property, collecting the tithes and taxes and preparing for the archiepiscopal visits. In those days great men travelled with such large retinues that they literally ate their way round their domains.

Becket, for instance, had Lympne to go to, if he wanted a change from Saltwood. As Hasted, the eighteenth century

chronicler of Kent, tells us, "The church of Limne was part of
the ancient possessions of the Archbishopric and continued so
till Archbishop Lanfranc gave it to the Archdeaconry, at
which time, or very soon afterwards, it seems to have been
appropriated to it, being the first possessions it ever had".

Thus the building, which in Saxon times had probably been
an abbey, was in Norman times rebuilt and fortified as a
residence for the archdeacon. Lanfranc, himself, may well
have been the builder, or rebuilder of this edifice and the
adjoining church, using material from Stutfall Castle, though
the much restored building which we see today goes back only
to about 1360, whilst the fireplace in the great hall was inserted
to replace the central hearth in 1420, when Edward III was
king.

The earliest archdeacon here was Anschitil, whose name
occurs in 1075 and again in Domesday book. The eighth was
Thomas Becket, who continued to hold the archdeaconry for
some time after he had become Primate of England.

Indeed, the early archdeacons were often regarded as rectors
of Lympne church, since they held the glebe lands and advow-
son of the vicarage of the benefice, and had no stall in the
cathedral at Canterbury. In fact, until after the dissolution of
the Canterbury priory, they had to be inducted into their
offices in one of their own churches. Before 1227 this must
have been Lympne.

The Church estates were certainly very widespread in Kent,
those in the south-east coming under the Archbishop, and
those in the north-west under the Bishop of Rochester. But
the dominance and exactions of Church rule were not always
liked by the people. Two centuries after the martyrdom of
Becket, the country was recovering from the Black Death.
Labour was scarce, and the common people felt free to break
their feudal ties and offer their services in the best market. In
these unsettled times the Lollards, as the revolutionaries who
followed John Wyclif's protests against Church dogma were
called, raised a flame of revolt, which culminated in the rebel-
lion of Wat Tyler.

One of the Lollards, William Thorpe, was imprisoned on
the ground floor of the tower on the north-eastern side of
Saltwood Castle, which is now called Thorpe's tower. He was

Lympne Castle

In 1829 (Engraving by George Shepherd)

Today, after restoration

tried for heresy and given life. But after sixteen years in this tower, he escaped in the confusion of an earthquake, which took place in 1380, and went on to live for another twenty-seven years.

An account of the trial of William Thorpe can be read in Foxe's *Book of Martyrs,* published after the burnings and beheadings of Queen Mary's reign. The year after Thorpe's escape from the Saltwood tower, Tyler and his Kentish rebels killed Archbishop Sudbury in London. His successor was William Courtenay, the best known of the Saltwood archbishops. A nobleman of the French connection, Courtenay was in marked contrast to the plebeian Becket. He enlarged the keep, and he had his architect, Henry Yevele, construct two new watchtowers in order to give his sentries a clear view of the pilgrim road to Canterbury, coming up from Hythe, which had become a well-frequented international highway after the growth in popularity of the shrine of St. Thomas, the martyr.

Courtenay also improved the inner bailey, now called the Essex ward, and built the encircling walls of the outer bailey. Son of Margaret de Bohun and great grandson of King Edward I, he was determined to be well protected and avoid the death at the hand of a common peasant, that had befallen his predecessor.

However, like Becket, he has not escaped censure as an overbearing prelate. Lambarde relates that he once took offence at some of his poor tenants of the Manor of Wingham, because they had brought their rent, in kind, of hay and straw to him packed conveniently tightly onto racks on the backs of their horses.

Courtenay thought of it as an insult, since they had been 'accustomed to bringing it spread out on carts to make a greater show. So he called them to Saltwood, where he was "as hot as toast with the matter" and gave them a penance. They were to march slowly behind his procession, bareheaded and barefoot, each with a sack of hay or straw over his shoulder and open at the mouth, so that everyone could see clearly what was in the sack.

No doubt, it was all part of a campaign to stamp out Lollardy and show who was master. The archbishops were to remain in possession of the castle for another century and a half, until Cranmer thought it politic to hand it over to King

Henry VIII before he was dispossessed of it by force. He was the last Church incumbent, later to be burned to death in Queen Mary's reign and take his place in the *Book of Martyrs* along with the Lollard, Thorpe.

Penance was, indeed, a favourite Church punishment in medieval times, when the Church had its own courts and meted out justice after its own fashion. An interesting example of it has come down to us in the annals of Saltwood church, which lies a few hundred yards from the castle across the green meadows.

In the year 1412, a certain Matthew Edenham was introduced there as rector under the patronage of Archbishop Arundel. But as he was standing in the choir of the church, holding the archbishop's mandate in his hand, he was assaulted by one of his parishioners, named John Maysham Esquire. Maysham rushed at Edenham, snatched the mandate out of his hand, and tore off its seal. The same squire later attacked and wounded Sir John Royton, who seems to have been the parochial chaplain at the time. He was assisted in this attack by a man named Nicholas Poteman.

Both Maysham and Poteman were excommunicated and given certain acts of penance. Part of Poteman's penance was to walk round the market of the town of "Hithe" on three separate days, clothed as a penitent and carrying a candle in his hands weighing one pound.

As already mentioned, this church of Saints Peter and Paul at Saltwood was senior to the parish church of Hythe. Like so many other country churches, it was rebuilt in Norman times, and the fine doorway, with the distinctive Norman zigzag pattern over the arch, has been very well preserved, as it is protected from the weather by the tower that was subsequently added.

The first recorded rector of this church was the Archdeacon of Totnes, Walter de Gray, who was appointed by King John in 1207, at a time when there was no Archbishop of Canterbury. In fact, the archbishop's patronage does not begin again until 1279, the time of Archbishop Peckham.

But in the intervening time, a rector was appointed, whose links with Hythe are clear. We do not know exactly when Master Hamo was granted the benefice, but we do know that it was under the patronage of Henry III, and that he resigned as rector in 1228.

The new incumbent was one, Henry de Bissopeston, who was to receive only one byzant a year from the benefice, whilst Hamo was to enjoy the residue of the emolument for life, although he had been presented by King Henry to the vicarage of Hythe. One suspects that Bissopeston was probably, like the Archdeacon of Totnes, more absent than present, since he is frequently mentioned in the Patent and Close rolls in connection with various public duties.

But Master Hamo, like the later Hamo, who became Bishop of Rochester, identified himself very much with local affairs. As he was Perpetual Vicar for life, it is probable that he was still holding office when the fine Early English chancel of Hythe church was built. If the Canterbury Registers for the years 1273 to 1279 were ever discovered, we would probably know more about this. But they were taken to Rome by Archbishop Kilwardby and never seen again.

In 1365 Alan de Sleddale was rector under the patronage of Archbishop Islip. Shortly after the archbishop's death in the following year, he procured royal Letters of Presentation to the benefice, probably being anxious to have the title confirmed. The letters begin thus:

> Alanus de Sleddale, clericus, habet litteras Regis de presentatione ad ecclesiam de Saltwode, cum capella de Hethe eidem ecclesiae annexa . . .

From this it is clear that, at that date, there was only one church in Hythe. Nevertheless, whilst eminent clerics came and went at Saltwood, Hythe was growing in size and importance. At the same time as the monks surrounded their hillside properties with high stone walls, the burgesses developed their medieval port, complete with bailiff, harbourmaster and barons.

The distance between the two places is small. Taking the footpath from Mill Road at the east end of Hythe, you will be up at the castle in twenty minutes, if the path is not too overgrown. From there, amidst the cries of the peacocks in the lee of the much restored walls, you can look back at the sea in the V made by the Saltwood stream, and enjoy the view that many archbishops must have enjoyed in times past.

5

The Cinque Port

SALTWOOD owed its importance not only to the commanding position of the castle on the road up from the haven of Hythe, but also to its focal position with reference to the ports of the south-east coast of England, facing France across the narrow seas. These ports, as we know, had been joined together since the time of Edward the Confessor in an association, which came to be called the Confederation of the Cinque Ports. Originally they were five in number, as the word *cinque,* being the French for five, indicates. But coming from the old Norman French, it is still pronounced as in "sink" and not as in the modern French word for five.

Counting from west to east, as was usual in the charter documents these five ports were Hastings, Romney, Hythe, Dover and Sandwich. A glance at the map of Kent and Sussex will show that Hythe thus occupies the central position.

Under a charter despatched in 1190 by Richard I from Messina in Sicily, whilst he was on his way to a crusade, Rye and Winchelsea, designated "antient towns", were added to the five. So the balance shifted westwards to Romney, although they were still called the Cinque Ports. Small places, which were in the locality of the principal ports, were called "limbs". Thus West Hythe became a limb of Hythe.

In return for certain privileges, the Cinque Ports had to give Ship Service, providing ships for the king's use. They had to maintain ships ready to transport the king, his retinue and troops to and from the Continent, and to defend the realm against enemy attacks.

When Henry III issued his instructions to the Cinque Ports in 1229, Hythe was required to provide five ships, each with a master and a crew of twenty men and a boy, known variously as a *gromet* or a *garçon,* for up to fifteen days a year free of charge. If the ships were required for a longer period, payment would be made. This was at the rate of sixpence a day for a ship's master and threepence a day for a member of the crew. The master of the ship was sometimes known as the governor, and there was also a constable on board, who maintained order and dealt with the victualling.

At this time Sandwich, Romney and Rye also had to provide five ships. But Hastings had to find six, and Winchelsea's share of the 57 ships the king required was ten. Dover provided the remainder—no less than twenty-one.

We may be sure that there was plenty of work for these ships. During the Norman period, the top people were constantly travelling back to their ancestral homes in Normandy. And later on, troops were continually on the move during the Hundred Years War, fighting for the king's possessions in France. In addition, crusaders frequently took the shortest sea route to start their overland journey to the East.

The ships, themselves, were not large, being of the order of fifty tons or so. The official shield of the Cinque Ports shows the sterns of three, with high poops and with ports for their oars, in its right half, and the heads of three lions joined on to them on the left.

But these rowing-boats were not typical of the vessels of Hythe in its heyday. The Common Seal of the Barons of Hythe, which dates from the thirteenth century, and the Hythe town crest, show a wide-bellied sailing ship, with a single mast and yardarm, and with castles at stem and stern. Two men are up aloft on the yardarm above the furled sail, and two men are in the hull, facing each other from either end, one of them blowing a trumpet, the other perhaps the coxswain. A cross surmounts the masthead, and seven fishes are seen swimming in the water below the ship.

This seal, with the inscription *Sigillum Commune Baronum de Hethe,* has been found on a document in the Public Record Office of Edward I, dated 1298. It, therefore, shares with Romney the distinction of being the oldest surviving impression of a Cinque Ports seal.

It shows a typical "round" ship of the twelfth century, with a hull shaped not unlike those of the boats, which the Hythe men launch off Fishermen's Beach to this day. It was steered

The East Wall of the Town Hall Council Chamber, showing the Cinque Ports Shield and some of the names of Hythe's mayors

The Jurats' Seal, now the Mayor's Seal

by means of a rudder let over the starboard side—the steerboard, which thus bequeathed its name to the right-hand side of a ship—and it had a single square sail of very little use for beating against the wind. The ports had to wait till Tudor times for an efficient rig for sailing up-wind to be invented, and by then there were ships with three or four masts.

The forecastles and aftercastles on these ships were an English idea. They could be fitted on to a vessel that was normally used for fishing, and turn it into a warship with platforms on the bows and poop to give the famed English archers greater height above sea-level. The timbers for the platforms were carried on board, so that they could be assembled quite quickly when the look-out in the detachable crow's nest on the mast gave warning of an enemy vessel in sight.

It was in the thirteenth century that the overall control of the affairs of the Cinque Ports was vested in the Lord Warden. From the time of Edward I, at the end of that century, this appointment was combined with that of Constable of Dover Castle. So it was natural for him to hold court at Dover, a place that William the Conqueror had considered so important that he had given it to his half-brother, Odo, to control. The warden was also Admiral of the Cinque Ports, and required to enquire into wrecks and whether they were lawful salvage or not, and to investigate allegations of piracy.

A long line of famous men have enjoyed the appointment of Lord Warden, which in our day has become more a position of ceremonial dignity than of actual power. Our wartime heroes, Admiral Blake, William Pitt, the Duke of Wellington and Sir Winston Churchill, all held it in their time. More recently there was a break with the tradition that an eminent man should be appointed when, in 1979, the Queen Mother was installed in the office. The following year she met the Cinqueportsmen in Hythe.

Ship Service varied according to the separate abilities of the ports to provide it. So did the lord warden's assessment of the total number of ships to be made available by all the ports combined. Hythe's regular quota was five ships. But in 1335, a survey of the potential of the Cinque Ports gave Hythe as having only three large ships available—the *St. Cross,* the *La Blythe* and the *Waynepan,* of 120 tons, 100 tons and 80 tons respectively. At the same time, Romney had a similar total tonnage of 320, whereas Sandwich was able to produce 650 tons of shipping. This was after the great storms of the previous century had done a lot of damage to the two ports bordering Romney Marsh.

But the disasters the town had suffered did not prevent Edward III, six years later, threatening to cancel the privileges of Hythe and Romney if they continued to fail to produce the required five ships. In spite of the lord warden's protest to the king that no more ships were available, the warning appears to have been salutary since, four years later, in 1345, Hythe sent six ships, manned by 122 men, to the seige of Calais.

Shortly after this, the town was prosperous enough again to have a town barge, some particulars of which may still be read in the archives. For the construction of the barge in 1378, some of the timber came from the Abbot of St. Radigund's near Dover. This was because the abbey owned a grange at the top of Blackhouse Hill in Hythe. 6 shillings were spent on laying the keel, 4 shillings on pitching the hull, and 26 shillings on one of the sails. But the town was again in trouble after another disaster— the great fire of 1400. It is recorded as having had to hire a ship from Small Hythe, the little port on the River Rother, to fulfil its obligations for Ship Service in 1428.

By the time of Queen Elizabeth I's survey of the Cinque Ports fleet in 1566, Hythe had only fishing vessels available— four crayers of 40 tons burthen and three of 30 tons, seven shotters of 15 tons each, and eight tramellers of 5 tons. They had been called out three times by Henry VIII. But the final effort, before Hythe Haven was blocked up for good, was against the Spanish Armada in 1588.

Hythe sent, or at least paid for, one ship of 50 tons, called the *Grace of God,* which must have been a mere mosquito against the great Spanish galleons, but probably had a good sting in it. According to a doubtful tradition, the town received in return the treasure chest of wrought iron, with an intricate lock and springs, which is in the parish church.

The privileges granted to the Cinque Ports in return for providing Ship Service are recorded in the various charters that have come down to us. These are principally the charters of Henry II of 1155 and 1156, addressed individually to each of the ports, and the charter of Edward I.

Hythe is the proud possessor of the original document, which the soldier king, Edward, sent to the town in 1278. He wanted more control over the ports, which is why he combined the warden and the constable in one man. But he was also prepared to perpetuate privileges, which the ports had clearly enjoyed before his time. This is how the charter, in translation from the Latin, begins:

Edward by the Grace of God King of England Lord of Ireland and Duke of Aquitaine, to all Archbishops, Bishops, Abbots, Priors, Earls, Barons, Justices, Sheriffs, Reeves, Ministers, and to all

Bailiffs, and to his faithful subjects.

Greeting.

Know ye that for the faithful service that the Barons of our Cinque Ports have aforetime rendered to our ancestors, Kings of England, and latterly to us in our army against Wales, and for their good services to us and our heirs Kings of England faithfully to be continued in time to come, we have granted and by this our Charter have confirmed for us and our heirs to the same our Barons and their heirs, all their liberties and freedoms so that they may be quit of all toll, and all customs, to wit, of all *lastage, tallage, passage, cayage, rivage, ponsage,* and all *wreck,* and of buying, selling and rebuying throughout our whole land and realm, with *soc* and *sac,* and *thol* and *them,* and that they may be *wreckfree,* and *wittfree, lastagefree,* and *lovecopefree.* And that they may have *den* and *strand* at Great Yarmouth according to the contents of our Ordinance thereof and for ever after to be observed.

These privileges enumerated in Edward's charter, which had already been verified in the earlier documents, were very considerable. But the unfamiliar medieval terms, which I have written in italics, are not easily understood today. *Lastage* and *tallage,* for instance, refer to duty on goods by weight and quantity respectively. *Passage* was a landing tax, *rivage* a wharf toll, and *ponsage* a bridge toll. *Wreck* was the right to take wrecked ships on one's coast without paying a salvage tax, and *wreckfree* was the freedom from the claims of others for the wreckage of their ships. *Lovecopefree* was the freedom to trade at will without paying market fees and unrestricted by guilds or monopoly interests.

The right of *den* and *strand* was of great practical importance, because it meant that they could dry their nets on the shore at Yarmouth, which was called the Den, and their catches there without paying a fee. They were thus able to go there and take their share of the profitable North Sea herring harvest, which was sold for the tables of East Anglia, then the most populous part of the country. But it did not fail to generate acute animosity between the Cinqueportsmen and the Yarmouth fishermen.

The charter then goes on to say that they may also have their *findals* both on land and sea, which means treasure trove. In other words, for them findings were keepings.

Soc and *sac* were obligations under feudal tenure. *Thol* was homage to any overlord except the king, and *them* was any claim of villeinage or serfdom. So they were, in effect, to be completely free men except for their duty to the monarch. This is reflected in the judicial matters that are mentioned in the charter. *Infangtheff* was the right to judge thieves taken in their jurisdiction, and *wittfree* was freedom from any amerciament by an outside court.

They also had *utfangtheff* "in the same way as the Archbishops and Abbots, Earls and Barons, have in their Manors in the County of Kent". This meant that they had the right to judge thieves from their ports taken outside their jurisdiction. It was a valuable concession when their men were away at Yarmouth and elsewhere. At one time the Cinqueportsmen had a fearful reputation for lawlessness, and it may well be that this right, like the right of the citizens of ancient Rome to claim trial by their peers, was a significant contributory factor.

Written in brown ink on yellowing paper, the charter goes on to describe the free ownership of property and goods that the Cinqueportsmen enjoyed, in marked contrast to the feudal bondage of most of the population. "And that as our Freeman they may be quit of all their goods, and all their merchandise. And that they may have their Honours in our Courts and their liberties throughout our whole land wherever they may come".

It is clear from this that the Freemen of the Cinque Ports had rights equivalent to those of barons, and so they were designated as such. The most conspicuous Honour at Court was the right to send barons to Westminster to carry the canopy over the king and or queen at coronations.

Thus we find in Shakespeare's play *King Henry VIII* instructions to the producer staging the coronation procession for Anne Bullen, the king's second wife. "A canopy borne by four of the Cinque-ports; under it the Queen in her robe". And in the script, one gentleman amongst the bystanders says to another, "They that bear the cloth of honour over her are four barons of the Cinque-ports".

There is also a stone in the vestry of the parish church in memory of Thomas Spratt, a mayor of Hythe and also three times bailiff at Yarmouth. He died in 1619 and was "one of

those that did cary the canopie over the Kinge at his coronation". The king must have been James I.

But the custom died, and the canopy has not been carried in
the coronation procession since that of George IV. After that
occasion there were second thoughts, as the elderly barons had
had considerable difficulty in holding it up over the royal
head.

However, the Barons of the Cinque Ports still have their
place. At the coronation of King George V in 1911, they
carried banners representing the dominions of the British
Empire. Nowadays, they line the west side of the screen in
Westminster Abbey, and receive the two standards carried
before the king or queen. At the coronation of Queen
Elizabeth II in 1953, Hythe's baron was Sir Frederick Bovens-
chen, a senior civil servant at the War Office, whose name was
known to millions during the Second World War as the man
who signed the Army Council Instructions. He wore the
costume that had originally been designed for the coronation
of King Edward VII.

There is a rather amusing sequel to the coronation of the boy
king, Henry VI, in 1429. Hythe and Sandwich appear to have
joined forces to pay for the canopy. After the ceremony John
Overhavene and John Godescalk were each paid 20d by the
Council for carrying the canopy and its staves from London.
On the way back, they had it valued in Canterbury, and then
went on to Sandwich with it, hoping that the Sandwich people
would keep it. However, Sandwich did not want it. So
Richard Rykedone had to go there, pay them 6s 8d, and bring
it back to Hythe.

The charter of Edward I also includes a description of the
freedom from the justice of the normal county and local
courts, which the Cinque Ports enjoyed, and of the arrangements for administering their own justice.

> And also that they may be quit of Shires and Hundreds so that, if
> anybody wishes to plead against them, they may not reply,
> neither may they plead, otherwise than they were wont to plead
> in the time of the Lord King Henry out great grandfather.

The charter continues with a reference to the Cinque Ports'
own court:

And that they shall not plead in any other place, save where it is
their right, and where they are wont to plead, namely at Shipway.

Hythe was, of course, the nearest port to this Court of
Shepway, which was established less than a century after the
Norman conquest, and handled matters which were beyond
the competence of each individual borough. It was usually
held in the open air on Lympne Hill, where Shepway Cross
stood and still stands today, and it had powers equivalent to
those of a shire court.

It was, in fact, the king's court, presided over by his deputy,
the lord warden, and the Cinqueportsmen cannot always have
regarded it with unadulterated pleasure. Judging from the
number of shells lying about in the vicinity, oysters seem to
have been one of the staple items of diet of those assembled
there.

Later, the Court of Brodhull and the Court of Guestling
came into being as the ports' own assemblies, to ensure that
the privileges granted in the royal charters were protected and
used to advantage, and to sort out local matters, such as the
appointment of the bailiff at Yarmouth.

It is not quite certain where Brodhull was located. But there
is a clue on the schematic map, called the *Card of the Beacons in
Kent,* which was printed in Elizabethan times to show the
early warning system to those whose duty it was to raise the
alarm on the first sighting of an invasion fleet. On this card,
the site of the beacon on the coast at Dymchurch, which
communicated with the one on top of Lympne Hill, appears to
be printed as *Brodhull* or *Brodbull.* Guestling is still a village
between Hastings and Winchelsea, which was conveniently
placed for the men of the three Sussex ports.

In its early days the Brodhull did, indeed, meet at Dymchurch, or *Deemchurch,* as it was then called, because the court,
or *deem,* sat there. But later, as the White and Black books of
the Cinque Ports indicate, the two courts were amalgamated
into the Court of Brotherhood and Guestling, which met at
New Romney, the place central to all seven ports, and later at
different ports at different times.

This court's most recent meeting in Hythe was in 1973, the
first time there for sixty-three years. Hythe's mayor, Christopher Capon, was on this occasion Speaker of the Cinque

Ports, and the court was held in the parish church, with the
gilded maces of the corporations assembled on a table at the
foot of the chancel steps.

But the records in Hythe show a bewildering vacillation in
the designation of the Brodhull. In the jurats' account book for
1413, we find four of the jurats and their servant being paid 3s
6d for riding, on July 20th, to the *General brotherhell,* and we
find John Maffay being paid 2s 3½d for writing the register of
the *Brodhell.* Yet again, sounding somewhat incongruously to
modern ears, we have three jurats and their servant going, five
months later, on the Monday before the Feast of St. Lucy,
Virgin, to the *General brothell.*

In July 1419 we are back to the *Brodhull,* and two jurats and
their servant go to *Romene* to attend it. But in 1432, it was
called the *Brotheryeld* or *Brothergild* as well as the *Brodhull,* and
in Elizabethan times the word *Brotherilde* is common. From all
this we can surmise the gradual transmutation from the original place-name to the idea of a brotherhood.

King Edward's charter also reveals the importance of the
wine trade in those days by making a specific concession:

> And that of their proper wines for which they trade, they may be
> quit of our Right Prise, that is to say, of one tun of wine before the
> mast, and another after the mast.

Indeed, as we shall see, it was hard for the Cinqueportsmen
in later centuries to give up their inherited right to "duty frees".

This important charter, a photograph of which has been put
on display in the Hythe Local History Room, was signed on
June 16th in the sixth year of Edward I's reign, and witnessed
by a cardinal, a prior, a dean, an archbishop, an archdeacon, an
uncle of the king and many other people. At one point the
charter says:

> And for the rest that they may have their liberties and freedoms
> better, more fully and more honourably than they and their
> ancestors at any time have had, as in the times of the Kings of
> England, Edward, William I and II, King Henry our great grand-
> father, and the Lord King Henry our father, by their charters, as
> those Charters, which our Barons themselves have, and which
> we have seen do reasonably testify.

This is a clear indication that the kings mentioned above, from Edward the Confessor onwards, all issued charters granting privileges to the Cinque Ports, although they have not all survived. In the same year, Edward I granted "to the Barons and good men of Hethe" the right to hold two annual fairs, and in the twenty-sixth year of his reign, he issued another charter giving the Barons of the Cinque Ports the right to purchase merchandise in Ireland.

Next in chronological sequence in the town's archives is the charter of Privileges granted by Edward II in 1313 specifically to "his men of Heia". Edward III's charter of 1328, in the second year of his reign, relates to the Barons of the Cinque Ports contributing from their "goods and chattels" towards the king's shipping, whether the owners of the goods were actually living in the ports or not.

Another document, specifically directed at Hythe, is a writ issued by the king in the same year, directing the "Mayor, Bailiff and Jurats of Hythe, and the proved men and all the commonalty of the Port of Hythe" to provide ships for the king's use. It is from this century that the surviving Hythe jurats' seal dates, displaying a bird of prey, which could be an eagle or a falcon. As the town did not have a mayor until 1575, the insertion of the word *mayor* in the writ must have been a mistake.

All these documents were written in Latin. But there is one in the archives written in Norman French, which is an agreement made at a session of the Brodhull. This meeting of the Cinque Ports was held at Romney in 1392, and the agreement concerns the future apportionment of dues payable to the Crown, and the summoning of a Brodhull at the request of any one of the Cinque Ports, which are called the *Cynk Portz*.

So, blessed with all the privileges enumerated in the charters, the men of the Cinque Ports played their parts. Naturally, the sea fights at which they were present during the Middle Ages have been remembered more than the less exciting business of transporting royalty and troops. For, though they could do little to prevent the Norman conquest, most of their seamen being away in the North Sea at the time, they were able to show their mettle on many subsequent occasions.

One of the best remembered naval engagements took place

in the reign of King John. There was an invasion scare. The king had signed Magna Carta in 1225, but the pope, whose friendship he had previously bought with a subsidy of a thousand marks a year, declared that declaration of rights to be invalid. So John went back on his word to his barons, who then made the mistake of turning to France for help. The French king, Louis, was actually offered the English crown.

The Cinqueportsmen, however, refused to support Louis. When, six months later, John died and the child king, Henry III, was hurriedly crowned in his place, their resolve to resist him was strengthened. But Louis, himself, was already in England by then, and he showed no signs of disbanding the invasion force, which he had been collecting.

Fifty or more ships were assembled on the French coast to bring reinforcements across the Channel. These ships came up, in the Straits, with those already blockading Dover. But the men of the Cinque Ports ships, getting up-wind of them, bore down on them from the south-west. They blinded their crews with quicklime, which they threw up into the air before closing with them. Then they showered them with arrows and made great slaughter off Sandwich.

The Battle of Dover, fought on St. Bartholomew's Day, 1217, is forgotten today. But in its time, it was no less significant than the defeat of the Spanish Armada over three hundred years later, since if Louis had become king, England would then have become a mere province of France. It ushered in a century of terrible storms, which smashed their way up the Channel, bringing floods and devastation, and ultimately radically altering the coastline around Romney Marsh. Violent hurricanes are recorded for the years 1250, 1252 and 1287.

Hythe provided special service for Edward I, when he went campaigning against Llewelyn in North Wales in the 1270s. If any ships were involved, it must have been a difficult business in view of the distance by sea. But the entry in the record of the Herald's Visitation of 1592 says that the coat of arms of three half-lions and three half-ships, similar to that of the Cinque Ports as a whole, together with the Common seal and the Mayor's seal, were granted by the King to "Hethe" for their "especial and faithful service done in Wales".

During this time the Cinqueportsmen had the king's permission to ravage the French coast, sparing only the churches, on condition that they remitted to him one fifth of the spoils. The French retaliated, sometimes rather nastily parading off-shore with a dead Englishman hanging from one end of the yardarm and a dead dog from the other. There ensued a challenge to the French seadogs from the Cinque Ports, with the result that, in 1293, in tune with the medieval concept of ceremony in conflict, a pitched battle was fought between them. The fight was strictly against orders, since King Edward I was now busy in Scotland, and had no wish for a quarrel with France behind his back. So the battle area selected was well out of sight, off the coast of Brittany. There were Dutch, Irish and Gascon ships on the side of the Cinque Ports, and the French team included some Flemish and Genoese vessels as well as the Norman ones.

The naval fight took place in an equinoctal gale, and ended with the Frenchmen being thoroughly worsted. This made the French king so furious that, after Edward had refused him compensation, he declared war on England. The Fench raid on Hythe, reported by Lambarde to have been in the same year, was probably after war had been declared:

> Before this Towne (in the reigne of King Edwarde the First) a great fleete of French men shewed themselves upon the Sea, of which one (being furnished with two hundreth soldiers) set her men on land in the Haven, where they had no sooner pitched their foote, but the Townsmen came upon them and slew them to the last man, wherewith the residue were so afraide, that forthwith they hoysed up saile, and made no further attempt.

It has been suggested that a number of human bones, which were dug up in the innings between Oaklands and Ladies Walk, were the remains of these slaughtered Frenchmen, who had no means of escape, as their ship had grounded and was set alight.

By the end of the century, the animosity between the Cinque Ports and the men of Yarmouth, which had sprung from the Cinqueportsmen's right of landing there, reached fever pitch. The Yarmouth fishermen not only resented the Cinqueportsmen's right of den and strand on their beach, they also fiercely objected to them having their own bailiff there and acting as if they were a law unto themselves.

All this came to a head in the year 1297, when Yarmouth and the Cinque Ports together had to transport Edward I's troops to Flanders, the destination being Sluis, which is now inland in Holland close to the Belgian border. The Cinqueportsmen attacked the Yarmouth ships, destroying about thirty of them and killing some two hundred of their men. What was more, after the slaughter they boasted of their victory, calling it the Yarmouth fair.

Naturally, His Majesty was not amused and told them so. Whereupon the barons of "Hethe", for their part, promised to accept the king's award, which must have been a fine, though the amount is not recorded.

In 1340 the Cinqueportsmen took part in a battle with the French off this same Sluis, which was one of the innumerable engagements of the Hundred Years War, and as an "especial grace" King Edward III bore half the cost of the twenty-one ships there. But the main naval occasion of the fourteenth century for Hythe was the siege of Calais five years later.

The Black Death of 1349 must have struck Hythe along with the other English towns, and Leland mentions a fire at the beginning of the fourteenth century burning down no less than three hundred and sixty houses, which must surely be an exaggeration. But these events are not what Lambarde refers to when he writes that Hythe was "miserably scourged".

The phrase is apt, since it was usual in those days to attribute disasters to the judgement of God for past sins. The Cinqueportsmen included many rough, independent characters, who were not above committing an outrage for the sake of loot, and no doubt their sins were many. For instance, when Edward I expelled the Jews under his edict of 1290, many were set upon in mid-Channel, plundered, and either slaughtered and pitched into the sea or left on a sandbank to drown under a rising tide. And in 1293, churchmen of the Cistercian abbeys dared not leave England at all for fear of the Cinqueportsmen.

The scourge was a double one. On May 3rd 1400, the disastrous fire already mentioned burnt down, according to Lambarde, two hundred homes in Hythe, probably accounting for most of the town. In the same year, and according to Lambarde on the very same day, five ships and a hundred men were lost at sea. It was the beginning of the reign of Henry IV, and the remaining barons petitioned the king to be allowed to leave Hythe Haven altogether.

Henry refused. But he did relieve them of their Ship Service for five years, reserving the right to call on them only in case of dire necessity. He also confirmed them, in his charter of 1403, in their immunity from summons before the circuit judges, who were called *justices itinerant,* and in exemption from "juries, assizes or recognizances".

In 1414 his son, Henry V, confirmed the release of the Port of Hythe from its services as one of the Cinque Ports, although his campaigns in France must have made him anxious to have as much cross-Channel shipping available as possible. Nevertheless, when Lady Clarence, wife of Thomas Plantagenet, the second son of Henry V, wanted to go to France in 1419, the town paid 40 shillings to John Bernevale for the hire of a ship, plus the large sum of £4 12s 6d for the victuals for her party, which were bought by the constable of the ship.

The town also provided part of a civic escort for the noble lady, since two of the jurats—Alexander Appelforde and John Overhavene—had to attend St. James Church, Dover, with other barons of the Cinque Ports, "to escort her over the sea" and were paid their own and their servant's expenses to the tune of 3s ½d.

However, after 1414 Hythe never again had to give Ship Service in full. The ship that the port furnished for the navy to fight the Armada was paid for by means of a special cess on all the inhabitants, and in 1596 Hythe combined with Dover to provide a ship of 160 tons to face the second Armada, that Spain was expected to send against England. After the end of the sixteenth century, the port was always paid for any ship the king used.

So the public expenditure in, for example 1419, appears to have been in spite of the recent release from service granted by Henry V. As well as giving Lady Clarence passage to France, the Council also paid Thomas Goldfynche Junior 32 shillings as "remuneration for his boat for eight weeks at the time when the King crossed over to Toke", which means Le Touquet.

But the governor of Lady Clarence's ship does not appear to have been above doing a little privateering on his own account. Another item tells us that four jurats and their two servants had to go over to Dover to St. James Church to be at the suit of John Bernevale, because "his goods were seized at a common suit for 4 marks 3s 4d from seventeen French prisoners, viz from each man 3s 4d for custom belonging to the town".

We are also told that Robert Hart "came to the Jurats to tell them to deliver up the goods of John Bernevale by counsel of the Lieutenant lest he should give the Jurats trouble before the Lieutenant at Dover" and was paid a shilling for his expenses. Somebody else was paid 4d for carrying a pipe of ale from John Bernevale's *balynger,* which was a kind of sailing ship fitted out for war.

The economics of chartering such a ship for a single voyage are clearly shown in the list of expenses for John Leghe's ship, "when he took Haukyn Mayshot". Bread and beef cost 9s 6d and 17s 10d respectively. Ale from four different suppliers totalled 15s. Cash delivered to Will Smyth, the constable of the ship, was 13s 4d. Only 6s 8d was paid to John Leghe, himself, for a charter of eight days, and the whole *fare* was thus 62s 4d. Another item in the books is 2d for a proclamation throughout the town for the men to prepare themselves for the ship.

Thus the ships came and went in Hythe Haven, the Cinque Port. But what of the people in the town itself?

6

Medieval Hythe

ONE of the reasons why we know so little about the Saxons in
Hythe is because they built mostly of wood, and their buildings have been destroyed. Furthermore, medieval Hythe suffered grievously from its great fire—two fires, if we are to
believe Leland—with the consequence that positive identification of structures preceding the year 1400 is limited to a few
walls here and there, as seen under the eagle eyes of the
experts, with the exception of two important buildings.

Some evidence of a fire was found during alterations to the
Manor House. When one of the floors was removed, some
pottery, iron instruments and a copper bowl, with fish bones
in it, were found, showing signs of incineration.

But there are nine houses, still wholly or partly in existence,
which were built shortly after 1400, of the type known as
Wealden, named after the Weald of Kent. They are character-
ised by their steep roofs, as on the one almost opposite the
Town Hall in the High Street. Originally, it seems, they had
no chimneys and few windows. Therefore, although they
probably belonged to the better-off citizens, they were still
quite primitive dwellings, built with wooden frames and lath
and plaster walls, which would be extremely vulnerable to the
risk of fire from the open hearth in the centre of the building.
The smoke from the fire would excape under the eaves and
between the tiles of the roof as best it could.

The best surviving example of these houses is the one next
to the White Hart Hotel, which is now occupied by Crun-
den's, the greengrocer, and Wood's, the butcher. One steps
down to enter the greengrocer's shop, and the old window
frame at the back retains the original building line.

The only existing buildings, that we can positively identify
from the pre-1400 period, are the church and the house called

Centuries, both of which have been much altered in the intervening years. The church, or strictly speaking the chapel, since it was not until 1844 that it was separated from Saltwood, was of supreme importance to the Hythe of the Middle Ages.

Domesday book described Hythe as a borough. But it was not a self-governing one, since the appointment of the bailiff was in the gift of the Archbishop of Canterbury. Some archbishops did allow the barons of Hythe to elect their own bailiff, but they were not obliged to do so.

In fact, we still have a number of the documents appointing the bailiff. For instance, in 1415 Archbishop Chicheley appointed William atte Mede to the Bailiwick of Hythe, and six years later the Duke of Gloucester, Henry V's brother, and the Earl of Pembroke, Constable of Dover Castle and Lord Warden of the Cinque Ports, were commanding obedience to him.

The appointment was for life. Later in the same century, Archbishop Morton appointed his "servant, John Michell" to be bailiff, addressing a letter to "my Neyghbours, the Juratts and Inhabitants hyn the towne of Hythe" from Knole in Sevenoaks. This letter to introduce a new bailiff reads as follows:

> My neighbours I commend me unto you. And where it is so that the office of the Bailiwick of Hythe hath been unrighteously occupied for a long season past to the displeasure of God and far from due order and good rule as ye know well Whereupon ye desired me at your last being in Canterbury with me to see a better provision for you on that behalf According to the which your desire I have assigned and deputed and ordained my servant John Michell this bearer to occupy and exercise there among you the said office Whom I pray you to assist to the best of your powers and as ye shall move do lawfully And to bear unto him your good will and favour on this behalf so as he may the better thereby occupy the said office of bailiwick I trust he will so behave himself in the exercising of the same that God shall be pleased And every man reasonably contented with him.

But in 1539 Archbishop Cranmer, handing Saltwood Castle over to the Crown, leased the bailiwick to the town for ninety-nine years, thus giving up his right of appointment, and in 1575 Queen Elizabeth's charter abolished the appointment altogether. From 1349 up to this time, the government of the borough had been vested in the bailiff and twelve jurats, who were sworn in as town councillors.

A great deal of the land, even in the town itself, belonged to Christ Church, Canterbury. It is the Church properties that were surrounded by the high walls, built of the local ragstone, which remain a pleasing feature of the old part of the town today. So it is not surprising that the town council, itself, used to meet in the church.

St. Leonard's Church, dedicated to the patron saint of prisoners and standing on the hillside above the high walls, which enclose the lower slopes, was thus the governmental centre of Hythe and also the focus of social life. It is a building that any small town might be proud of, and an indication of the affluence and prosperity of the Old Cinque Port in its prime.

Leland says that "It evidently apereth that wher the paroch chirch is now was sumtyme a fayr abbay . . . In the top of the chirch yard is a fayr spring, and thereby ruines of howses of office of the abbey".

There is no record of an abbey in Hythe, and no memory of it, unless it be in the property opposite the southern side of the church, which is called the Priory. But since monks were accustomed to going out from the mother priory in Canterbury to tend the lands and properties of Christ Church, it would not have been surprising if they had had a house in Hythe. It is possible that the fine Norman doorway, with the chevron decoration, which leads directly from the vestry into the north transept of the church, was at one time the entrance for the community of monks, as described by Leland. Certainly he was no casual observer, since he was right about the spring, located half-way up the west wall of the churchyard, which has now been stopped up.

What is certain from documentary evidence is that, in the twelfth century, there was a small priory up Blackhouse Hill on one of the ways to Saltwood. The place was named Blackwose, after the famous ooze that has already been mentioned. It is called St. Nicholas, and occupied by monks following the precepts of the Abbey of Prémontré in France. Being a cell of the priory of Lavendon in Buckinghamshire, it was a small house with only five canons and one lay brother in it. One of its benefactors was Arnulf, Lord of the Manor of Newington, who gave the canons a mill, with the lands and rents belonging to it, which amounted to 7s and 1,000 herrings a year.

Nevertheless, it was too small to prosper, and at one stage the white canons had to wander about the district begging for their food. Not being Buddhists, the barons of Hythe considered this to be a great scandal, and complained to the Abbot of Prémontré, who had it attached to the Premonstratensian Abbey of St. Radigund near Dover for more effective supervision. Today Blackhouse Hill and Cannongate, spelt with two 'n's instead of one, are reminiscences of the old foundation, gate meaning a road or path in Old English rather than a gateway.

Whether the parish church of St. Leonard was built on the site of a former abbey or not, it clearly goes back to the early Norman period. This fact is firmly impressed on the visitor, as he makes his way up the steps of the porch to the south door, which is the one in general use today:

> Welcome to this church dear visitor.
> God has been praised here for 900 years.
> Come and join us in our worship of the Lord.
> He is waiting with love for you.

It is an indication of the church's fame and popularity that the vicar has had this welcome repeated in French, Dutch and German.

The original Norman chapel was built at the beginning of the twelfth century, and was not very large, probably not more than half the length of the present church. Traces of the old chapel can still be seen on the inside wall of the north aisle, where there were two clearstorey windows, now blocked up. But the finest remnant of the Norman period is the doorway of the north transept, which was built towards the end of the century.

It was probably through this doorway that the bailiff entered to join the jurats in the meetings of the borough council, which were held in this part of the church, called St. Edmund's Chapel after England's martyr king. Nevertheless, there is evidence that there was a Common House, a sort of

St. Leonard's Church

The living church . . .

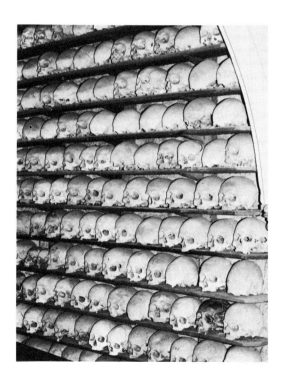

. . . and the dead
in the crypt

Moot Hall, as early as 1370, since the records mention the supply of rushes for the floor and candles for a meeting. And again, in 1412, paper, ink, parchment and a form were purchased for the "Common House", as well as rushes and candles. It has been suggested that this was the old Wealden house in the High Street, which has already been mentioned—the next building but one to the present Town Hall.

Be that as it may, the tradition of holding civic meetings in Hythe's splendid church has never completely died. In the sixteenth and seventeenth centuries, and in the eighteenth century up to the time when the new Town Hall was built, the mayor and jurats used to meet in a special room built over the south porch.

It was called the Parvise because there is a circular window in it, through which one can look into the body of the church, and it was probably originally constructed as a priest's chamber. But that this room was considered to belong to the town is clear from the fact that, until very recently, the church paid a peppercorn annual rent for it of a shilling. As we have seen, as recently as 1973 the Court of Brotherhood and Guestling met with traditional pomp and ceremony in the nave.

In the thirteenth century, the church was greatly enlarged, and it is to this time that it owes its chief splendour, the Early English raised choir and sanctuary, built when Master Hamo was the vicar. The communicant reaches it up a noble flight of steps. But in addition to being raised above the nave, the chancel itself is lofty, having a triforium gallery with three clearstorey windows above it on either side.

This is a most unusual feature for a parish church, and yet the name of the architect is unknown. But surely he must have had the great cathedral at Canterbury in mind, when he made his plans for the church at Hythe, which resembles it so much in miniature. In any case, St. Leonard's was fortunate in having one of the archbishops' favoured residences in nearby Saltwood, and several of these archbishops were Lord Chancellor of England as well. Stephen Langton, archbishop from 1207 to 1228, could well have been in the Cathedral at the time when these great works were undertaken. Nevertheless, we may pause to note that the vaulting of this much admired chancel was not actually completed until the late nineteenth century.

There is a turret beside the choir, with a circular staircase in it, which formerly led to the old rood loft, from which the cross was suspended over the chancel arch. Continuing upwards, the staircase gives access to the gallery, and finally to the roof, thus giving the effect of a round tower with a miniature steeple. Underneath the raised choir there is a most unusual crypt. It has two doors, north and south, just as the stepped porch has two doors, east and west, so that on feast days processions can go right round the church without leaving consecrated ground. Though why it was not possible to take in a little more ground from the pathway at the eastern end of the church is not clear.

The crypt is, therefore, often termed an ambulatory. But this is not its strangest feature. What makes is unusual is that it is about the only charnel house, or ossuary, left in England today, although it was not specifically designed as such.

The piles of bones stored there represent the remains of some 4,000 people, if we can judge from the number of femurs, which are the most numerous. This is a good deal more than the total population of Hythe up until recent times. In 1910 the bones were restacked on shelves, from which the skulls stare out at you as you enter the cavernous vault.

Because of their great number and the rare way in which they have been preserved, many legends have grown up concerning the origin of these bones. When the compulsive traveller and raconteur, George Borrow, was alive, the sexton was regaling visitors with the story that they were the relics of a great battle between the resident Saxons and the invading Danes, which took place in Alfred the Great's time. This was, perhaps, an echo of the raid up the River Limen, mentioned in the Anglo-Saxon Chronicle, and Borrow recounts the tale in *Lavengro* with his customary embellishments:

We were, if I remember right, in the vicinity of a place called Hythe, in Kent. One sweet evening, in the latter part of the summer, our mother took her two little boys by the hand, for a wander about the fields. In the course of our stroll we came to the village church; an old grey-headed sexton stood in the porch, who, perceiving that we were strangers, invited us to enter. We were presently in the interior, wandering about the aisles, looking on the walls, and inspecting the monuments of the noble dead. I can scarcely state what I saw; how should I? I was a child not yet four years old, and yet I think I remember the evening sun streaming in through a stained window upon the faded tints of an ancient banner. And now once more we were outside the building, where, against the wall, stood a low-eaved pent-house, into which we looked. It was half filled with substances of some kind, which at first looked like large gray stones. The greater part were lying in layers; some, however, were seen in confused and mouldering heaps, and two or three, which had perhaps rolled down from the rest, lay separately on the floor. "Skulls, madam" said the sexton; "skulls of the old Danes! Long ago they came pirating in these parts: and then there chanced a mighty shipwreck, for God was angry with them, and He sunk them; and their skulls, as they came ashore, were placed here as a memorial. There were many more when I was young, but now they are fast disappearing. Some of them must have belonged to strange fellows, madam. Only see that one; why, the two young gentry can scarcely lift it!" And, indeed, my brother and myself had entered the Golgotha, and commenced handling these grim relics of mortality. One enormous skull, lying in a corner, had fixed our attention, and we had drawn it forth. Spirit of eld, what a skull was yon!

It is possible that the monster skull, mentioned by Borrow, is the one now preserved in the museum of the Royal College of Surgeons in London. But it is not likely to have belonged to a Dane, or even to one of the Frenchmen killed in the raid of 1293.

In the early nineteenth century, on the other hand, the sexton was telling people that the bones had come from a fierce fight between the old Britons, deserted by their Roman masters, and a wave of Saxon marauders in the fifth century. The bones, he said, had become bleached through lying about on the beach for a long time before being gathered up for decent interment. It was about this time that Richard Chamberlain was being paid £1 in addition to his salary of £4 a year for the "privilege" of showing the bones.

However, at the time of restacking, the bones were examined carefully by F. G. Parsons, who was then Professor of Anatomy at the University of London. He declared that most of the cuts and fractures in them had been made long after death, not by swords in battle but by the spades of gravediggers.

Furthermore, the Rev. H. D. Dale, who was vicar of Hythe at the time, had certain relics, which were found amongst the bones, examined by experts at the British Museum. They declared them to belong to the fourteenth and fifteenth centuries, thus indicating the era in which the bones were likely to have been put there. So the Black Death of 1349, and the pestilence recorded as having hit Hythe at the same time as the double disaster of fire on land and loss at sea, are more likely than warfare to have been the originators of many of the skeletons. But the last word has not yet been said on these mysterious bones. In the year 1932 they were re-examined by Dr. G. M. Morant of University College, London, who declared that they were the skeletons of men and women who were considerably shorter than the people of today, and did not belong to any English type at all. He said that they were more likely to be the remains of Italian, Central European or even Balkan folk, presumably the descendants of immigrants from the polyglot Roman Empire. Were these then, in actual fact, the last of the Romans?

During medieval times, the only Church in England was, of course, the Catholic Church. Churches were the centres of social life. They were full of colour, as were the feast day processions, in which most people took part. Statues of the saints abounded, and were the focal points for people begging the spirits of the saints to intercede with the deity for them in their troubles.

The patron saint of the fishermen of Hythe, and indeed of fishermen throughout the Christian world, was St. Nicholas. So there was a chapel to this saint on the waterfront between Hythe and Seabrook. It was not on the present shore, but on the long arm of the sea that used to run close to the present line of the Military Canal.

Many of the reformers of the sixteenth century called the worship of the saints "filthy idolatry", and Lambarde was amongst them, referring to King Henry VIII as the English Theodosius, after the famous Byzantine destroyer of idols. He says that the chapel was still standing in his day, and remarks that "although it may now seeme but a base Barn on your eie, yet was it sometime an Imperiall seat of great estate and maiestie":

For it was Saint Nicholas chappell, and he in Papisme held the
same Empire that Neptune had in Paganisme, and could both
appease the rage and wallowing waves of the Sea, and also preserve from wreck and drowning so many as called upon his name.
And therefore this is one of the places
   Servati ex undis figere dona solebant.
Where such as had escapde from the Sea
were woont to leave their guifts.

This chapel, which Lambarde says was actually in the
neighbouring parish of Newington, lying to the east of Hythe,
is not to be confused with the one dedicated to the same saint,
which lay to the west of the town. The land at the Hythe end of
Seabrook Road, known in the deeds as Chapel Fields, is no
doubt a reminiscence of this place.

Of course, it is natural that, from an age in which the words
cleric and *clerk* were synonymous, the written records that have
come down to us are largely concerned with Church matters.
Thus we have considerable information about one of the best
known medieval citizens of Hythe and his benefactions—
Hamo, Bishop of Rochester.

This Hamo was born in Hythe in the year 1275, reputedly at
the house called Centuries, which still stands at the corner of
Church Hill and Bartholomew Street. It had been built in the
previous century, with an arched entrance that can still be
seen, and was on the main highway up the hill from the haven
to Canterbury via Saltwood.

Hamo served his novitiate under the Benedictine monks,
who looked after St. Leonard's Church, and later studied for
the priesthood at the Priory of St. Andrew in Rochester.
Becoming private secretary and chaplain to the Bishop of
Rochester, he was well placed in the corridors of power, and
so became bishop himself in 1319. Styled "Hamo de Hethe",
he retained the appointment until he resigned it in 1352.

During this time he had the family house at Hythe enlarged.
He bought farm land nearby, and created a hospital, or almshouse as we would call it, for ten needy men and women,
who had been born in the town and fallen from affluence to
poverty through no fault of their own.

Hamo called his hospital St. Andrew's after his own priory

St. Bartholomew's Hospital

The Great Seal of
Hamo of Hythe

The house called Centuries and Clyme Hill

in Rochester, intending to establish it in his own residence in Hythe. But for some reason he changed his mind and set up in Saltwood, where his farm was located. There was consequently a Hospital Lane in Saltwood, which changed its name to Bartholomew Lane after 1685.

There had already been a hospital in existence here since 1276, called St. Bartholomew's and founded for thirteen poor people. In the event, Hamo's establishment appropriated the name, and the Great Seal of St. Bartholomew was granted to the Prior Brothers of the hospital. From the charter of 1336, granted under the King's Licence, we learn how it was conducted.

Hamo ordained that the Master and Mistress of the hospital, selected from amongst the ten inmates, and the Brethren and Sisters, should all wear russet clothes and recite three hundred Pater Nosters and Hail Marys every day for their founder and benefactors. The hospital was endowed with an income of twenty marks a year, and each inmate received fourpence a week. We may note that there was no segregation of the sexes in different houses in this pre-Puritan England.

In 1334 Centuries was enlarged by Hamo, who was himself an architect of no mean repute, having been responsible for the construction of the main tower of Rochester Cathedral and other ecclesiastical buildings. For a while he used the house as a summer residence, which is perhaps why he did not accommodate his poor folk there.

In the Hundred Court books of the fifteenth century there are several references to St. Bartholomew's. In the year 1409, John Sherwynd, "hospitular" of St. Bartholomew's, and two others were accused of having "thrown dung at the Spytal corner, to the public nuisance". Then, in 1429, there was a complaint that one, William Cheseman, had stopped up a lane called Porg Lane near the land of the Hospital of St. Bartholomew, and also that, through the making of a dam between the land of Richard Rye and Robert Rye and that of John Rye, the "common water of Hethe" had overflowed the land of the Brethren and Sisters of St. Bartholomew, and had also overflowed the King's highway leading from the Marsh to Hethe.

In 1685, after further extensions to Centuries had been carried out, the almshouse at last moved there. At the same time the trustees of the charity had a coloured map, or plan, prepared by Thomas Hill, showing the lands of St. Bartholomew's and St. John's, which is valuable evidence for the condition and appearance of Hythe at the time, in addition to the St. John's Hospital map, or "plott", made by Hill the previous year by order of the mayor and jurats.

The final extension of Centuries, with the neo-Gothic exterior that is most apparent today, was carried out in 1811. From then on the house was in continuous occupation by needy folk until the occupants were evacuated to Worthing during the Second World War. After that, the small number of inmates who remained were transferred to Hythe's other almshouse, St. John's.

This almshouse was originally a hospice for lepers. We know that it was already in existence in 1336, since it is mentioned in Hamo's charter, so that he was able to specifically exclude lepers from his own foundation. It could well have been on a spit of land projecting from the waterfront and thus isolating the lepers to some extent. But it now stands in the High Street, having undergone the same kind of Gothic facelift as Centuries, in the year 1802

It is not known when the last leper lived there. But certainly by the mid-sixteenth century its inhabitants had changed. In 1562 Archbishop Parker's visitor valued its revenues at only £6 a year, and stated that "there were kept daily and maintained eight beds for the needy and poor people and such as were maimed in the wars".

It is clear that the archbishop's visitor was not altogether happy about the way it was run. In 1573 he noted that it is "not used and ordered according to the foundation . . . the goods of the same almshouse is bestowed upon rogues and beggars contrary to laws". And as for St. Bartholomew's, "It is not used according to the foundation, for where the poor of that house should all saving one be of the town of Hith, such as have the order of that house do place therein foreigners for money and such as are able of themselves to live otherwise".

The numbers sheltered in the hospitals may seem small by today's standards. But they do show that some care was taken of the poor and destitute, since Hythe, itself, was also quite small. At the time of Queen Elizabeth's survey four years later, there were only 122 inhabited houses in the borough.

Another example of Hythe folk's care for their less fortunate brethren was the Fraternity of the Assumption of the Blessed Virgin Mary, one of the few charitable societies of the kind, whose records have survived from medieval times.

Though it was called a fraternity, both men and women were members, the numbers increasing from 22 in 1466 to 102 in 1471. They had an annual dinner of plain food, and provided wax for the candles that burned in front of the numerous images of the saints, which stood in the church in those days. Out of their annual subscriptions, they also paid for rushes to be strewn on the floor of the church, and for its interior decoration.

But there was, in addition, money to pay for the funerals of poor people and making loans to people in distress. For instance, there was one item—"lyyng yn Thomas Callo's hands iij li. vj s. iij d. of yower lady bredered"—which probably means, "£3 6s 3d of Our Lady Brotherhood lying in Thomas Callo's hands".

Unfortunately this excellent organisation had to be dissolved in 1532 at the Reformation. No doubt many of its members acted in the religious plays put on by the Hythe Players in those days, with themes such as the Passion and the Resurrection—themes which are still tackled today, from time to time, by the St. Leonard's Players.

In 1412, after the various disasters, there were only 134 ratepayers. According to the memoranda of receipts in the jurats' book for that year, there were 30 in the East Ward, 25 in the Middle Ward, 37 in the West Ward, 21 in Market Ward and only 8 in West Hythe. There were also 13 *advocantes,* who appear to have been relatively well-off people, living outside the town.

The numbers were only slightly higher for a "Cess on the whole Commonalty for the New Port and Navy for the service of our Lord King Henry in the 13th year", which would have been 1412 or 1413. There were 175 people, who were assessed according to the value of their possessions. They included 16 advocantes and 11 in West Hythe.

It is, therefore, interesting to see how this community of probably less than a thousand souls managed their affairs.

Every activity seems to have been quite carefully regulated since, in addition to the rates, the town received various dues, called *maltotes,* which included a sort of local income-tax, a value-added tax on sales, and fines for misdemeanours. Tailors, cobblers, braziers, smiths and wheelwrights had to pay a halfpenny a week to the Council, whilst coopers, curriers, water-carriers, tailorsmen and cobblersmen paid a farthing. Even a labourer had to pay a farthing a week for exercising his "art of labourer".

Thus,, when Thomas Marchal went to settle his account with the Council on January 20th, 1413, he was "charged 13½d maltote for his art of labourer. And 4d for a cow going over the Slip. Sum of this account 17½d. Thereafter he asks to be allowed for a Proclamation made throughout the town, 2d. And for carrying a barrel of ale, 1d. And so he owes a clear 14½d. He paid and is quit".

The "slip" is presumably the slipway for the boats, since we continually read of men being fined for allowing their livestock to stray on it. When we consider the sales tax, we find Thomas Clement making his account "in the Common Hall before the Jurats" on the same date in the previous year:

> He acknowledges for maltote 8d for woollen cloth sold this year, value £4. He also owes 3d for 6 quarters of malt sold, ½d for 2 quarters of barley, 1d for a heifer, 2d for 2 barrels of herrings, and 2½d for 4 shillings rent from letting.

Included in Henry Tropham's account, made in the Common Hall on the Sunday before the Feast of St. Luke the Evangelist, is the sum of 25 shillings for a dole of herrings. A dole was a part of the catch apportioned to a member of the crew of a fishing-boat. As he also paid 1d for 2 lasts of sprats and 3s 8d for 11 lasts of herrings, it appears that he was a regular fisherman, since a last was made up of ten barrels, each of which might contain 1,000 fish.

As the water was, in those days, generally unwholesome, the people of Hythe, like most folk in medieval times, drank a great deal of ale. They also drank beer long before the proverbial introduction of malt liquor in 1530, as in the proverb:

> *Hops and turkeys, carp and beer,*
> *Came into England all in a year.*

Thus, in 1413 we find the Council spending on bread and ale for the subsistence of people engaged in all sorts of activities. They spent 10d on men sent to *Boterbregge* (now called Botolph's Bridge) to choose men there to arbitrate in a dispute between the town and a certain Thomas Newman. 5d was spent on bread and ale in the house of William Condy, the bailiff, entertaining a Hollander, who had "come to see and make a new *slow* by the Hermitage", which was probably a sluice.

Then they spent 3d on ale "at the firing of the guns, when the Commonalty made a demonstration". Furthermore, we find certain breweresses being brought before the court for selling ale and beer before it is lawfully aged, and for breaking the assize and selling ale for 2d.

The bailiff frequently entertained with bread and ale. But the legal fraternity had, it seems, to be regaled with wine. In the accounts for 1419, we read of wine being given to a man named Gwodred "for his good counsel against the next session", to John Dreyland, and to Thomas Adam in Appledore, who was counsel in the tiresome dispute with Thomas Newman, a suit having been filed alleging encroachment by some men of Hythe, which was to be heard in London.

Sometimes, however, it was apparently better to warm someone's heart with plain cash. For instance, in 1413 Robert Long, the Lord Archbishop's messenger, was paid 20d "to carry a good report concerning this town". Then, in 1419, we find the Council paying sweeteners to the staff at Dover Castle—13s 4d to the steward "for his good counsel this year", 10s to the clerk of the exchequer at Dover "for his friendship" and 8d to the sub-clerk of Dover Castle.

It was all according to one's status in the hierarchy. The Lieutenant of the Castle often received gifts of fish, as in 1412, when he was given whiting, haddock and salt mackerel, costing 3s 11d in all, on his way through the town to Romney. But when a porpoise was caught, it was sent to the Archbishop of Canterbury on a horse.

The lieutenant also had to be entertained by the bailiff on his occasional visits to the town itself. In 1419 the civic breakfast cost 17s 11d, and the major item was horsemeat, provided by six different suppliers, including the host, William Condy.

Other items on the bill of fare were four capons, mutton and other meat, bread, and of course ale, most of it from the bailiff's own store, but some of it provided by an alewife named Juliana Maket, about 28 gallons in all. It was midsummer, and perhaps a really hot, thirsty day.

In addition to all these expenses, bearers of writs had to be paid, since the rule of payment on delivery made it much more likely that the letter would, in fact, be delivered. In 1413, 6d each was paid to the bearers of writs. One was for the arrest of a certain Peter Nappe, at the suit of the men of Folkestone. Another notified that Parliament would be held at Leicester, and another that all strangers should depart from the kingdom unless they had "safe conduct". A special 8d was paid to the king's messenger instructing the navy to put to sea.

About this time, soon after the leaders of the Hythe community had petitioned King Henry IV to move somewhere else and start afresh, the scourged port does, indeed, appear to have been in poor shape. The court records of 1409 tell of lanes being choked up and dung thrown haphazardly:

> The King's highway from the church of St. Nicholas, itself a ruin, to *Crowolle* is blocked up by overgrowing hedges, and the way from *Estflete* to the church of West Hythe is in a state of nuisance through default of repair. So are the roads near *Brokhull* and *Walteryswelle,* whilst the King's highway near the *Pype* is blocked by the overflow from William Canne's house.

It was the responsibility of the owners of the land through which the roads passed to keep them in good order, and they were presented to the court if they did not do so. The dumping of dung was always a problem before the advent of modern sewage pipes. So it need not surprise us that some people were presented for "throwing dung in the Delf" near the West Bridge, and others for dumping it in the King's highway in the lane near the North Steps.

But the throwing of dung into the Holy Well of the church-yard must surely have been an act of idiocy. At all events, it would appear that the problem of the town's sanitation had not been very well taken care of before 1473, when John Edwey left the sum of 3s 4d in his will "to making of one common latrine in the town".

We have to remember that it is only the misdemeanours that appear in the records of the Hundred Court. Neglect of land and property, petty theft and breaking the peace bring people to the court.

Thus, in 1428 the High Street near the church of St. Nicholas is "in a state of nuisance to the King's people, by reason of the want of cleansing of a gutter by John Skinner and John Prylle, on land near the pigeon house". And in 1427 Lettice Coltys is up before the court for breaking into the house and close of John Malyne Junior and stealing a skein of woollen thread, and Lettice Emota is in trouble for receiving it. Katherine Pecchinge and her daughter, Emota, are up for being "common scolds and brawlers, against the Statute proclaimed, and they often do this". Furthermore, the wives of Roger Carpenter and Thomas Burgeys spoil the water of *Jowet Pette,* with which all the neighbours there make their dinner.

The dykes are called *pettes.* In 1445 we read that the land is in a state of nuisance near *Pettispette* through neglect on the part of the widow of John Overhavene, and that the King's highway between the gate of Alexander Appelforde and the bridge called *Tukkeresbrygge* is "drowned" through default in cleansing the pits upon the land of the said Alexander. In 1427, by default of cleansing the pits in the land of the heirs of John Wolvyne, the lands of the Archbishop were "drowned".

The mentions of widows and heirs tell their own tales of decease. And with dykes blocked, streams have been diverted. The *Strodewelle* and the *Molendwelle* are both out of their courses in 1427, and in 1411 the watercourse running from *Shipweye* by *Perksyde,* from *Lyme* to *Westhethe,* was turned out of its right direction by default of Hamon Dene. Thirty-four years later, it is the stream called *Schepweywelle* that has been turned out of its course. But *Shipweye* and *Schepwey* are not necessarily the same place.

In fact, most of the lanes and springs mentioned in these record books are now lost to us, with some notable exceptions. Jury's Lane, Wheel Street, Butcher Street, Hog Lane, Pork Lane and Prison Lane are lost for ever. But Duck Lane was the old name of Bartholomew Street until the hospital moved there, and Pennypot is probably the place meant by *Bettispette* or *Pettispette.*

The records of the local court represent the small coin of the troubles of town and country life in the Middle Ages. But the evidence from the archives as a whole is that Hythe was a well-ordered community, with all the details of the town's life as a port and centre of local affairs constantly under the eyes of its various officials. There was a strong sense of the dignity and tradition of a borough, which bore a special relationship with the Sovereign, and there were to be great efforts to thwart the forces of nature that brought about the Haven's inevitable demise.

7

Port of Stranded Pride

As we have seen, the great days of Hythe as a Cinque Port were during the twelfth to fourteenth centuries. In the fifteenth and sixteenth centuries the port was in decline, and in the seventeenth century it no longer existed as a haven. The St. John's Hospital map, displayed in the Local History Room, does not even show a dent in the shore where the harbour used to be.

Precisely how this radical change in the coastline took place we do not know. But we do know what were the contributory factors. The assault on the waters of the haven, which ended up in their complete disappearance, was from both land and sea.

During the fourteenth century, West Hythe was still a limb of Hythe in the Cinque Ports organisation, and may still have had its own outlet to the sea. But in the sixteenth century the situation was quite different. Both the *Card of the Beacons* of 1570 and Symonson's map of 1596 show an arm of the sea going in a north-westerly direction from in front of the town. But this arm appears to be going up the Slaybrook in the deep chine where the London road now runs instead of towards West Hythe and Lympne. So we may probably conclude that, by then, the only contact West Hythe had with the sea was down the narrow, winding channel of the Willop Gut past Butler's Bridge to its outlet near Dymchurch.

The factors involved in filling up the old channel would be the silting up with earth brought down by the streams from the ragstone ridge, and the mysterious earthquakes, which are mentioned twice in Hythe's history. In fact, it is probable that the earthquake of 1380, which shook Saltwood Castle, and the well documented one of 1580, which again damaged the castle and made the bells of St. Leonard's Church ring, were not

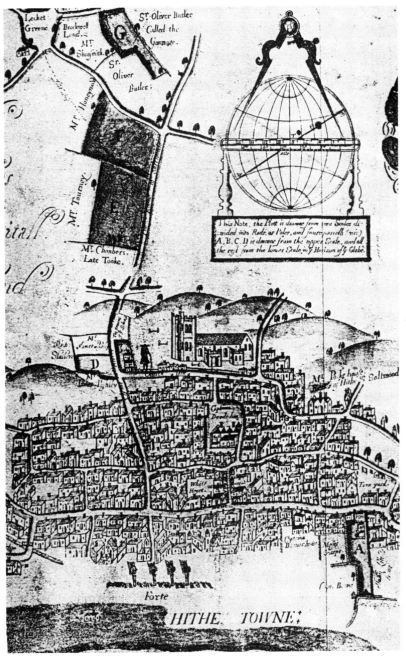

Part of Hill's St. John's Hospital map of 1684

true earthquakes of deep seismological origin, but local land-slips.

The sixteenth century farmhouse a mile to the west of Lympne, known as the French house because of its magnificent view across the Channel to the other side, was the victim of one such landslip in 1726. This splendid timber building was originally built on the top of the cliff. But one night it slipped down fifty feet so gently that, according to Hasted, the farmer who lived there, and his family knew nothing about it until they woke up next morning and looked outside.

Such landslips, large and small, to which the geological formations known as the Hythe beds are particularly prone and of which the uneven slopes of the sheep pastures above the Military Canal provide ample evidence, even allowing for the quarrying that has taken place there in the past, would be enough, over the years, to fill the shipping fairway from the landward side. A simultaneous attack came from the sea. The great shingle bank, on which the military ranges are now located, was steadily building up eastwards with the prevailing current and winds, thus tending to block the harbour mouth.

The Symonson map shows two islands in the harbour, and a long arm of the sea extending between the shingle bank on the eastward side of the entrance and the cliffs as far as Seabrook. This is what Leland calls the "large mile".

> The haven is a prety rode and liith meatly strayt for passage owt of Boleyn. Yt croketh yn so by the shore a long, and is so bakked fro the mayn se with casting of shinggil, that smaul shippes may cum up a large myle toward Folkestan as yn a sure gut.

Which being interpreted reads:

> The haven is a pretty harbour and lies nicely opposite for passage out of Boulogne. It curves in along the shore and is so protected from the open sea by banked up shingle that small ships can go a sea mile towards Folkestone in a safe channel.

The name of the Seaway cottages at the eastern end of Mill Lane was, no doubt, a memory of this time, and gardeners living in any of the houses on Seabrook Road will tell you that they do not have to dig far before reaching shingle.

However, the exact line the foreshore took in front of the town is by no means clear. At an early date it was probably broken by a number of creeks besides the two major indentations of the Slay and Salt brooks. Digging for drainage works anywhere along the line of the High Street produces shingle at no great depth, and it is a tradition in the town that the curiously indented square stone that stands embedded in the ground outside Centuries was once a mooring-post. At that time Bartholomew Street, formerly known as Duck Lane and continuing along Dental Street, could have been the waterfront road. The actual entrance to the haven, at any rate during the later stages of its life, would have been between Stade Street to the west and Twiss Road to the east. The stade at the end of Stade Street was, itself, the landing-place after the interior of the haven had become too shallow for ships to enter.

The good people of Hythe were very upset at the way their harbour was vanishing before their eyes, and did all they could to prevent it wasting away. In the year 1287, the last of the violent storms of the thirteenth century banked up the shingle to such an extent that the mouth of the harbour was nearly closed, and the seaway was only kept open with difficulty. Dumping of ballast from ships in the harbour may also have contributed to the problem.

So, in the year 1412, after King Henry IV had refused the petition of the people of Hythe to move elsewhere, following their triple disaster of fire, pestilence and shipwreck, the barons made a last determined effort to keep enough water in the haven for it to be serviceable. A Hollander was hired to make a survey, and the whole population was put to work digging for four days. There were fines of fourpence a day for those who shirked it.

The records show that John Lucas was paid 3s 4d per rod for digging 19 rods in the new harbour, 1s 8d a rod for 106 rods from the haven to *Estbregge,* and 12d a rod for 380 rods from the Hermitage to West Hythe. He was presumably the principal contractor. The Council also spent 2s 5d on bread for the workmen and 9s 3d on ale, which comes to no less than 74 gallons at the set price of 1½d a gallon. 7d was paid for carrying the ale to the work sites.

A rod, pole or perch was equal to five and a half yards. So the distance cut from the Hermitage, which was situated to the west of the town, to West Hythe was over a mile, and from the haven to the East Bridge one third of a mile. The long stretch to West Hythe is likely to have been a channel to link up with the waters of the marsh, which would thus flow into the harbour at low tide and help to keep it scoured out. This would account for the fact that the contractor was paid less per rod for it than for the work in the harbour itself, where a deeper, wider excavation would be necessary.

One, Stephen Marshe, was paid 6s 8d for digging between the two bridges, which must mean in front of the town. But where was the new harbour? The maps already mentioned show that the actual mouth of the harbour was where Leland said the haven "crooked in", at the eastern rather than the western end of the town—the end served by the Bell Inn. One of the sixteenth century maps shows the outline of the harbour actually in the shape of a shepherd's crook, forming a sort of S bend before going off eastwards up the "large mile" towards Seabrook.

At all events, the opening of the new harbour was definitely considered to be a noteworthy occasion by the townsfolk. We are told that at least eighteen gallons of ale, provided by the Council, were consumed during the celebrations.

It is probably to this time that belongs the third of the old seals of the town that have come down to us. The fact that the Cinque Ports were free of customs duty did not make it unnecessary to have an officer to control the comings and goings in the harbour. There had to be a Portreeve or "harbour magistrate" to carry out the duties of harbourmaster and customs officer.

The seal of Hythe's portreeve is unique amongst the Cinque Ports, and was discovered in unusual circumstances in 1868. A workman was digging in the main road of Goudhurst, when he discovered the small object, 1½ inches high, at the level of the original turnpike road about three feet below the surface. It bears the demi-lion and demi-ship of the Cinque Ports, surmounted by a crown and surrounded by little crosses, together with the inscription *Sigillum Custum de Hethe*.

This seal was acquired by Sir Edward Watkin, Hythe's

M.P. from 1874 to 1895, and presented by him to the town. Today, a replica of its impression forms part of the mayor's chain, which was put together piece by piece during the late nineteenth and early twentieth centuries, and is a permanent reminder of the great days of Hythe's activity as a port.

The central link of this chain is a golden falcon, presented in 1872 by H. B. Mackeson, who was mayor for nine years and a member of the Hythe brewing family that has been known in the town for three hundred years. On either side of it are the Cinque Ports coats of arms, which he presented in 1877 and 1878, linked to it by two white horses of Kent, with the motto *Invicta,* which he added in 1873 and 1874.

The large pendant medallion on the chain, bearing a replica of the same ship as is shown on the Common Seal, was presented by Watkin in 1879. The words *Burgus et Portus de Hythe* mean Town and Port of Hythe. A final large medallion of a Cinque Ports ship was added by William Cobay, who was mayor throughout the First World War, in 1919.

However, in the long run the effort to restore the harbour was to no avail. Hythe dwindled as the harbour dried out. Camden, writing the Kent section of his *Britannia* in 1586, says ". . . its name signifies a port or station: though at present it can hardly maintain that name against the heaps of sand which shut out the sea for a great way".

As a result of all this, when King Charles I called for Ship Money in 1636 for the second time, Hythe was assessed for only £40 out of the total £8,000 that the towns of Kent were expected to raise, whereas New Romney and Old Romney had to pay £180 each, Sandwich £250 and Dover £330. By this time it was indeed, to quote the words of Rudyard Kipling, one of "our ports of stranded pride":

> *And east till doubling Rother crawls*
> *To meet the fickle tide*
> *By dry and sea-forgotten walls,*
> *Our ports of stranded pride.*

At this time, in the middle of the seventeenth century, more land was inned from the dried-out harbour. It was town land, which was then leased by the Corporation to individuals, though the first inning that we know of was done in the previous century by John Knight. The year was 1555, and it was called Knight's Innings.

Then, in 1651, the Corporation leased five acres of land, known as the New Innings, to the mayor, Austen Greenland. In 1664, two acres of the harbour were leased to a man named John Matson, from Dover, which he was to "in" himself and enclose out of the 500 acres of salt and beach lands belonging to the town. But the rights were reserved there for the townsmen to catch shrimps and lobsters, and for ships to land goods on the beach.

At the same time, a final effort was made to maintain some sort of a harbour at Hythe. In 1654 it was resolved that "This Assembly taking into consideration the general decay of this town in the want of hade (sic) whereby it is much impoverished, and that the apparent ground or cause hereof is by reason of the swarming up of the Haven or harbour belonging to this Town, Have ordered and decreed that the haven shall be cut out with all convenient speed".

Contributions were pledged by the mayor and members of the Corporation, and Edward Beane agreed to contribute ten shillings more than any other fisherman, except for Elias Bassett and John Cheeseman, and was consequently admitted a freeman. The Corporation also appointed six surveyors from amongst their number, and agreed to borrow £100 on the security of the town lands to buy timber for a sluice gate. In 1656 the mayor went to London to ask the Lord Protector for a contribution.

The result was probably what was called the Channel of the Hoy. We read that, in 1677, John Terry got a lease from the Corporation of "outlands along the main channel of the Hoy" and in 1686 John Lambert was leased outlands and beach land from the Hoy and the Stade towards Romney Marsh.

Thus, leasing of both the old and the new innings continued. The Stade, or beach landing-place, is often mentioned, and was probably located at the end of Stade Street, where a slipway still exists. There was a mark-post at the Old Stade, for in 1698 a fisherman, named Thomas Chapman, took a lease on "the land and gravel grounds" 320 rods in length, extending eastwards from this point, which he could use as a landing-place and where he had the fishing rights. But the mark-post had gone by 1716, for in that year John Ramsay got beach land lying from Sir William Honeywood's wall eastwards to where "the old mark post of the Stade formerly stood".

One rather strange lease, at this time, was drawn up in 1709. Ralph Hutton, a tailor, received no less than a mile of beach from high-water mark to low-water mark westward to the limit of the town liberty for fifteen years at fifteen shillings a year. One wonders what he did with an area that is usually thought of as belonging to the public and where the townsmen's rights were still reserved.

By 1784 there was no alternative for ships but to come up to the beach. Kenneth and Jacob Spicer owned hoys, and they had to pay twenty shillings a year for the use of the town anchor, whilst colliers and other vessels had to pay half-a-crown each time they lay on the shore. What is more, this beach was a mile from the town, though the Stade is only about a third of a mile from the High Street. It seems, therefore, that the last channel was the remains of Leland's "large mile" and had its outlet at Seabrook, where the sluice gate of the Military Canal is now located. Certainly Stockdale's map of 1805 has "Hithe Haven" marked at Seabrook at a time when there was a weekly hoy from London calling at Hythe.

In the sixteenth century, although her importance as a Cinque Port had diminished, Hythe was still a trading port, as the Customs Port books of that time show. Apart from other items, there appears to have been a thriving export trade in horses to France. In Henry VIII's time Hythe was victualling the garrison at Calais, and the passenger traffic continued.

But during the following century, this commercial traffic faded. However, the old occupation of the majority of the population continued. This, of course, was fishing. In the 1566 census of shipping it was recorded that 160 of the occupants of Hythe's 122 houses were engaged in this occupation in one way or another.

The whole business, or industry as we would call it today, was organised systematically, and the year was divided up into fishing "fares" or seasons. In the Shotnet season, from April to June, the medium-sized boats like the undecked, square-rigged, single-masted shotters of around 15 tons, went to sea in the Channel to catch mackerel. This was followed by the Skarborow fare from June to September, when the bigger crayers of 30 to 40 tons went deep-sea fishing for cod off Scarborough.

Back in 1412 John Leghe is recorded as having paid local customs dues on five lasts of herrings of *Shardeburgh fayre*. But the main centre for the North Sea herring fishery was Yarmouth. The *Yarmothe* fare lasted from September to November. So it was possible for the same ships to take part in both fares in a single voyage lasting nearly half the year. The typical crayers were clinker-built, with a raised deck or cabin astern, and they did duty as passenger and merchant ships as well, if necessary.

The fish caught on the deep-sea voyages were salted to preserve them. But there was also an overland trade in fresh fish even in the days of rough travel before the turnpike roads were brought into use. Indeed, some of the fish consumed in London was supplied from Hythe. The rippiers carried it via Ashford on pack horses, and speed was of the essence.

The main season for the small tramellers of 5 tons or so was the Tucknet fare from February to April, when they went out for plaice and sprats. These and the shotters were the Stade boats, hauled up the beach by means of capstans, as the fishing boats are today, except that the capstans have been replaced by an electric winch. Many of the wills of the Elizabethan period refer to *vernes* or capstans, and *lodges* on the stade. There was also a certain William Rust, who had seven "sea horses", which were no doubt used to turn the capstans.

A boat, or a share of one, was the most valuable item bequeathed in a good number of these wills. Usually two or three people shared the cost of a new boat, and it is clear from the reference to "the house where the shipwright dwells" that some of them were built locally. On the other hand, in 1487 John Clarke bequeathed his share of a boat that had been built in Normandy. This was in spite of continual quarrels with the folk on the other side of the Channel over fishing rights as well as political disputes.

Thus the fishing continued even after the harbour had become blocked up. The boats were launched on the tide down the shingle beach, and returned on the tide, as they still do. And today the conflict of interest with the men across the water is as acute as it ever was. So long as the twelve mile limit remains uninvoked, and the foreigners from Belgium and France, and from up North come into the Channel with their large beam trawlers, scraping off the sea bed everything that moves, it will continue to be so.

One of the old gravestones in St. Leonard's churchyard has an endearing epitaph to the fishermen engraved on it:

> His net old fisher George long drew,
> Shoals upon shoals he caught;
> Till Death came hauling for his due,
> And made poor George his draught.
> Death fishes on through various shapes,
> In vain it is to fret;
> Nor fish nor fisherman escapes
> Death's all enclosing net.

It is a fitting epitaph to the decline of local fishing as well. Nowadays there are only three or four fishing smacks in regular commission, supplying local needs through the Griggs family, plus half a dozen smaller craft, all registered in Folkestone. It is nothing compared with the armada that puts to sea from Boulogne all the year round. Blackman, the other Hythe fishmonger, fishes from Dungeness.

In the meantime, the old privileges were dying too. In 1575 Queen Elizabeth I granted the town a new charter. It was to have a Mayor, elected by the people, instead of a Bailiff, and a Corporation with the right to own land and hold a fair. These three concessions are recorded for posterity on the brass plaque fixed to the wall near the south door of the church above the grave of John Bredgman, who was last bailiff and the first mayor:

> *Whylst he did live which heare doth lie,*
> *three sutes gatt of ye Crowne,*
> *The mortmaine, fayer and mayraltie,*
> *for Heythe, this auntient towne.*
> *And was him self the Baylye last,*
> *and Mayer fyrste by name.*
> *Though he be gone, tyme is not paste*
> *to preayse God for ye same.*

From the date of this charter up to the time of the Municipal Act of 1836 the Corporation under the Mayor consisted of twelve Jurats and twenty-four Commoners, or common councillors. The mayor was chief magistrate with jurisdiction exclusive of the county justices, and he was also President of the Court of Session, convened to try all kinds of offences. The jurats were also magistrates with similar jurisdiction and assisted at the Sessions. They were, therefore, something akin to a jury in function as well as in name. A Court of Record was also appointed, but it fell into disuse in 1777.

As well as the principal officers, the Corporation was allowed two chamberlains, two sergeants, a billet-master, two key-keepers, a gamekeeper, a pound-keeper with two assistants, a hog-driver, a gaoler and a town-crier. We do not know where the hogs were driven, but Pound Cottage, a few yards down Seabrook Road on the left-hand side, indicates the location of a pound at some stage in Hythe's history.

It may appear that the town was doing well out of all this. But in fact, Queen Elizabeth was simply bringing Hythe into line with other towns without its special rights and privileges as a Cinque Port. In 1587 she announced that she did not "meane to suffer them (the Cinque Ports) in suche fruitless manner to enjoye so great privileges without doing any service, but to resume them into Her Majesty's hands and to reduce them to the same terms that the rest of her subjects bordering upon the sea are in".

As is well known, the queen made it her business to travel extensively in her realm, and there are many houses which boast that "Queen Elizabeth slept here". As for Hythe, we can at least say that Queen Elizabeth possibly passed through here. It was in 1573 that she decided to visit Kent, with a baggage train of no less than four hundred "caravans", some of them drawn by six horses.

She left Westenhanger on August 25th and dined that day at Sandgate Castle, which had been built by her father, King Henry VIII. This means that she may have come down through Saltwood, since from Sandgate she went up to Folkestone Down, where she received several hundred men of Kent. Lord Burghley commented that the way was so rough and steep that it was as dangerous as the Peak in Derbyshire, and that the baggage train was so long that the rear of it was still toiling up Folkestone Hill as the queen entered Dover.

A few years later, it was probably with a sense of the enhanced dignity of the town that Thomas Torney presented the moot horn to the Corporation in 1582. He was the great grandson of the Tournay who had come south from Lincolnshire in 1498.

This horn mysteriously disappeared for some years in the nineteenth century until it was fortunately identified in an antique dealer's shop and recovered for the town. It now hangs below the Cinque Ports shield in the council chamber of the Town Hall. Made of brass, it has a zone of ornament on it, which includes the date, written as 158Z, the name of Thomas Torney in capitals, and a quartered shield incorporating the coat of arms of the Torneys (three bulls) repeated, that of the Sellinges, who had set the family up at Brockhill (three wolves' heads), and that of the Brockhills of Saltwood (a cross dividing four groups of three crosses).

It was the custom to blow the horn on the admission of the freemen to the Assembly, when voting was to take place, new freemen having paid 15 pence for admission. And it is still blown nowadays on ceremonial occasions, Wakefield Day in 1957 being an example. More recently it was blown in 1975 on the 400th anniversary of the granting of the charter of Queen Elizabeth I.

That the horn was not merely a symbolic object is corroborated from some of the old records. For instance, in the account of Edward Baker, who doubled as town sergeant, and pound-keeper in the year between the candlemasses of 1763 and 1764, we read that his fee "for blowing the horn" was one shilling. As town sergeant, he looked after the gaolbirds as well as the animals impounded on the Green, and charged a pound "for looking after the prison", six shillings "for emptying the prison tub three times" and one shilling "for whipping Henry Turrell".

The first mayor had been a member of parliament some years earlier. So he was clearly an important public servant of the borough. As far as Parliament was concerned, he was heir to a tradition that was already lengthy, because Hythe can fairly claim to have been one of the first towns in England to send representatives.

As we know, representative parliamentary democracy began in England after King John had signed Magna Carta, the basis on which the clever Frenchman, Simon de Montfort, was able to summon Parliament after his victory over his brother-in-law, King Henry III, at Lewes in 1264. In the warring between the king and the barons the Cinque Ports had sided with the barons, thus backing Simon. Indeed, the battle at Lewes, in which the barons had been supported by 15,000 Londoners, had been mainly to save the Cinque Ports from the king's wrath.

Therefore, after the king had been taken prisoner, and his son, Prince Edward, had surrendered, de Montfort sent a writ to each of the Cinque Ports to call together his first parliament in 1265, saying:

> We greatly need your presence and we command you by the faith and affection with which you are bound to us, putting all other things aside, you do send us four of the most lawful and discreet men of your port.

In the same year, Simon was killed and the barons were defeated at the battle of Evesham. So the Cinque Ports were badly placed, having supported the losing side. They had to make their submission to Prince Edward, who was then Lord Warden, and were not invited to send members to Parliament again until 1322, after they had somewhat redeemed their position by sending men to the wars in Wales and Scotland. This time, Parliament was to be at York, and the writ said:

> We command you, firmly enjoining, that from each of the Ports, you shall cause two Barons of the most discreet and best able to travel, to be elected.

A later writ for another parliament said that the barons were "to be conversant with naval affairs and dealing with merchandise". And another, in 1342, directed that "two of the best and most discreet mariners of each Port be returned to give their advice to the King's Council". By this time there was no need for the electors to limit their choice of M.P.s to those capable of travelling long distances, since from 1338 all parliaments had met at Westminster.

But Hythe paid its M.P.s and kept a careful record of them. In 1411 Henry Philpot, a woollen cloth merchant and already a jurat, was paid 53s 4d for attending Parliament for thirty-two days, and eight years later John Skinner, who had been a member of parliament at the same time as Philpot and also a jurat, received 44s 8d for carrying out his parliamentary duties, together with his expenses in entertaining the Lieutenant of Dover Castle to breakfast, itemised as 15d for six rabbits, 12d for two capons and 9½d for ale. In 1446 the M.P.s were Nicholas Brockhill of the old Saltwood family, son of the Sheriff of Kent, and John Honeywood, who was also bailiff.

In those days voters were few, and the ballot was not secret. Indeed, it could at times be very dangerous to show one's true belief. Amongst the "noble martyrs" of Kent, who were burnt at the stake during the pogrom of Protestant activists in Queen Mary's reign, four from Hythe are listed on the memorial at Canterbury. They were George Catmer and Robert Streater, who were killed in 1556, George's widow, Joan, who was burnt the following year, and William Hay, who also lost his life in 1557. According to witnesses, Joan presented such a sweet and beautiful appearance, that those who fed the flames turned aside their heads and wept.

Only landowners of a certain substance were eligible for the voting register, and sometimes there were no more than fifty men in the electorate. In these circumstances it was not difficult for a powerful man to influence the result, and after the town had exchanged its bailiff for a mayor and corporation under Queen Elizabeth's charter, it became common for one of the M.P.s to be nominated from above.

Thus, in 1584, we have Sir Francis Cobham writing from Cobham Hall to the Mayor, Jurats and Commons of the Town and Port of Hythe and telling them to choose Sir Thomas Bodley, the founder of the Bodleian library in Oxford University:

> I commend me unto you. According to my speeches uttered unto you, Mr. Mayor, and to one of your Jurats at your late being with me, I have now received answer from the Court, whereby I am required to recommend unto you Thomas Bodley to be chosen by you for a burgess to the Parliament with some other person of

your own town, whom you shall know to be sufficient for the place, and namely well affected in religion and towards the present state of this governemnt. Wherein I would wish that good consideration should be had of the man, who shall be so elected, for the party whom I am willed to nominate, besides the commendation which is delivered unto me of him, I am persuaded that he is such a one as may and will be ready to pleasure you and your town, and of that credit as may stand you in stead. So fare ye heartily well.

But John Collins, who was a "burgess" of Parliament as well as being mayor in 1588 and 1589, and again in 1595, was one of the local men. He had the distinction of being commemorated by Epiphanius Evesham, a noted engraver of his day. As the plaque in the St. Katherine's Chapel of the parish church tells us, he had two wives and children from each, and he had been appointed mayor for the fourth time when he died at the end of 1597, aged only forty.

In the following century the patronage of the Lord Warden of the Cinque Ports was the understood thing. We have a letter to the town of Hythe written in 1625 by the influential Duke of Buckingham, who was then Lord Warden. Modernising the spelling, it reads like this:

I shall be very ready to preserve and increase the privileges of the Cinque Ports, so I am unwilling to let pass the remembrance of those respects by my predecessors, which makes me at this time to recommend unto you to serve in the first place as Burgess for your Town in this next Parliament, Sir Richard Weston Kt, Chancellor of the Exchequer; his office enables him with power on all occasions to effect the good of your Town. By your free and cheerful embracement of my desire herein, I shall be able to judge of the measure of your love and esteem for me, and accordingly be ready to requite it when occasion shall be offered. And so I rest your very loving Friend.

Thus candidates sought election who had no previous connection with the town at all, as is the case in modern times. On the other hand, the townsfolk might feel that they had the advantage of a man of influence representing their interests. As another of Buckingham's nominees wrote:

In respect I am a mere stranger to you all, and thus deserve nothing from you, if it please you to favour me in this my desire your courtesy is the greater, and engages me so much the more to endeavour by all the good means I can to do something that may be advantageous and profitable for that Town in general, and to every one of you in particular.

Certainly electioneering promises are nothing new. But clearly there were some people who were not bothered by a life of stress and lived to a ripe old age. According to his epitaph, Captain John Ward, whose black tilting helmet, crowned with a leopard, is fixed above the doorway in the west wall of St. Edmund's Chapel in the church, lived to be ninety-six before expiring in the year 1601.

8

People, Pirates and Politics

IF the Borough of Hythe was thought to be in Buckingham's pocket in 1625, the first year of Charles I's reign, this was certainly not so during the Civil War, which broke out less than twenty years later, after the arguments about Ship Money and other grievances. Although Royalist Kent rose up to fight for the King in 1640, in the Bishops' War, by 1643 the whole of the south-east was held by the rebels.

In 1648 country Kent rose again, and after presenting the Kent Petition to no effect, stormed Maidstone. Their leader was William Brockman of Beachborough near Hythe, who was a stout Cavalier and devoted supporter of the Royalists. But he and his eight hundred men were ousted by Fairfax on June 1st, and the final success of the Roundheads was not long delayed.

It seems, for Hythe, to have come none too soon, since the town's picture of *The Burial of Charles I* is dated 1648, whereas he was not, in fact, executed until the following year. However, the apparent anomaly is explained when we recall that the king was executed on January 30th, asking for another shirt lest the spectators should think he was shivering from fear rather than from the cold, and that, in those days, the year began on April 1st.

Cromwell's forces considered themselves to be fighting for God as well as for Man and, though never a walled town, Hythe had its own defences at this time. When it was still an active port there had been cannons, probably positioned at the eastern end of the town to command the harbour entrance.

We read in the jurats' accounts for 1413 that the town paid that year for eighteen cannonballs, called *gonnestonnys,* eighteen gun *tampones,* which plugged the barrels, five gun *touches,* which were the fuses, and other items of equipment. Nine of the stone balls were made by William Scriveyn for 13d, and the other nine by a woman, named Isolda Cleokes, who only received 5d.

These warlike stores may have been prepared because the king was about to go campaigning in France, and the town armament may have fallen into disuse after Henry VIII had built Sandgate Castle. But in the seventeenth century there was a gun battery on a platform in front of the town, which is recalled in the name of Mount Street, once known as Library Lane.

The St. John's Hospital map shows four guns in the "forte". Later, according to Hasted, there were six. The remains of the mounting for one of them were discovered during the construction of the building at the corner of Prospect Road, which became the Hythe Institute. The arc of gun metal on which it traversed was found deep in the ground.

At this time, the invasion scare was from the Dutch. When Admiral Blake was appointed to the wardenship of the Cinque Ports in 1651, he began to demand salutes from all vessels passing up and down the Channel. The Dutch refused to comply, and the following year, under Admiral Van Tromp, they challenged the British fleet to battle. The contestants met off Dungeness on November 30th, and Van Tromp, having mustered seventy-five ships, was able to trounce Blake, who had only half that number. He then fixed a broom to his masthead and swept the Channel in triumph.

But next year, 1653, Blake's fleet put to sea again with new heart, and this time, in a running fight in the Channel, which lasted for three days, they were able to defeat the Dutchmen. So Hythe's guns never had to fire in anger.

Blake then went on to trounce the Spaniards as well. After that, our Lord Warden led the first British fleet ever to enter the Mediterranean, for, in 1654, the government of the Commonwealth despatched him to exact reparations from the Moorish pirates. This he did with his usual vigour, by attacking their lairs on the coast of North Africa. Algiers submitted, and after being submitted to a bombardment, Tunis did the same. We are thus reminded of some rather surprising alarms and excursions at a time when the stranded port had become, perhaps, a backwater in the metaphorical sense as well as being left high and dry.

At the turn of the century, the nest of pirates at Dunkirk had been the main menace to English shipping in the Channel. We read in the minutes of the meeting of the Court of Brotherhood and Guestling of October 5th, 1596 that six of the Cinque Ports and their limbs agreed to find one ship each to fight this threat to their lawful occasions. Hythe's ship was to be a 60 tonner, carrying an armament of 3 *mynions* and 4 *falkons,* 5 hundredweight of powder and 20 pieces of shot of all kinds for each gun.

Now, in the seventeenth century, the Barbary pirates from the Moroccan and Algerian coasts had become bold enough to actually sail into English waters. At times they raided the coast, as the Vikings had done centuries before. But more often these Corsairs seized ships at sea and sold their crews and passengers into slavery. In the ten years between 1609 and 1619 over four hundred and fifty English ships were taken in this way.

This is the background against which a deed was drawn up in the reign of James I between the Barons of Dover and Hythe, under which they agreed to provide a warship to fight the pirates from Algiers, who were infesting the English Channel and capturing British subjects. It was also the reason for Charles I's insistent demands for Ship Money, which were constantly resisted as examples of royal tyranny.

After Admiral Blake's expedition, the Corsairs resumed their kidnapping expeditions, for in 1670, in the reign of Charles II, there was a proclamation to be read out in church, describing the sufferings of people captured by those who:

Sold their captives like beasts in the market, made them work in chains, beat them constantly upon the soles of their feet, and made their lives worse than death, and attempted to make them renounce their Christian faith.

The congregation was urged to contribute to the ransom of these unfortunate people. For, as Samuel Pepys, Secretary for the Navy, had complained in his diary, there was never enough money.

By this time there was a new element in Kent life, provided by the Huguenot refugees from the Catholic kings of France. After the St. Bartholomew's Day massacre in Paris in 1572, and after their defeats in the France of Cardinal Richelieu in the early seventeenth century, and later on, when Louis XIV had revoked the Edict of Nantes, Huguenot refugees came into England in considerable numbers. They brought their skills at weaving and lace-making with them, as well as wits sharpened by the need to survive in a new environment.

It has been said that the name of Dental Street, running into Bartholomew Street behind the High Street, is derived from the French *dentelle,* meaning "lace". There was a spring or stream hereabouts, called the Denthalle water, that could have served the lace-makers' needs. But since it is recorded by that name in the Presentment of the Hundred Roll of Hythe for 1408, the ninth year of Henry IV's reign, it predates the Huguenot boat people by a considerable period of time.

Perhaps it was weavers rather than lace-makers who used the spring. In the records we find that Henry Matlow had to pay tax on 800 ells, or about 1,000 yards, of woollen cloth and 500 ells of linen, which were woven in 1412, and we know that Edward III made strenuous efforts to get Flemish weavers to settle in the country in the fourteenth century, when he banned the export of wool.

The period after the Restoration, when the religious tolerance promoted by Charles II was followed by the supremacy of Parliament under the Dutch and German kings, was also the period during which a limited number of local families established their continuing influence over the stranded Cinque Port. The names of Deedes of the Manor House, and from 1800 of Sandling Park, of Boteler of Saltwood Castle, of Brockman of Beachborough, and of Hales, figure repeatedly in the records of the town's assemblies, as well as the Tourneys, who have already been mentioned.

Members of the Deedes family were twenty-two times mayor of Hythe between 1640 and 1795. The Manor House is described as "Captain Deedes' House" on the St. John's Hospital map of 1684, and the oldest part of it was built about thirty years earlier, in 1658, though it is clear that the actual site was inhabited long before that, since part of a Norman wall had been discovered inside it. It was known as St. Leonard's House, appropriately enough, since it stands facing the church only a few yards down the steep hill. At the end of the eighteenth century, it had a facelift, which gives it a Georgian appearance, and in fact, one of the bricks of the similarly styled adjoining building, which was once the vicarage, bears the date 1785.

John Deedes, who built the house for his family, was Captain of the Trained Band of Hythe volunteers, who were paid to muster by the Council, and then Major of the divisional organisation. He was also "Baron" in Parliament three times and Mayor three times before his death, aged fifty-eight, in 1692. A plaque in his memory was placed behind the pulpit in St. Leonard's Church.

At this time, members of parliament were still elected annually, and voters were few, frequently not more than a couple of dozen. For instance, in August 1679 Captain Edward Hales was returned by twenty voters, consisting of the mayor, four jurats, five commoners and ten freemen, and the freemen were not necessarily residents of Hythe.

Hales was Lieutenant of Dover Castle and son of the Edward Hales, who had been prominent in presenting the Kent Petition of 1648. It was therefore apt that the father should have been one of the first M.P.s after the restoration. But he was a Catholic, and when he was granted a colonelcy in the infantry, he became liable to a penalty of £500 under the Test Act for holding an official position.

When James II came to the throne, it was arranged that his coachman, Godden, should sue him for this penalty, and judgement was obtained against him. Thereupon he pleaded special dispensation under the Great Seal, and a judge of the King's Bench found in his favour, giving it as his opinion that the king could dispense with such penal laws in certain cases, and overturning the judgement of the assizes.

His son of the same name was close to James II, who wanted to restore Catholicism in England, and was identified with him when he fled the country. But he was caught and thrown into Maidstone gaol. He remained there and in the Tower of London for eighteen months before being allowed to go into exile and join the ousted king in France.

In March 1689, Sir Philip Boteler and William Brockman were returned by only sixteen voters, comprising the mayor, five jurats, six commoners and four freemen. Four years

The Manor House

before this, in 1685, Julius Deedes had been elected by only twenty-three voters. But his election was declared void by the House of Commons since, being mayor, he had voted for himself. As he had already surrendered the office of mayor on being elected a member of parliament, he found himself out of both offices. But he was returned again without fail the following year.

The narrow voting base was further restricted by the fact that the Lord Warden of the Cinque Ports considered that he had the right to nominate, personally, one of the two barons to serve in Parliament. But objections to this were vindicated by an Act of Parliament of 1689, which specifically withdrew the patronage.

After this, votes appeared to have greater value in the eyes of the public, with the consequence that it was not unknown for them to be treated for. In 1710, the mayor was Henry Deedes. The members elected were Lord Shannon, Lieutenant of Dover Castle, and the Honourable John Fane, who later became seventh Earl of Westmorland, served under Marlborough, reached the rank of Lieutenant-General, and was appointed Chancellor of Oxford University. Lord Shannon was not even present at the election, nor had he been sworn in as a freeman of the borough. So it was decided to send a commission to him to administer the oath, if he did not turn up within a month.

The local men, John Boteler, brother of Sir Philip, and William Berners, who were runners up in the election, objected strongly, claiming that there had been manifold irregularities. They petitioned Parliament, saying that some of the voters, who were entitled to be freemen, had been refused the right, and others had not received the sacrament or paid Church poor rates in Hythe.

Furthermore, they claimed that there had been irregular soliciting for votes, including treating and bribery. The mayor, they said, had not only gone out with his staff—or in other words in his official capacity—from house to house soliciting votes for the sitting members, he had also treated the whole Corporation to a dinner, costing forty pounds, five days before the election, at which he had solicited votes. There had also been other treats, mostly attended by a certain Colonel Marsh, who had subsequently stood on the steps of the church, soliciting voters on their way up to vote.

It was not all one-sided, however. During the subsequent enquiry one witness said that he had been promised an interest-free loan of twenty or thirty pounds for two or three years, and another that he had been offered one or two of the best bullocks on Romney Marsh, to vote for Boteler.

The upshot of all this was that the noble lord and the young honourable were unseated. But Berners died within two years, and Lord Shannon was again returned in 1712. Some years later, one, Henry Stoakes, was foolish enough to write in a letter that he was prepared to sell his own, his father's and his elder brother's votes, and was removed from his office as a jurat in consequence.

In 1713 Jacob des Bouverie, one of the Huguenot family that had immigrated from Flanders in the sixteenth century, was returned with Boteler. He had prospered as a Turkey merchant and obtained the manor of the Earl of Folkestone, and was an ancestor of the Earl of Radnor, whose name is still well-known in the nearby seaside town today.

It was the year in which James Butler, second Duke of Ormonde and hereditary Butler of Ireland, was appointed Lord Warden after a distinguished career in the War of the Spanish Succession, first as Queen Anne's Commander-in-Chief and then as Captain-General. The destruction of the French and Spanish fleets at Vigo Bay was his doing. Yet, on the accession of George I in 1714, he was attainted as a traitor, and spent the rest of his life in exile in Spain.

Of course, it is as well to remember that such wars cannot be prosecuted without money. In 1702, the first year of Anne's reign, Parliament passed an Act "for Granting to Her Majesty a Land-Tax for carrying on the War against France and Spain". For "the Town and Port of Hith and West Hith within the Liberty of the said Town and Port" the contribution was set at £246 2s. This compares well with Folkestone, which was only required to pay £144 19s, and is about the same as New Romney at £249 17s, but very much less than Dover at £1,923 13s 9d.

In those days M.P.s were expected to do something practical for the town as well as protecting its interests at Westminster. The old East Bridge once bore an inscription to say that it had been built at the expense of "Hercules Baker Esq., one of the Barons in Parliament of this Port, in the year 1728". Thirteen years later, the same member paid for new water pipes from the town cistern.

Indeed, it was not unknown for candidates to promise to carry out public works as an incentive to the voters to vote for them. Thomas Hales, one of the candidates in 1727, promised that, if elected, he would build an arched stone bridge at the west end of town, and would improve the church with stone steps leading up to the south doorway, new jurats' and commoners' seats, and a new pulpit. He also engaged to provide maces for the town's sergeants and pay off a Corporation debt of fifty pounds.

However, in spite of all these promises, Hales was unsuccessful and had to wait for Baker's death in 1744 to get the seat he coveted. He then redeemed his promise of maces for the sergeants. There were two of them because, up to the time of the Municipal Corporation Act of 1836, Hythe had a mayor's sergeant and a town sergeant instead of just the town sergeant of today. This is clear in the minutes of the Assembly for July 5th, 1716:

> At this Assembly John Iggulden, the Town Sergeant, made report to this House that on Tuesday night last and following morning he spoke to and warned George Bennett to appear there this day in order to be sworn a Freeman of this Corporation if he made good his Claym to which he then made answer both times that it was very well, but not appearing here this day William Carter, the Mayor's Sergeant, was sent downe to his house or Shopp to call him up. And his Mother returned answer to the said William Carter that her said son, George Bennett, was gone to work at New Romney as she was informed by the post, and he not appearing, it is ordered that the House shall be adjourned till tomorrow at six o'clock in the afternoon and that the Town Sergeant leave notice for him, the said George Bennett, to attend then.

Whilst donating the silver maces, Hales made sure that his family would be well remembered. The maces were made by Paul Lamerie, one of the best known London silversmiths of the day, and their hemispherical heads consist of a coronet of fleur-de-lys supporting an orb and cross, with the arms of George II below it. It is on the mace heads that the family is perpetuated. Divided into four panels, the under parts of the heads display Hale's coat of arms, his crest—a mailed arm holding an arrow—and a quartered shield, displaying the arms of his mother, his grandmother and his great grandmother as well as his own. The fourth panel contains the inscription, "The Gift of Thomas Hales Esq., Lieut. of Dover Castle and Member for this Port 1744".

From 1705 until the inauguration of the new reformed Corporation in 1836, the office of Town Clerk was held by a Tournay for all but twelve years, in addition to a Tournay being nineteen times mayor from 1712. This did not go without comment. T.H.B. Oldfield, writing in his *History of the Boroughs of Great Britain,* remarked that:

> The Corporation of Hythe are under the absolute discretion of Mr. Robert Tournay who is, every other year, chosen Mayor, and in spite of legal incapacity unites with the office of Town Clerk that of Chief Magistrate.

By then the Tournays had become mainly professional middle class—lawyers, parsons and doctors, who mixed more with graziers and farmers than with the "County" families. Thomas Tournay had been a declared Cromwellian, and must have lost caste because of it when the Restoration came. But after the reform of the Corporation, the Tournays took no further part in it.

Instead of Hales, it was William Glanville, the successful candidate of 1728, who built the church steps. He also presented one of the galleries in the nave, which have since been taken down. They were a source of revenue for the church, because people paid an annual rent for the privilege of having their pews in them.

Glanville's fellow M.P., Baker, built another of the three galleries in the same year, 1734, although they were not an unmixed blessing. The sexton had orders to "constantly attend Divine Service every Sunday in Church and sit in the great gallery among or near the boys and shall take care that they behave themselves with good order and decency".

The other member for 1728 was James Brockman, son of William Brockman, and there is a curious clause in the father's will to the effect that he should never again stand for Parliament as Member for Hythe. On the other hand, he was enjoined to lay out the sum of £100 at such time as the local inhabitant freemen should be successful in getting two candidates into Parliament, and distribute the money amongst them in "such manner and proportion as shall appear most meet and beneficial towards restoring and recovering the Native and National Rights and Libertys of the said Corporation, Town and Port of Hythe, together with their freedom of election".

Alas, it is unlikely that Brockman ever had to spend his money, since from that time until the representation was reduced from two to one by the Reform Bill of 1832, it was usual for an outsider to hold at least one of the seats, and the patronage of the Lord Warden continued unabated in spite of the Act of 1689. In 1761 Lord George Sackville, Vice-Treasurer for Ireland, was elected. He was a son of the Lord Warden of the Cinque Ports, the Duke of Dorset. In 1766 it was William Amherst, son of Lord Amherst, and in 1768 William Evelyn of Ightham, Kent, who was Captain of Sandgate Castle and a son of William Glanville, although he had a different surname.

Evelyn was the nominee of the new lord warden, Lord Holderness, and a collection of letters of the Deedes family reveals very clearly the kind of wheeling dealing that went on before the election to unseat Lord Sackville, the previous lord warden's nominee.

William Deedes supported Evelyn and reckoned he could count on Brockman, but Tournay would be against him. In 1766 Evelyn wrote to Deedes to say that he had seen Lord Holderness, who had spoken to the Duke of Grafton, who now desired to see him. "Upon the whole I have not at present any reason to doubt his intentions of taking me as his Man." He asked Deedes to do everything in his power to prevent Lord Sackville choosing the next mayor.

In this he was unsuccessful. As the secret ballot had not yet been introduced, voters were very vulnerable to undue pressure. The following year Lord Sackville wrote to General Irwin, saying:

> I carried my Mayor by 51 against 34, and I had the pleasure of seeing most of those in Custom House employment vote for me, and all those who were under the Lord Warden, tho' they were assured in the most positive manner that they would be immediately dismissed from their offices.

However, in spite of the fact that Lord Sackville had his mayor in position, he did not retain the seat. The same year, 1767, Evelyn wrote to Deedes saying:

> The Duke of Grafton is determined to stand by me. I rather think that when he (Lord Sackville) finds that we are determined to Stand him out, he will think it not worth his while, when he can be chose at Grinsted for naught, to be at great expense at Hythe.

Against this background of personality politics and patronage, the actual inhabitants of Hythe were steadily pressing for their rights and taking up their freedom, which was restricted, as today, to the sons of freemen, those married to the daughters of freemen, and those who received it by gift from the Corporation. In 1774 sixty-two freemen voted, in 1780 seventy-six, and in 1784 eighty-six. But in 1790, 1796 and 1798 candidates were returned unopposed. In 1802, in the first election of members of parliament of the United Kingdom, after the Act of Union the previous year, thirty-seven men claimed their freedom and were sworn in and admitted as voters, a total of 357 votes being cast.

On the whole, eighteenth century life in Hythe under the ruling families was quiet and peaceful. Only one accident is recorded, which could have had fatal consequences, but fortunately did not. In the year 1739, the steeple of the church, which had possibly been weakened by the "earthquake" of 1580, fell down. The General Evening Post of May 31st tells us what happened:

> We learn from Hythe that on Thursday morning last, about eleven o'clock, the Steeple of their Church fell down, and that they have been very busy since in digging out the Bells, being six in Number. About ten Persons were present when it fell, waiting for the Keys in the Church-Porch to go up the Steeple for a View. But some Delay being made in bringing them, they all happily saved their Lives, and had no other Damage than being terribly frightened.

The accident should not have been entirely unexpected, since three years previously a vestry meeting had warned that the north and west sides of the tower were in a "ruinous and dangerous condition". A few days after the occurrence, another vestry meeting was held to decide what to do about it, and the minutes in the Vestry Book record the following:

> After thanks returned to a merciful Providence that no Life or Limb hath been lost by the fall of the Steeple, it is resolved that the Churchwardens shall take all possible care that the Bells and all the broken parts of them, together with the Lead, Iron, Timber, parts of the Clock etc, be secured and kept without any Embezzlement for the use and Benefit of the Parish. And that the Arch at the West End of the Church shall be boarded up with such Boards as we have as soon as it can be done, as far as they will go. And that

one Bell shall be hung up in the most convenient place to give Notice unto the Parishioners of the time at which they shall assemble for Divine Service.

It is clear that by 1745, six years later, little had been done to restore the tower, since the minutes of the vestry meeting of April 30th in that year record that "We do not agree to have the remaining part of the ruinous Steeple, now standing in a dangerous manner, taken down out of hand to the foundations".

It will have been noticed that these two excerpts from the Vestry Book both refer to the "steeple" of the church, whereas the church depicted on the St. John's Hospital map of 1684 shows a square tower with a flat roof and crenellated parapet, not dissimilar in shape to the present one, which was ultimately erected in 1750.

Since ancient times, a "steeple" has meant a spire in the form of a cone, and such a steeple is shown at Hythe on the *Card of the Beacons in Kent,* which has already been mentioned. As in modern Ordnance Survey maps, the churches, which were significant landmarks of importance for such a card, were drawn on it to show whether they had a steeple or a tower. It seems, therefore, that at some stages of its life, St. Leonard's Church did have a steeple, perhaps superimposed on the tower.

This was clearly so in the fifteenth century, since we have the churchwardens' accounts, written in a mixture of Latin and medieval English, for the year 1480. One of the items is 6s paid to John Hame, and two men working with him for two weeks "in takynge downe of the olde frame of the stepulle".

Other items are 2s 4d for victuals for men carrying new timber for the said steeple, and 5s paid to Hame and two men for ten days' work making the new frame for the steeple, plus 3s for four gudgeon-pins and other iron-work for the said frame. At the same time there were sundry disbursements for mending the clock, making the chime of the clock, and buying new clappers for two of the bells.

A subscription was raised for this work, since we have a list of the receipts from certain men and women, who contributed "for devotion's sake, towards the bells of Hethe, and other works pertaining to the steeple of the said church". First on the list are the subscriptions of the twelve jurats, the largest sum being 10s. Then comes a long list of commoners, with two of them outdoing the jurats, one with 12s 6d and the other with £1 from the estate of a deceased person. At the other end of the scale, Richard, a labourer, contributes a penny, and five other men and women do the same.

In any case, the year 1750 was obviously one of major church restoration, since in that year the south transept, which is shorter than the north one, was completely rebuilt. Julius Deedes footed the bill, as he did for a great part of the expense of the new tower. In return, the Deedes family, who still lived in the nearby Manor House, were allocated a private chapel in it, with a vault beneath it for their burials.

The marble plaque commemorating Julius, who lived from 1692 to 1750, notes that, "His high regard for his native place was his motive to use his utmost Endeavours for the Service of it, which will be known to posterity by the many public works procured for it in his Time, in particular the rebuilding of the Tower of this Church, which he lived not to see finished".

The Mackeson family, well known in Hythe in later years as brewers of the famous stout, were given a vault to the east of that of the Deedes, with access through the retaining wall of the church, in return for providing the choir stalls and altar rail.

A little later, a long overdue Town Hall, also called the Guildhall, was built in the High Street, then known as King's Street, thus ending the necessity for holding the assemblies in the church, and making a definite division between the civil and ecclesiastical. The new building was put up in 1794 on a collonade where the old arcaded covered market-place had stood, and obviated the need for special seats for jurats and commoners, or as we should say, councillors, in church.

There had been dissatisfaction for some time. In 1791 a committee was appointed to study the question, as it was stated that "The Court Hall is in a very ruinous state and the common goal (sic) is neither a safe place of security for prisoners nor a fit place for the prisoners to be any length of time confined".

Some time later, concern was expressed because "Upon a late trial of a prisoner the said town hall was found to be in such a dangerous state that much mischief might happen should there be such another crowded court, and that the prisoner in the goal was obliged to be watched during his confinement".

Consequently, contracts were awarded to Henry Tritton, a riding officer in His Majesty's Customs, who happened to be Mayor, to provide a new gaol, or gaoler's house and prison yard, and to William Tritton, who also happened to be on the council, to build a new Court Hall or Guildhall.

The Corporation was also concerned, at this time, to clean up the town, and a sum not exceeding £15 a year was set aside "to carry filth and dirt from the streets to certain beachy outlands". In addition, a notice was set into the wall under the new Town Hall exhorting people to "unite in their Endeavours to keep this place clean, and to prevent Boys and other from dirting the same".

Hythe had now been a port without a harbour for some two hundred years. But the maritime tradition was still there amongst the local inhabitants, if not amongst the strangers who represented them in Parliament. The fishing boats were launched off the beach, as they are to this day, and in due course a lifeboat was included amongst them in its own house, which can also still be seen at the eastern end of Fishermen's Beach. The very idea of a purpose-built boat for saving life at sea, specially constructed to ride the roughest waves, came from the brain of a Hythe man. He was Lionel Lukin, whose grave lies near the west door of the church, ten yards to the left of it next to the lamp-post.

Lukin was originally from Essex, as the epitaph on the front of his gravestone makes clear. But he settled at Elm House in Hythe in his later years. Under the motto *Mediocria Firma,* his life is described in the measured phrases of Georgian England:

> In this grave is interred the Body of Lionel Lukin—born at Dunmow in Essex on the 18th of May 1742—In 1767 he became a member of the Coach Maker's Company of London, and after 60 years of Various Success in that Business—settled in Hythe in 1824 with the Humble Hope that the same Divine Providence which had been his Guide and Protector during a long and Chequerd Life would permit him to Conclude it in Ease and Tranquillity and finally remove him to a better and Eternal Inheritance Through the merits and Intercession of Christ Jesus our

Redeeemer—died the 16th of February 1834.

The whole gravestone has recently been cleaned, and on the back of it, facing the grave itself, we are given the information that:

This Lionel Lukin was the first who built a Life Boat and was the original inventor of that Principle of Safety by which many lives and much property have been preserved from shipwreck and he obtained for it the King's Patent in the year 1785.

Hythe High Street—Wealden House, White Hart and Town Hall

But William Brockman of Beachborough composed his own epitaph, as anyone may see for himself by visiting St. Nicholas Church of Newington next Hythe. On a marble plaque on the wall of the Lady Chapel of this ancient church, which is full of the Brockman memorials, we can read a really fine example of the balanced prose of the Georgian age:

> I have always thought that the true Christian religion, accompanied with humanity, not loaded with superstition, mankind's glory; that hope of futurity is our present support; that natural liberty without a licentious deluge is most amiable; that the wife understand government is more for protection than domination; that magistrates are ordained as well for chastising the wicked as for rewarding the good; that traitor's impunity is a nation's most baneful scab; that ecclesiastical wiles, no less than the courtly, are detestable; that retirement is more eligible than the publick stage; and that a course of life serious, calm and undisturbed, all showiness apart, is still to be preferred to an ambitious, dependent state of giddy popularity—W.B.

This Brockman died in 1741, and his wife eleven years before him "Dorcas-like full of good works", and well might he prefer his home two and a half miles inland from Hythe to the hurly-burly of London politics, for he lived in what was one of the finest examples of an English country estate anywhere in the land.

There is an engraving still in existence, which shows the large Tudor house with its tall chimneys, and the landscaped park with its stately avenue of trees reaching out towards Peene, that is now intersected by the B 2065 road to Etchinghill and Lyminge. An artificial lake was constructed in the re-entrant in the downs behind the house, and a circular gazebo, with columns supporting an ornamental roof, was placed on the very top of that isolated outpost of the downs, which is still called Summerhouse Hill.

The legend, passed on by Igglesden, is that the Brockman, who built it, was even more addicted to strong language than the average eighteenth century squire. So he had the gazebo built as a refuge when he felt a swearing fit coming on—until he laughed himself out of the whole idea.

And indeed, who would want to swear at that delightful look-out point, which dominates the shore line? The whole sweep of the coast from Dungeness to the seafront at Hythe is in view, with Folkestone to the left beyond Newington Church, and the broad swathe of the M 20 in the foreground. On a clear day Cap Griz Nez and the hills around Boulogne look hardly a stone's throw away. According to the sundial fixed to the wall, 1813 was the date of the reconstruction of the Tudor mansion. It was done in the simplest Georgian manner round a central portico, confident in the belief that the danger of invasion by the French was over for good.

After William Brockman came the squiresons—men who were both squire and parson at one and the same time. For James Brockman, who died in 1767 aged seventy-one, was a bachelor, and willed the estate to his vicar, the Rev. Ralph Drake, Clerk D.D., who had married the youngest daughter of his Cheriton cousin, Henry.

The new bailiff's house, which stands on the right-hand side of the Elham and Lyminge road and was recently restored, was built by Ralph Drake-Brockman, himself, in the neo-Gothic manner, using stone from the old mansion at Brockhill, which had been acquired by the Brockmans. But the reconstruction of the main house was undertaken by Ralph's son, and it was the Rev. Tatton-Brockman who restored the porch of St. Leonard's Church in 1863.

The great house prospered in the nineteenth century, with a staff of a dozen or so to keep it going. But the First World War, when it became a hospital for Canadian soldiers, was the beginning of the end. Between the wars it was a preparatory school, called Beachborough Park, and the hilltop gazebo was burnt down in the 1930s by some people celebrating Guy Fawkes night—too enthusiastically. The building was again taken over by the army in the Second World War, ending it in poor shape. In 1960 a careless workman set fire to it with his blowlamp, whilst it was being converted into flats. This resulted in the disappearance of the central portion of the house, with the exception of the stone portico, which has oddly survived.

Walking past the house today, and up to the little lake, now clogged with fallen trees and enclosed by rusty and twisted five-foot railings behind a Ministry of Defence notice saying

"Trespassers will be prosecuted", one needs an effort of the imagination to match the scene with the magnificent prospect depicted in the painting, which is now in the art gallery of the city of Melbourne in Australia. Certainly such well-groomed men, women and children as are shown in the picture, dressed up to the nines and elegantly decorating the landscape, will never be seen again. But the view from the top of Summerhouse Hill endures for ever.

Some of the members of the "D-B" family still reside in the vicinity, and of these, Lt-Col. R. F. H. Drake-Brockman, sometime Royal Artillery officer and sometime Government Officer in Malaya, is the most prominent in Hythe affairs, being President of the Civic Society as I write. But there are many more in Western Australia, whither they emigrated, taking their breeding stock with them.

The Windmill in Park St. and the Hope Inn

9

Invasion Scare

HYTHE must have been quite a sleepy little town in the eighteenth century. It was almost a rotten borough, still returning two M.P.s to Parliament with a population of only about a thousand. The making of the three turnpike roads to Ashford, Folkestone and New Romney between 1750 and 1780 will have improved its communications with the rest of Kent, but hardly turned it into a place of bustling activity.

The pike itself was near the present terminus of the Light Railway, and its memory was preserved in Turnpike Camp until the 1970s, when the wartime hutments there were pulled down. But the Gate Inn, situated just before you reached it on what used to be called Market Road, still survives. There is a little rhyme on the inn sign, which says:

> This gate hangs high and hinders none.
> Refresh and pay, and travel on.

Near it, on the other side of St. Nicholas Road, stands Rock Cottage, one of the older houses of Hythe, which was built in 1711. And at the point where the roads to Dymchurch and Ashford parted company, there was something a good deal more sinister. It was the gallows, and before the roads were widened and realigned after the First World War, the road junction was always known as Gallows Corner.

But the *Hythe and Sandgate Guide*, "embellished with a new panorama picturesque plan, containing engraved likenesses of these places, with the towns and antiquities which are contiguous", which was published in Romford in 1803 and sold by William Lee at the Library, Hythe, described pleasanter things:

The most agreeable walks in the immediate vicinity of Hythe are called the Marine Grove and Sir William's Walk, in which the

visitors and townspeople sometimes form fashionable prom-
enades; others choose the footways which lead from the main
street, and, passing Quarry Hill, arrive upon the spacious heights
of Saltwood, the walks of which give a most comprehensive view
of the inland country, capacious sea, and busy shore beneath.
The rides of pleasure that are usually chosen by those fashionable inhabitants who know the neighbourhood are as follows: In
the chilly seasons of spring and autumn they commonly prefer the
sheltered lowland ways, which I have described to be traversing
near the sea strand, between Hythe and Sandgate; in more conge-
nial weather they prefer the uplands; and where the highways of
the county do not afford a road through the downs, they are
intersected with those of the landholders, which are commonly
sufficiently spacious for any carriage, and are open to the public.

However, this peaceful atmosphere was changed when
Napoleon Bonaparte, having conquered most of Europe,
decided to mount an invasion of "the nation of shopkeepers".
After two centuries of relative obscurity as a seaside town with
a small body of inshore fishermen launching their boats off the
beach, the ancient Cinque Port sprang to life again in the front
line of the defence of our shores. In the ten years from 1801 to
1811, the resident population nearly doubled to 2,287, apart
from the temporary influx of soldiers and labourers.

The projected invasion was no idle threat. The Peace of
Amiens, which had been signed in 1802 after nine years of
hostilities, was broken in the middle of May 1803, the casus
belli being a dispute over the Mediterranean islands. The
French then built a vast number of barges, which they
stationed on their side of the Channel, 1,500 of them being at
Boulogne and the neighbouring seaside places. Altogether,
they were intended to transport an army of over 100,000
seasoned soldiers across to the English beaches.

The strategy was to lure the main British battle fleet across
the Atlantic, and whilst it was far away, to select calm weather
after a storm. Hopefully, the frigates guarding our shores
would be blown off station and then becalmed. At this
moment, the barges would be rapidly paddled across to land
the troops on our side of the Channel.

The flat stretch of coastline between the cliffs of Folkestone
and those of Hastings, with the broad sands of Littlestone Bay

at the end of the short sea passage from Boulogne, would be the obvious part of the shore for the French to aim at. So the grand old Duke of York, Commander-in-Chief of the Army, had to look urgently to his defences.

At the same time the poet, William Wordsworth, safe in his Lakeland retreat, wrote his well-known sonnet "To the Men of Kent" urging no parleying:

Vanguard of liberty, ye men of Kent,
Ye children of a soil that doth advance
Her haughty brow against the coast of France,
Now is the time to prove your hardiment!

The famous soldier, Sir John Moore, was in command of Kent. At the end of May 1803, he took over the brigade at Sandgate, and with it the responsibility for the defence of the coast from Deal to Dungeness. His Commander, Royal Engineers was Colonel, later Brigadier Twiss.

It was Twiss who recommended the construction of the Martello towers, which can still be seen, here and there, along the coast from Folkestone to Rye. They were based on a type of tower that had been defended very effectively by the French at Cape Mortella in Corsica during a seaborne attack on St. Florent. The word means "myrtle" in Italian, but to English ears it was very like *martello*, the "hammer" used to strike a gong and raise the alarm in the coastal towers of Italy, when sea raiders came into sight. Thus, though the official designation was "Mortella", they came to be known everywhere as Martello towers.

Colonel Twiss' proposals were taken up by the Duke of York, in view of the fact that "these works from their construction require but a feeble garrison for the defence, nor viewing the permanency of the work, are they considered to be expensive".

As the winter of 1803 approached, the danger of invasion receded, and Sir John Moore wrote to his mother, "I consider invasion over for the winter and therefore probably for ever . . therefore send me your recipe for mince pies . . ." So nothing further was done about the towers. "Towers as sea batteries appear to have little or no advantage over any other battery of the same number of guns", reported a committee in 1804.

But spring came, and the number of troops in camp on the cliffs above Boulogne, espied through English telescopes, was seen to increase. So there was again a need to do something urgently. William Pitt emerged from retirement in May 1804, and formed his last government to prosecute the war. He was, himself, Lord Warden of the Cinque Ports and in favour of the towers.

In order to breathe a suitably warlike spirit into the populace, posters were distributed describing the consequences if Bonaparte were to succeed in his invasion plans— Universal pillage; men of all parties slaughtered; women of all ranks violated; children murdered; trade ruined; the labouring classes thrown out of employment; the remaining inhabitants carried away by ship loads to foreign lands. Nothing seems to have been left out in this catalogue of horrors.

Meanwhile, the Emperor of the French was seen to make a personal visit to the invasion forces on the occasion of his birthday. In anticipation of success, the erection of a monument on the hills behind Boulogne was commenced. It can still be seen, when visibility is good, from the opposing hills behind Hythe.

However, even with Pitt's drive behind it, the scheme for the construction of the towers was not finally adopted until October of that year. This was after Pitt had personally selected some of the sites with Colonel, later Brigadier Hope, who has left his name to a public house in Stade Street, though Whitbreads later attributed it to A. J. Hope, Marquess of Linlithgow and Viceroy of India.

Fifteen months had gone by since the original recommendation. But the Hope family motto was *At Spes non Fracta*— Hope is unbroken—and in the event, twenty-seven Martello towers were built on the Kent coast between 1805 and 1808.

No. 1 was, and still is, on Folkestone's East Cliff, and No. 27 was at St. Mary's Bay. As can be seen, they are massive, round buildings, tapering slightly towards the top. Their brick walls were solid enough to withstand the firing of a twenty-four pounder gun, which was mounted on the platform on top. There was a small door on the landward side, twenty feet above the ground, with a retractable ladder to give access. The accommodation for one officer and twenty-eight men was on this level, the lower storey being a store for ammunition,

Fishermen's beach and Martello towers

Restored Martello Tower No. 13

provisions and water. The circular wall was eight feet thick at
the base and six feet thick at the top, and within its thickness
there were steps leading up to the gun platform.

Of the Martello towers in Hythe, No. 10 stood beside what
is now the golf links of the Imperial Hotel. Nothing remains of
it except, perhaps, the gun, a cannon with the date 1790 on it,
which now stands opposite the landward entrance to the hotel.
No. 11 was between South Road and Marine Parade, where
the Hythe swimming-pool now lies.

Between these two towers, at the end of Twiss Road, stood
Twiss Fort, with its battery of guns and accommodation for
up to a hundred men, as can be seen on some of the old prints.
No. 12 was at the seashore end of Stade Street and, like No. 11,
has been lost without trace. But No. 13 has been excellently
preserved. It has been converted into a private house, tidied up
and whitewashed. Its cannon is mounted in the garden, point-
ing at the parked cars in West Parade.

The next eight towers were on the shingle bank of the
Hythe military ranges, built at intervals of a quarter of a mile
to ensure that the whole beach could be covered by their guns.
Numbers 14 and 15, near the Fisherman's Beach, are quite
recognisable, and so is No. 19. But the rest are either rubble or
reduced to nothing.

Sutherland Fort, the second of Hythe's redoubts, was at this
end of the town, its name recalled until recently by the Sutherland Hotel. The third fort, now within the ranges another mile
towards Dymchurch, was named after James Moncrieff, the
distinguished military engineer, who was killed at the siege of
Dunkirk in 1793.

Whilst these defence works were being constructed, Hythe
was also invaded every summer by a Royal Artillery field park
for gunnery and mortar practice on the beach land between the
town and the forts. Then Nelson won his epic battle against
the French at Trafalgar, and the immediate invasion scare
appeared to diminish once again.

But it was not for long. Once more, Napoleon showed who
was master of Europe at the battle of Austerlitz, and the
invasion fleet remained awaiting orders at Boulogne. The
unfinished Colonne de la Grande Armée on the cliffs above the
town was still surrounded by encamped mcn.

So the two other parts of the defence plan for the Dungeness to Shorncliffe coastline remained under active consideration. One was, if necessary, to flood Romney Marsh by opening the sluice gates to the sea at high tide. The other was to construct a canal cutting off the marsh, which would be both a defensive ditch and a communication channel. The Royal Military Canal was the brain child of Lieut-Colonel, later Major-General John Brown, who had been constructing gun batteries in Ireland before becoming Assistant Quartermaster-General.

On September 11th, 1804 the Kentish Gazette reported that:

> On Thursday last Mr. Pitt, accompanied by Generals Twiss and Moore, met the Lords and Bailiffs of the Level of Romney Marsh, at New Hall near Dymchurch, to consider of the best mode of inundating the Marsh in case of invasion, when it was determined that, on the appearance of the enemy on the coast, the sluices should be opened, to admit the sea so as to fill the dykes, which might be accomplished in one tide, and in the case of actual invasion remain open another tide, which would be sufficient to inundate the whole level. The wall of course would not be injured, as the space of 24 hours will be fully sufficient for the intended effect.

But the Duke of York was in favour of the canal. In a letter written in the same month, he wrote:

> In regard to the proposal of cutting a canal betwixt Hithe and the River Rother, for the purpose of military defence, by separating an enemy landed upon the coast of Romney Marsh from the interior of the country, I am to press this measure most earnestly upon the consideration of His Majesty's Government.

The advantage of the canal was that inundation of the marsh would be rendered unnecessary. The costly flooding would have to be set in motion the moment the enemy appeared to be leaving port, and could thus be easily triggered off by a mere feint on the enemy's part, resulting in great damage to the countryside for nothing.

A civilian adviser was engaged as consulting engineer. He was John Rennie, who had built the old London Bridge, which was taken stone by stone to Arizona in the U.S.A. during the 1960s. Brown and Rennie went down to Hythe, dined at the

White Hart, met Sir John Moore at Sandgate, and talked to the
civilian contractors who were to undertake the work.

Sir John was still inclined to play down the threat of invasion. Nevertheless, the work went ahead. The canal was to
cover twenty-eight miles from Shorncliffe, or Seabrook, as
we would say today, to Cliff End below the village of Pett in
Sussex. It would be sixty feet wide, with a towpath and a
drainage ditch on the seaward side, and a rampart, or parapet,
a military road and another drainage ditch on the landward
side. The canal was of particular significance for Hythe, since
it is the only town it actually passes through.

The section from Seabrook to three miles beyond Lympne
was to be cut first, and a timely leak to the Kentish Gazette did
much to persuade the local population that it would be a good
thing for them as well as for the defence of their country. Even
if never used in the nation's defence, the article said, it would
bring great benefit to the region when it was linked up with
the existing waterways in Kent and Sussex.

It was even said that Portus Lemanis, the old Roman harbour of Lympne, would be reopened, and Hythe would get a
new harbour where it went out to the sea. The railway age had
not yet dawned, and canals were still the main means of inland
transport for heavy goods.

Brown was appointed commandant of the Royal Staff
Corps as well as being the Quartermaster-General's principal
staff officer. But this corps was not a body of staff officers, as
might be supposed. It was originally a company of Pioneers,
which was expanded to construct field works for the army,
which the Engineer Department was unable to undertake on
its own.

So, when the civilians failed to come up to scratch, a decision was taken by the highest authority, the Duke of York
himself, to remove the project from the control of Rennie, the
civilian engineer, and place it entirely in the hands of Brown
and his army men.

Thus, from the middle of 1805, troops were employed to do
the work under the direction of the officers and N.C.O.s of
the Royal Staff Corps, whilst the Royal Waggon Train, the
precursor of the Royal Army Service Corps, carried the materials required. The soldiers were employed mainly on building

the rampart and manning the pumps, with locally engaged labourers doing the actual work on the canal, and the whole waterway was completed in 1809. It consisted of straight stretches with bends every third of a mile, even if the next stretch went straight ahead. This would allow guns to be mounted on the bends, which could fire along the length of the canal, enfilading any of the enemy attempting to cross it. In Hythe, Rampart Road was, in effect, a section of the military road behind the rampart on the landward side of the canal, though the parapet itself was taken down when improvements to the A 259 trunk road were undertaken in 1980.

In spite of the long-term advantages promised, Hythe was still reluctant to give something for nothing. The pebbles which were being used as top dressing for the military road, were being taken from the shingle banks near the town, and in due course the Town Clerk wrote to point out that the land belonged to the Corporation, and to demand a penny a ton for the shingle. After various negotiations, Brown bought a beach area of seven acres for £105 instead.

In March 1806, Sir John Moore left for overseas service, whilst the canal was still only half completed. But in August of the same year, the Duke of York was able to inspect eighteen miles of it in a small boat, towed by relays of horses. Before the end of the year, the elm trees were being planted, which had to be felled in the 1970s when they became victims of the Dutch elm disease. In the meantime, the Royal Army Ordnance Corps had only completed six of the Martello towers.

Naturally the local landowners, though no doubt just as patriotic as anyone else, wanted to get the best deal they could out of the government. In 1807, they held a meeting in the Guildhall under the chairmanship of William Deedes, one of the members of parliament. The complaints registered included unsatisfactory fencing of the canal, insufficient compensation for damage to property, and loss of tax revenue from land taken up by the canal.

Deedes was, himself, Colonel of the local Home Guard, called the South Kent Volunteers, and not a man to be trifled with. He died in 1834, at the age of seventy-three, and as his epitaph in the parish church reminds us, "when the coast was threatened with invasion, he remained at his post in the fearless discharge of all his public and private duties". The family motto *Facta non Verba*—Deeds not Words—was entirely appropriate.

The same year, on August 13th, a high-powered body of Canal Commissioners was appointed to administer the waterway. It included the Prime Minister, the Commander-in-Chief and the Lord Warden of the Cinque Ports. In fact no canal, including Suez, has ever had more V.I.P.s on its board of control. But by this time the great prime minister, William Pitt, who had hurried on the work of both the canal and the towers, was dead.

These defence works, though never put to the test, brought great activity to Hythe, which was the centre of operations, and increased its population both temporarily and permanently. Barracks for the Royal Staff Corps were built in Military Road, and there were more barracks on the cliffs of Saltwood behind the town.

The headquarters of the Royal Staff Corps moved from Chatham, the home of the Royal Engineers, to Hythe in 1805, and Brown immediately pressed for a permanent home there for them. So, after two years, an Act of Parliament was passed granting the authority to purchase the necessary land. The Corps then built their own barracks and the Canal Commissioners footed the bill for the land and materials. The two-storey blocks were completed in 1810, the year after the canal itself was finished, and stood between the cliff behind Military Road and the canal at the western end of the town. Here the members of the Staff Corps had their home until it was disbanded in 1838 in the careless years of peace.

It was at this time that Hythe had its final fling as a one-time port of importance. In 1810 a Letter of Marque, or in other words a commission to go privateering was received. It was for fitting out a small ship of six guns, called the *Venus,* to serve against the Batavian Republic, which was the name given to Holland under Louis Bonaparte.

During the years of war, Hythe was full of soldiers, and of navvies, the professional diggers of navigation canals. Although there is only one memorial to an officer of the Royal Staff Corps at St. Leonard's Church—to Major-General King, who died in 1864—the lower ranks frequently made their

presence felt. There are a number of references in the records
to deceased children, father unknown, and the Kentish
Gazette of March 15th, 1805 recorded that:

> Last week the wife of one of the men employed in cutting the
> canal at Shorncliffe, was conducted by her husband to the market
> place, at Hythe, with a halter round her neck and tied to a post;
> from whence she was purchased for six pence by a mulatto, the
> long drummer belonging to the band of the 4th regiment, lately in
> barracks at that place—She was a young woman, apparently not
> more than 20 years of age, tall, and of a likely form and figure; her
> face, however, exhibited evident marks of incompatibility of
> temper; vulgarly, she had a pair of black eyes; notwithstanding
> this, the new partner led her away, with much apparent satisfac-
> tion from his bargain.

Whether this was the incident or not, which gave Thomas
Hardy the idea for the opening scene of his novel *The Mayor of
Casterbridge,* such a transaction might be called one of the
sordid effects of war. And of course, there was a sordid
underside to the heroics. No war is complete without prisoners, and this war with France was no exception. Naturally,
some of the French prisoners in England tried to escape, as was
their duty unless they were on parole. But it is surprising to
find a man of Hythe, which was then full of British soldiers,
aiding and abetting some of them to do so.

Yet it was related in 1811 in the Kentish Gazette that two
Bow Street police officers, named Lavender and Vichery, had
found four French officers hidden in the Hythe house of a man
named Webb, whom they had suspected for a long time of
helping French officers to escape across the Channel.

After receiving information that Webb had arrived home at
night with his covered cart, they raided his house and found
the four Frenchmen in bed there, two of them having made
their way from Crediton in Devonshire and two from Merton
Hampstead. Webb was also in bed, but rudely aroused and
taken, with the prisoners, to the barracks.

It seems amazing that Webb had travelled some five
hundred miles in the fourteen days he had been out with his
cart. But the two sleuths had received a tip-off, and had been
expecting to run into escaping Frenchmen, crossing Kent on
their way to the Channel from the west country. The previous
week they had caught two in Oxfordshire in a cart that was

known to belong to a Folkestone smuggler. After capturing
Webb, they went off in pursuit of another man, whose habit it
was to take his covered cart to fairs, selling gingerbread, in
order to allay suspicion.

Prisoners could, of course, belong to either side, and the
new gaol, built in 1801, must have been occupied mainly by
our own men. A four-square stone building in Stade Street,
now neatly whitewashed and disguised as Rock Cottage, it
was once the army guardroom, and the cottages to the right of
it were officers' quarters.

However, the upper classes thought more of the heroics of
war. At any rate this was certainly the case with a lady who
had her verses printed by Tiffen of Hythe in the year 1819.
Modestly referring to herself as "the wife of an officer", she
"gratefully and humbly" dedicated her slim volume of *Poems
founded on the Events of the War in the Peninsula* to "Field-
Marshal the most noble Arthur, Duke of Wellington, of
Ciudad Rodrigo, and of Victoria, Prince of Waterloo, KG,
GCB, KGF, GCTS, GCTM etc etc etc".

Her *Sketch written in the year 1814* was penned at a time when
Sir John Moore had been killed at Corunna in Spain, and
Arthur Wellesley, Duke of Wellington, who had already made
his name in India, had gone into Spain via Portugal to retrieve
the situation and emerge victorious:

> *Deserted all the long contested shore,*
> *And silence dwelt around the tomb of Moore,*
> *Spread o'er the subjugated hills of Spain,*
> *And reigned o'er hapless Lusia's lost domain.*

Then came Wellington, the defeat of Napoleon and his exile
on the island of Elba:

> *What guardian angel hovers o'er the coast?*
> *Vimeiro's hero leads a British host!*
> *O is it he, the victor chief sublime,*
> *The conquering warrior from Hindostan's clime?*
> *Behold the martial air, the lofty crest,*
> *The piercing eye, 'tis Wellesley stands confess'd.*

And finally:

> *O Albion! ever blessed be thy sod:-*
> *"Blest is the land that calls the Lord her God."*

Wellington returned to a hero's welcome. But there were many who did not. One of them was Lieutenant Henry Brockman, third son of Sir James Drake-Brockman, who died of typhus at Elvas in Portugal, aged twenty:

> *Forgive, blest shade, the tributary tear*
> *That mourns thy exit from a world like this;*
> *Forgive the wish that would have kept thee here,*
> *And stayed thy progress to the realms of bliss.*

It was said that, six years later, the guns firing at Waterloo could be heard on the Kent coast. But there were Hythe men who heard them thundering in their ears much closer than that. One of those who returned was Philip Sandilands, who commanded a troop of the Royal Horse Artillery in the battle, and later became Lieut-General, Royal Artillery. He lived at Elm House in Hillside Street, as Lionel Lukin had done before him, and he left a diary of the part he played in the events of 1815, which was discovered by his son, Philip Henry, after his death in 1869.

"June 18th," he relates, "was a very wet morning. Captain Hay arrived from Brussels and brought us a roast fillet of veal and wine". Later in his account he says that:

... the action during the whole day seemed as if the Artillery was to decide it, so great was the cannonade, but it was tremendous about 4 p.m. The French, having failed in all their attacks, began again to menace our centre. Bonaparte collected the principal part of his Infantry upon the Brussels road, and about seven o'clock p.m. he moved them forward expecting to cut through our line. Notwithstanding his columns advanced under a very severe fire from our Artillery, they steadily arrived on the ridge of our position, and our Infantry, who were now in line, poured into them such a fire that they were put into the utmost disorder and flight.

After the battle, young Sandilands moved on, passing through several villages that had been plundered by the Prussians, and eventually reached Paris on July 9th, where he saw the King of Prussia and the emperors of Austria and Russia in their victory parades, and also met his elder brother, Patrick, who had fought at Waterloo in the Coldstream Guards. There was sightseeing at the Luxembourg gardens, the Zoo, called the *Jardin des Plantes,* and the Gobelins tapestry factory, all of which appear to have been functioning quite well in spite of the war.

Philip Sandilands was Mayor of Hythe for the three years 1852 to 54, and the family continued to produce notable military men. His son, Philip Henry, finished his army career as Major–General, Royal Artillery. One of Philip Henry's sons was a brigadier in the R.A., and another was in the Royal Scots.

Francis Sandilands, great grandson of the Philip who fought at Waterloo, became Chairman of the Commercial Union Assurance Company, and in 1976 he was also Chairman of the British Government's Inquiry into Inflation. Perhaps the wheel had come full circle. For it was the printing of paper money to service the National Debt that was the chief cause of the severe inflation immediately after the Napoleonic wars, and consequent increase in taxation and smuggling.

After Waterloo, the whole nation rejoiced at final victory, and Napoleon's column behind Boulogne was left unfinished, not to be completed until 1841. But Hythe had already glimpsed two of the royal victors before the hundred days between Napoleon's escape from Elba and his final defeat. On June 26th, 1814 there was a right royal visit from no less a person than the Emperor of Russia.

The whole town was en fête not only for the Emperor, but also for the King of Prussia. Both of these allied monarchs were returning to the Continent after a triumphal visit to London. Houses were decorated with branches of oak and laurel, and the Swan Hotel displayed a particularly large white flag, with a blue cross on it and a motto alluding to the joyous occasion. Mine host, Mr. Knott, had thirty post horses in readiness, and several sets of artillery horses at his disposal.

The first to arrive was the King of Prussia, who got there at half past four in the afternoon. But he went straight on without getting out of his carriage. The Emperor of Russia did not arrive until after eight in the evening. Nevertheless, he stayed long enough to take refreshment in the Swan and meet the mayor. The "fair and accomplished" daughter of William Deedes helped to serve the coffee, and after about an hour the Emperor left for Dover, which he reached at eleven o'clock at night.

10

Soldiers and Smugglers

WHEN Napoleon was defeated at Waterloo in 1815, and peace finally returned, Hythe got no new harbour, nor was the Military Canal linked up with any other canal system in Kent. In due course the powers-that-be might have got around to it. But the railway age was dawning, and all eyes were on the new iron horse instead.

Nevertheless, there were ways in which the canal was put to good use. In 1807, an Act had been passed authorising its use for commercial purposes, and the old coaching inn, the Swan, ran a packet-boat service, which went as far as Appledore and back, a distance of fourteen miles each way. It departed at 10.30 a.m. and got back at 5 p.m., and in winter there was a fire in the boat's saloon to keep the passengers warm. But it was discontinued when the railway line was put through from Ashford to Hastings, via Appledore and Rye, in 1851. There was also a certain amount of barge traffic, for which tolls were charged, and the canal authorities even made a small profit at times.

The canal had already been stocked with tench in 1806, and now its bridges were improved. A new bridge, called Marine or Ladies' Bridge, was built in 1813 to connect the town with Ladies' Walk, a footpath down to the shore that had been laid out to commemorate the jubilee of George III in 1810, and flanked with elm trees like the canal itself. In the same year, a new Duke's Head bridge was built, which now carries the main A 259 trunk road to Dymchurch.

Of course, now that the danger of invasion was over, there was no lack of people to say that both the Military Canal and the Martello towers had been a complete waste of time, money and effort. When the Master-General of Ordnance was told to take over the administration of the canal in 1832, he

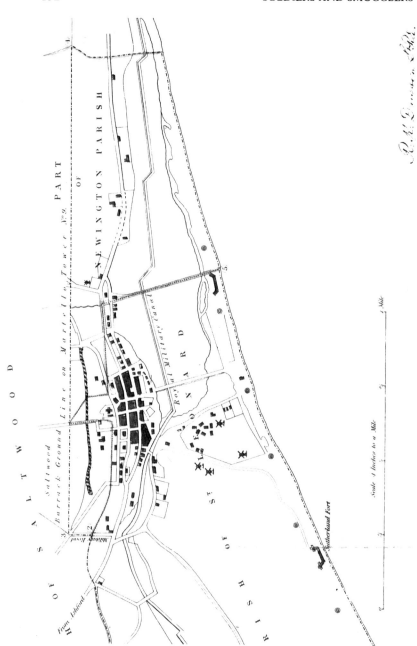

Early Nineteenth Century Ordnance Survey, showing the Military Canal and Windmills

declared that "the work was of as little advantage as a canal as it was absurd as a means of defence". And when the radical M.P., William Cobbett, took one of his rural rides through Hythe to Folkestone in 1823, he had this to say about the towers and the canal:

I think I have counted along here upwards of thirty of these ridiculous things which, I dare say, cost five, perhaps ten thousand pounds each . . . Hythe is half barracks; and barracks most expensive, most squandering, fill up the side of the hill. Here is a canal, made for the length of thirty miles to keep out the French; those armies who had so often crossed the Rhine and the Danube, were to be kept back by a canal, made by Pitt, thirty feet wide at the most! All along the coast there are works of some sort or another; incessant sinks of money; walls of immense dimensions; masses of stone brought and put into piles. Then you see some of the walls and buildings falling down; some that have never been finished.

And again, writing about the towers:

These towers are now used to lodge men, whose business it is to sally forth not upon Jacobins, but upon smugglers! Thus, after having sucked up millions of the nation's money, these loyal Cinque Ports are squeezed again: kept in order, kept down, by the very towers, which they rejoiced to see to keep down the Jacobins.

Cobbett, like most propagandists, was inaccurate in many respects. But he was right to stress the military presence in Hythe. As well as the Royal Staff Corps, the main part of the Royal Waggon Train had moved there, though it was disbanded shortly afterwards in 1833. Tiffen, in his *Sandgate, Hythe and Folkestone Guide* of 1823, says that:

Continuous to the western extremity of Hythe is a handsome range of substantial brick buildings erected by the government in the years 1807 and 8 for the reception of the Royal Staff Corps, permanently stationed here, and from that circumstance called the 'Staff Barracks'. Besides the officers' apartments there are accommodations for about three hundred men, and a number of comfortable rooms for married soldiers. Near the spot is also a remarkably pleasant and commodious house, at present occupied by Colonel Sir B. D'Urban KCB, Deputy Quarter-Master General and Commandant of this respectable corps.

Ireland copies Tiffen in his *History of the County of Kent,* published in 1828:

> Hythe has a neat little theatre, some good and spacious inns, a subscription reading-room and an excellent public library. The shops as well as the dwellings belonging to the superior classes of inhabitants, speak the opulence, respectability and commercial importance of the place. There are many pleasant houses upon ledges of the cliff above the town, commanding delightful and extensive views both of the sea and neighbouring country, as well as numerous convenient habitations appropriated for the use of strangers during the bathing season. Others are occupied by the families of officers of rank in the army stationed at this place, who greatly contribute to, enliven and improve the society constantly frequenting the town of Hythe.

In fact, the military brought a bustling life to the town that it had not known since its great days as a Cinque Port. Punters who nowadays go up to the Folkestone races at Westenhanger to place their bets, may be surprised to know that, in this period, Hythe had its own racecourse, complete with a raised box for the stewards at the starting and finishing post.

According to a poster, which has survived, there were five "matches" on each of the two days of the garrison races, which were held on June 1st and 2nd, 1813. Each match was between only two horses. But the prize money of fifty guineas was considerable, and one match, between Sir John Tylden's horse "Jack" and Captain Gubbins' "Yorkshireman", had a prize of eighty guineas. The stewards were both military officers—Col. Sir N. Peacocke and Lt-Col. Thornton.

With the advent of the soldiers, the amenities of the town also increased. The new public houses to augment the refreshment offered by the older hostelries included the Hope in Stade Street, which had been the canteen for the Waggon Train before it became a licensed premises in 1827, and the Gate beside the old toll gate opposite the barracks. A detachment of the 29th Regiment was there in May 1842 after the men had been shipwrecked off Dymchurch Wall, and there were also companies of the Rifle Brigade and the 30th and 50th Regiments.

However, by the mid-century it began to look as though Cobbett was going to have his way. The two original units had gone, the barracks at Saltwood on the cliffs had been demolished, and the "neat little theatre" had closed in 1837. In the meantime, Twiss Fort and Sutherland Fort had become coastguard stations, with a Royal Naval officer and six or seven men in each.

But in 1853 a radical change took place when a corps of instructors in musketry was formed in the barracks, and the old Waggon Train barracks, in the triangle between the canal and the Dymchurch road, were demolished to make room for a parade ground. The following year the School of Musketry was opened. Its first objective was to train officers and N.C.O.s in the use of the new Enfield rifle. They would then return to their regiments and instruct their men.

The curriculum of the courses held at this school developed to include the operation of machine-guns, range-finding and fieldcraft with some knowledge of the capabilities of the small arms used by foreign armies. A firing range, called by some a shooting gallery, was established on the shingle of the seashore, which became the nucleus of the military ranges still very much in use today.

The courses lasted six or seven weeks, and about four hundred officers and six hundred non-commissioned officers passed through the school each year. After the musket had been superseded by other weapons, the name was changed to the Small Arms School, which remained in Hythe as a vital component of the army's strength until 1968, when it moved to join the rest of the School of Infantry at Warminster. The first Commandant, Lt-Col. C. Crawford Hay, who rapidly rose to the rank of Major-General, laid the foundations of modern weapon-training here, and may well be considered to have been the father of modern rifle shooting.

Sadly, the Commandant's white house, which is now hidden from view by the large office block of the South-Eastern Electricity Board, is all that remains of his school in a dark-red jungle of small houses and flats that has sprung up around it. The memory just lingers on in Sir John Moore Avenue and Corunna Close.

The numbers passing through this unique school built up gradually. In the year 1858 to 59, for instance, about 195 officers were trained there, thirty of whom had no previous instruction at all in rifle shooting. At this time another war with France was feared, and great efforts were being made to form a peacetime body of part-time soldiers, called the Volunteers, who were the forerunners of the Territorial Army. Captain V. A. King, a volunteer in the 2nd Cheshire Rifles, has described his experiences at the School.

On the first day, the officers assembled in the barracks tent to be addressed by the general, who told them that 2,000 volunteers, who could shoot, were better than 200,000 who could not. He added that the great object of the instruction at Hythe was to raise the intelligence of the soldier and to make him consider himself a unit and not a machine.

The officers were told that the less practice they had previously had with a rifle, the better shots they were likely to become, because the carefully organised position drills and exercises in range-finding and aiming, produced better results if there were no bad habits to eradicate. The British rifleman now had a much better weapon than the old musketeer, who had fought Napoleon's troops with the inefficient "Brown Bess", and Hay was determined to make the most of it. Hence his system of registering every shot and keeping detailed statistics of the scores reached on the range.

General Hay was undoubtedly an original character, and as such he was the subject of many stories. One was that he had his own personal target set up on the beach, and used to fire at it from the churchyard a mile away. But the *Illustrated London News* of February 18th, 1860 described the scene on the ranges in winter in not very attractive terms:

> For those who love gunnery there is nothing more pleasant than a trip to Hythe, albeit a more desolate seaside place can scarcely be seen. The town nestles snugly enough under a long range of hills . . . but the beach has a most bankrupt, dreary air, with a set of baths (shut up), one row of lodging houses and a large, half-finished shell of another. It bristles at intervals, as far as the eye can reach, with Martello towers, where the Volunteers are exercised, and from which danger flags are waved to the mariners when the practice commences in the butts. The musketry ground is a long, deep shingle, fearfully trying to walkers who are not quite up to the mark, and about half a mile broad. It is sadly windy, and, as they are obliged to shoot towards the sea, there is no suitable

Badge of the
Small Arms School
Corps

Hythe Ranges, showing General Hay's personal target

background for the eye; but still, many first-class shots are trained
there. The eighteen foot target of General Hay, the Commandant, is a very prominent object, and on each side of it are ranged
the targets for the men, with little cast iron huts, from which the
effect of the shots is telegraphed by means of different flags, held
in different positions.

The following year, Admiral of the Fleet, Lord Fisher,
attended a course at the School when he was a young lieutenant. Later, he recalled that he had had "a lovely time there".
"The British Army was very kind to me," he wrote, "and I
loved it. The best shot in the British Army at that date was a
confirmed drunkard, who trembled like a leaf, but when he
got his eye on the target, he was a bit of marble and got bull's
eyes every time!"

Thus the military presence in Hythe remained considerable,
although the ten to fifteen thousand men in the vicinity at the
height of the Napoleonic wars had melted away. The army
was not only in town but also on the nearby cliffs at Shorncliffe Camp. And soon after the establishment of the School of
Musketry, there was even a body of troops, called the Foreign
Legion, which had its bell tents strewn across the "Roughs"
between Hythe and West Hythe. They were destined, poor
fellows, for the Crimea and were mostly Germans.

So it was scarcely surprising that the thoughts of the young
men of the stranded port should turn to a career on land in the
army instead of adventure on the sea. And in this period of
ever-growing empire, it was to the Indian Army that many of
them turned—an army in which an officer could live on his
pay.

St. Edmund's Chapel in the parish church, which is also
known as the Soldiers' Chapel, contains some most interesting wall plaques concerning those who went off "to fight the
good fight" and never returned to be buried in the churchyard.

There was Lieutenant R. G. Hart of the 23rd Regiment,
Madras Light Infantry, who died at Saugor in 1851, aged
twenty-five. He would have been serving the East India
Company, and indeed India, itself, was called the "East
Indies" in those days.

Then there were those who died in the Indian Mutiny—
Captain H. D. Hart of the 39th Madras Native Infantry, who

was killed at Vellore "by a mutinous sepoy" in 1858, aged thirty-five, and Colonel John Finnis of the 11th Regiment, Bengal Army, who was killed by mutineers of the 20th Regiment, Native Infantry at Meerut in 1857, aged fifty-three. John Finnis was born in Prospect House, which still stands on Prospect Road, and so was his brother, Thomas Quested Finnis, who was Lord Mayor of London in 1856. The entrance to the family vault is next to that of the Shipdems in the retaining wall on the south side of the church.

Indeed, the Finnis family was one of those that built up a tradition of service in India, and many of them died there. Colonel Finnis' elder brother, Stephen, was a lieutenant in the Bengal Army, and died before him at Dinapoor in 1819, aged only twenty-one. His son, John Finnis, joined the Punjab Frontier Force and became a lieut-colonel before dying in Mussoorie in 1884, aged forty-four. *His* eldest son followed the family tradition by becoming Commanding Officer of the 53rd Sikhs in the Frontier Force. He died of wounds received in action whilst leading his regiment in an attempt to relieve the garrison of Kut in Mesopotamia during the First World War. The date was January 13th, 1916, and he was forty-five years old. Another commanding officer in the Indian Army, Lt-Col. Oliver Holmes of the 4th 6th Rajputana Rifles, was killed in action at Keren, Eritrea in the Second World War, aged twenty-seven.

Not all the members of these army families served in the army, however. Robert Francis Finnis, brother of the Punjab Frontier Force officer who died in Mussoorie, joined the Indian Navy, and died in South America, aged twenty-nine. And Captain Robert Finnis RN met his end in a war that is nowadays almost completely forgotten—the war of 1812 between the United States of America and Canada. He was commanding I I.M. sloop of war *Queen Charlotte* on Lake Erie, when he was killed in an engagement with an American squadron in 1813, aged twenty-nine. He must have joined the Royal Navy as a boy, since he already had sixteen years' service.

Of course, after the government of India had been transferred from the East India Company to the Crown, service in the British Army might involve a tour of duty in India as well. Thus Lieut. H. M. Rose of the 1st Bn, the East Surrey Regiment, died of enteric fever at Agra in 1894, aged twenty-five, and had a brass plaque donated to the church by his brother officers.

Another officer of the British Service, who never returned, was Lieut-Colonel Henry Deedes of the family that had moved from the Manor House to Sandling Park. He was in the 34th Regiment and died on H.M.S. *Bellerophon* in 1848, aged forty-eight, whilst he was on passage with his regiment from Corfu, then a British colony, to Gibraltar. Yet another was Julius, the eldest son of Julius Drake-Brockman, a captain in the 15th Infantry Regiment, who died of cholera in 1833, and was buried at Fort Bellary, Madras, but remembered in St. Martin's Church, Cheriton.

Two other Brockmans, named James and Thomas, are remembered in the same place, the former killed in 1845 in the war against the Sikhs, aged thirty, and the latter dying in 1846 at Wadi Beni Jaber in Arabia Felix, which became the Aden Protectorate. They were the tenth and sixth sons of Julius Senior.

Many others went out from Hythe and the nearby estates to serve the Empire. No less than four of the sons of William Mackeson died serving their country, three of them in India. First to go was his fifth son, Thomas, who fought the Turks at the battle of Navarino in 1827 as a lieutenant in the navy, and then went on a survey expedition to West Africa, on which most of his fellow officers died of disease, only to die, himself, in Malta, aged twenty-eight. Second was his seventh son, Adjutant of the 19th Regiment, Bengal Native Infantry, who died in Bombay in 1842, aged twenty-six.

The third son to go was his eighth son, Julius, who served in the Afghan War of 1842 and the Sikh War of 1845-6, subsequently to die in Neemuch, aged twenty-nine. And fourthly, there was his fourth son, Frederick, who is commemorated in Peshawar and Canterbury as well as in the Cavalry Chapel of Hythe's church, which stands above the Mackeson family vault. He died in 1853 of "a wound inflicted by a Mahometan fanatic", aged forty-six, after serving on the North-West Frontier from 1838 and becoming a Lieut-Colonel in the Bengal Army and Commissioner of Peshawar, which meant that he was virtually ruler of the province.

So it may seem strange, in view of its "respectability and opulence", that there was an underside to Hythe life at this time. But so it was. Smuggling had always been a semi-respectable occupation on the coast of the marsh ever since the Cinque Ports had lost their duty-free privileges, and now, far from being thrust into the background by the new military garrison and the canal, it was on the increase. The canal's accountant, Alexander Swan, reported to the Canal Commissioners in 1816 that the smugglers had become extremely audacious, not only round the more remote parts of the waterway, but also near Hythe. More cavalry patrols were suggested as a remedy.

The reasons for this upsurge in lawlessness are not far to seek. The high excise duties imposed on liquor and tobacco to help service the National Debt run up during the war provided the incentive, and men discharged from the war without a job to return to provided the rank and file of the smugglers.

Hythe has its own smuggling stories, some legend, some fact. Beneath the floor of the Bell Inn, at the eastern end of the town, there is a tunnel close to the millstream. It was a legendary hiding place for the casks of brandy, that comprised one of the smugglers' favourite cargoes, and mine host will show you the hook in the attic that was used for the hoist to get them out when the coast was clear.

Another hiding-place was in the millstream itself, which flows from the mill wheel in a capacious culvert underneath the mill house. When the Military Canal was constructed, the engineers extended this underground waterway in a tunnel that led to the canal, and for many years it was the dare of Hythe children to go right through it from end to end. They were able to do this because there is a ledge on one side of it, which was very convenient for the storage of contraband goods.

In addition, on the topmost platform of the watermill there is a protruding alcove with a seaward facing window under the steep roof. The story that Jack Swain, the old carter, used to tell is that the window was used for signalling out to sea, and whenever the preventive men were near, the sluice of the millrace was opened to the full, so that no one could get into the tunnel past the churning wheel and the rushing waters.

At the other end of the town, beside the sheep and cattle market, the Duke's Head also had the reputation of being a smugglers' retreat. There they were politely known as the free-traders or the fair traders, and on one occasion a smuggler escaped capture by the revenue men by hiding in a sewer.

In the High Street there was a Jacobean house, unfortunately demolished in 1908 in spite of fruitless attempts of townsfolk to save it, which was called the Smugglers' Retreat. It had a small tower on its roof in which it was said, a lantern would be placed to signal to the smugglers at sea. A similar use is attributed to the look-out tower on the roof of the Manor House itself.

In Regency days smuggling was rife on the marsh, as Mr. Swan noticed, and it was to be expected that Hythe would have its share. Kipling paints the picture in his distinctive style in *Puck of Pook's Hill:*

> *If you wake at midnight, and hear a horse's feet,*
> *Don't go drawing back the blind, looking in the street.*
> *Them that asks no questions isn't told a lie.*
> *Watch the wall, my darling, while the Gentlemen go by!*

Some of the "gentlemen" were in the Ransley gang, whose headquarters were in the Walnut Tree Inn in Aldington. Betrayed by one of their number, named Spratford, for £500, sixteen of them were captured by a detachment of troops from Hythe and put on board a revenue cruiser. Their leader, a man called Quested, was hanged at Maidstone, but his body was released for burial at Aldington.

In his "Dr Syn" novels, Russell Thorndike has given a good picture of the smuggling activities of our locality. In *Dr Syn Returns* dragoons set out from Hythe to arrest the murderer of a riding officer from Sandgate, which is where the excise office was located in those days.

On another occasion, Hythe troops were out on a rescue mission. The magistrates at New Romney had convicted a man named Walker, and had sought assistance from Lieutenant David Peat R.N., whose vessel was lying at anchor near Dungeness, because there was a mob threatening to release him.

Peat hurried to the scene with a small party of marines, and a magistrate read the riot act. But the mob persisted, and it looked as though they might succeed in getting Walker away. On the magistrate's instructions, Peat ran Walker through with his sword and killed him, and when he went later to New Romney for the inquest, the mob surrounded the building where the jury had assembled, and shouted for his blood. So the son of one of the magistrates crept out to the stables, saddled a horse and galloped off to Hythe for help. In the end, it was a troop of dragoons that quelled the furious crowd.

In 1821 the Customs House in London offered a reward of £100 "to any person or persons who shall discover or cause to be discovered any one or more of the said offenders". What had happened was that a smuggling boat, carrying foreign spirits in small casks had been seized by the Coast Blockade

Hythe High Street—Smugglers' Retreat

near Hythe. But the smugglers, themselves, had put up a fierce fight and fired at the revenue officers and seamen, one of their balls going through the shirt of the Chief Officer. They had then escaped across the Military Canal by means of one of the barges that lay in it.

Then, in 1829, the justices of the peace, William Deedes and James Brockman, convicted one, William Sampson, of smuggling 133 gallons of brandy and 34 gallons of gin. He was sentenced at Hythe to five years in the navy!

Later in the century, in 1877, a smuggler was caught almost red-handed in Hythe itself. A small boat of about ten tons, called the *Wasp,* had been run ashore at Hythe, and at the same time five bales of tobacco, each weighing about 300 lbs, had been washed up at a spot which, allowing for the tide, they would have been likely to reach if they had been thrown overboard from the boat on its way in. Later, five bales, each of 56 lbs, were washed ashore at Sandgate, and as the crew had been seen throwing the bales overboard, the captain was arrested and given a year in prison in default of payment of a £100 fine, his boat being sold for the benefit of the Crown.

But it was not only "brandy for the parson" and "baccy for the clerk" that the smugglers dealt in. There were bigger pickings to be had in the so-called Guinea Trade, which was masterminded by some of the highest financiers in the land.

The smuggling of gold, ·which occurred during the Napoleonic era, has been much misunderstood, to the extent that the local people have been accused of lack of patriotism for taking part in what appeared to be a process of draining funds from Britain into the enemy's coffers. But that is not the whole truth, and anyone wanting to know more about the business should read the life of Nathan Rothschild, the naturalised Englishman of the five famous banking brothers, who came to manipulate the money markets of Europe.

In the year 1810, as our gallant poetess noted, Wellington was with his army fighting the French marshals on the Spanish peninsula. He was paying his expenses by issuing drafts on the British treasury to Sicilian and Maltese bankers, which they cashed at enormous discounts, Rothschild bought £800,000 worth of gold belonging to the East India Company in London, and offered his services to the British government in

getting the actual coinage out to Wellington through his
brother, James, in Paris.

It seems that the French treasury knew about this move-
ment of cash, but held the view that Britain was being
weakened by such a drain on her reserves, and did little to
prevent it. On the contrary, the French welcomed certain
British goods, which were in short supply on the Continent,
and at the little port of Gravelines near Dunkirk, there were
special facilities for admitting them.

Nevertheless, such valuable cargoes as golden guineas
would still be shipped secretly from the English coast to avoid
the attentions of pirates as well as customs officers, coast-
guards and enemy vessels. Some of the subsidies to the European allies went the same way.

Unimportant Folkestone was chosen as the centre for these
activities, and it is not known for certain whether Hythe men
were involved. But what is certain is that it is from this period
that the interest of the Rothschilds in this south-east corner of
England stems, and that of the other Jewish families linked to
them by marriage—the Cohens and the Sassoons.

These sophisticated operations were a far cry from the
activities of the "owlers" described by Defoe in the seventeenth century, who smuggled wool out of the country in
defiance of the government monopoly. It is pretty certain that
some Hythe men took gold across the Channel and returned
with brandy and silk goods, though they may have been
dealing independently of the clandestine government operation, since gold was at a premium in Europe because the
French had the same problem as the English over paying their
soldiers in cash.

Till recently it was possible to see a ten-oared rowing-boat,
which was kept under the long counter of the baker's shop on
the corner of Windmill Street and Albert Road. It was typical
of those used by the smugglers. As much as £10,000 in gold
might be carried on a single run, and the captain of the revenue
cutter Orontes said that trying to catch them was like a tortoise
chasing a hare.

Since an English guinea would fetch the equivalent of thirty
shillings in France, it was not surprising that some smugglers
operated on their own account. Napoleon, reminiscing in his

exile on the island of St. Helena, once said that many of his bills to pay his troops were discounted in London for a ten per cent commission. They then gave some of the bills on different bankers in Europe and the rest in gold, which was brought over to France by the smugglers.

Thus international financiers kept the war machines going on both sides, and Hythe played its small part. A postscript was provided in August 1945, when it was again profitable to smuggle sovereigns into Europe in contravention of the Defence Finance Regulations of 1939. A craftsman of the Jewish Infantry Brigade, returning to his unit in Italy from leave, was fined £50 in Folkestone for attempting to smuggle sixteen sovereigns and two half-sovereigns to the Continent, and this was considered by the prosecution to be only the tip of the iceberg.

In the meantime, whilst the smugglers carried on their clandestine activities, the old Cinque Port revived for the last time. It became quite popular for a few years in the middle of the century for making the passage to Boulogne, which was thought to be somewhat shorter than the voyage from Folkestone. The ships were paddle-steamers, and presumably there was some kind of landing facility, which has since disappeared, where coal for the new seashore gasworks was also unloaded.

With the enlarged electorate, Hythe was once again able to elect a local man to Parliament. He was William Deedes, a baron of Hythe, who was returned in 1807 and held his seat until 1812. However, in 1826 both members were again outsiders. One of them was Sir Robert Townsend Farquhar, who was a director of the East India Company and had been the first governor of the Indian Ocean island of Mauritius after it had been taken from the French. The other was Stewart Marjoribanks of Berwick, uncle of Lord Tweedsmouth and an important shipowner, especially of East Indiamen.

Indeed, the pictures of two of these ships, presented to Hythe by Marjoribanks in 1831, still grace the Town Hall. The Kent and the Hythe are shown going into Macao roads and passing through the Sunda Strait between Java and Sumatra.

During the eighteenth century the Irish connection in Hythe's parliamentary representation was noticeable. One of

Dublin's principal streets was called Sackville, whilst the
Botelers, or Butlers, were linked with the Duke of Ormonde,
a title taken from the old name of County Tipperary, which is
perpetuated in the name of a road of modest terrace houses in
the new Hythe by the sea.

Now in the nineteenth century, it was the turn of the East
India Company to descend on the little Kentish seaside town,
for in 1830 another director of the company, who had been
twice chairman, was elected. He was a captain in the Royal
Navy from Midlothian, named John Loch, who was Marjoribanks' son-in-law.

These gentlemen were Whigs, which is why the Town Hall
possesses a picture of the famous Whig prime minister,
Charles James Fox, which was also presented by Stewart
Marjoribanks. During the furore of 1831, when the Whigs
were trying to push through the Reform Bill, Marjoribanks
and Loch stood firm, and when, in 1832, the borough had only
one member to elect instead of two, Marjoribanks was able to
defeat the Tory opposition by 226 votes to 198.

The enlarged constituency was extended from the Old
Borough of Hythe and parts of West Hythe and Aldington to
include the rest of West Hythe, Saltwood, Cheriton, Folkestone and most of Newington. This was in spite of the protests
of many of the Hythe burgesses, since the voters of the Old
Borough were now outnumbered, and now no freeman could
vote who lived more than seven miles from the polling centre.

In 1836 Marjoribanks resigned his seat. Like Baker and
Glanville in the eighteenth century, he and his fellow M.P.,
Samuel Lloyd, had had a gallery built in the nave of the
church. It was for "families of resident Freemen". On his
resignation he was given a eulogy by the mayor, the aldermen,
of whom there were now four, and the town council for "the
manner in which you have discharged your duty as a Member
of the British Legislature". Thus the Liberal tradition was
established, which continued right through the Victorian age,
when Hythe became a popular resort of the quieter and more
dignified kind.

11

Victorian Splendour

BEFORE the Victorian era, the town of Hythe was largely confined to the landward side of the Military Canal. A painting done in the year 1829, and now belonging to the Local History Room, shows Stade Street as the only road going down to the shore. So the topography of this area had not developed materially from what is shown on the St. John's Hospital map of 145 years earlier, with the exception of the stream running alongside the road, made up of the two streams coming in from east and west, which were subsequently captured by the canal.

At this time, the main feature of the land south of the canal was the windmills. There were four of them. One was a post mill at the seaward end of St. Leonard's Road, close to the two small rock-built cottages, numbers 38 and 40. It ceased operating in 1832, and was demolished by Horton in 1835, but without the consent of the Corporation, which owned it. Consequently, he was required to build a row of cottages, Numbers 6 to 12 in St. Leonard's Road, in compensation.

A smock mill, which was near Rockdene, the house built in 1803 by the mill-owner, Joseph Horton, stood in the same road. It was struck by lightning in 1817, and although it was undamaged, Stephen Brown, the miller, was killed. However, it was demolished in 1832, leaving its iron windshaft as its memorial for a while.

In Cobden Road, there was another mill, called the Lower Mill, but it was closed in 1858 and removed to Cheriton in 1877. Being close to the shore, it commanded a good view of the sea from its upper stage, and boys used to stand there on watch for the coal brig. The one who spotted it first got sixpence as a reward.

The fourth mill was in Park Road, and operated right up to

1902, as early photographs testify. People in the new houses nearby continually complained about the noise of the machinery. But "No noise, no flour for bread", was the answer they got, and at least the local cottagers were able to use the waste hot water, which they much appreciated on washing days. Known as the Stade Mill, it was worked for nearly a century, though in 1857 there was a big sale of equipment, including sail cloths, sack chain, regulator straps, grindstones, a scale beam and iron rope. There was a fifth windmill, called Albion Mill, near the bottom of Blackhouse Hill, which operated in the first half of the nineteenth century, and is featured in a picture of Hythe, painted in 1806.

All these mills postdated by many years the old Hevywater watermill, which was at the bottom of Hythe Hill by the London road. But now it is only in Windmill Street, a turning to the west off Stade Street, that their memory lingers on. The only remaining mill in Hythe is the watermill at the eastern end of the town, which is still inhabited.

This mill was probably built in place of Damer's Mill, which stood on the site in the seventeenth century. One of the bricks of the mill house has the date 1773 on it, and in 1832 the building was taken over by George Burch, who also ran the Stade Mill later on. Standing astride Hythe's eastern stream, the Saltwood brook, it must have looked magnificent in its prime, with its great wheel, twenty-one and a half feet in diameter and six feet wide, driving four pairs of millstones.

A feature of the mill was the dam enclosing the millpond in the fork of the deep chine. By this means, a constant source of water, pouring into the millrace from a useful height, was assured. However, the silting up of the millpond made it necessary, in the mid-nineteenth century, to augment the power from this great piece of machinery of the early days of the industrial revolution with the installation of an auxiliary steam-engine.

Known to everyone as Burch's Mill, Hythe's only surviving watermill was run by the Burch family for nearly a century. When it was sold in 1932, it was still a going concern. But unfortunately, the purchaser, Mr. Stuart Brown, who was in his hundredth year when he died in January 1982, was unable to maintain it in good repair. So, unavoidable neglect,

Burch's
Watermill
in Mill Lane

together with the damage suffered from the bomb, which fell
in Mill Road in 1941, has now reduced it to a sad spectacle.

The derelict machinery, dried out and overgrown millpond, and broken sluice gate, are fascinating to look at, but
give a poor idea of what the place must have looked like before
the war. Yet the problem of reactivating the mill has, so far,
proved too formidable a task for the local residents who would
like to preserve it as an example of industrial archaeology.

As we have seen, the Corporation had been selling, or
leasing out land from the dried-out harbour since the sixteenth
century, and now that Hythe was attracting more residents
and holidaymakers, this land was being built on. In 1854 a
bathing establishment was erected at the Corporation's
expense where the Hythe Sailing Club now stands. It had a
domed roof, rest rooms, and living accommodation for a

guide, and it cost £2,000, the price of quite a luxurious building. The Corporation made sure that the nearby bathing-
machines would be used by forbidding changing on the beach
anywhere between the Imperial hotel and the gasworks between 8 a.m. and 8 p.m.

An important reason for the town's growth was its new
accessibility. The South-Eastern Railway Company got Parliament to pass an Act giving them the authority to construct a
railway line from London to Dover. This line, via Tonbridge
and Ashford, was completed as far as Folkestone in 1843.

A single-track line was then built, branching off the main
line at what came to be Sandling Junction. Prince Arthur,
Duke of Connaught, cut the first sod in 1872. It passed close to
Saltwood Castle on its way down to Hythe Station, which
was built on a high stone wall that can still be seen on the
eastern side of Blackhouse Hill beside the abutment of the
bridge, which was demolished in 1966.

This branch line descended the cliff and went as far as
Sandgate Station, which is now the bus depot at the bottom of
Hospital Hill in Seabrook. In fact, the two bridges over Horn
Street and Hospital Hill are still standing.

The original intention had been to run the line through to
Folkestone along the foot of the cliffs, so that boat trains
would be able to go straight down from the main line at
Sandling instead of reversing down to Folkestone harbour
from the high level east of the Folkestone viaduct. The company even bought Sandgate Castle from the War Department
with the intention of using it as the next station along the line.

Although the project was never completed, the regular
service on the branch line, which was begun in 1874 and was
inaugurated by the Duke of Teck, benefited Hythe greatly.
The trains ran to Sandgate until 1931, and to Hythe until they
were discontinued in 1951 in the Beeching cuts.

From this it can be seen that they ran to Hythe for 77 years,
and it was a real loss to the town when the last one climbed the
hill to Sandling. As recently as 1981 there was a hope of a
resumption of the service by the East Kent Railway Society,
using two redundant steam engines from a colliery near
Dover. Unfortunately, thoughtless destruction of bridges and
track has made their task a very difficult one.

However, the town's unique contribution to the age of steam was, appropriately enough, in shipping rather than in railways. Sir Francis Pettit-Smith was born in Hythe in the year 1808, and lived until 1874. He became renowned as the inventor of the screw propellor for steamships, which became a very much more efficient means of propulsion than the old paddle-wheels. In 1839 the S.S. *Archimedes* was the first ship to be equipped with this new device. It proved so successful that the *Great Britain* was fitted with propellers in 1843.

Hythe commemorates the memory of Pettit-Smith with a plaque on the house at the corner of the High Street and Three Posts Lane, which was his birthplace. But it must be admitted that, across the water, Boulogne has done rather better. No day tripper from Folkestone can fail to notice the bronze statue there of Frédéric Sauvage, who was also amongst the first to use propellers in steamboats, since it stands at the end of the bridge which takes you into the town across the basin from the packet-boat quay.

After the construction of the branch railway-line, Hythe's local transportation system was improved as well. This was largely due to Sir Edward Watkin, a Cheshire man, who was Chairman of the South-Eastern Railway, and an ardent advocate of the Channel tunnel a hundred years before his time. Sir Edward viewed with some disfavour the keen competition provided for cross-Channel passengers by the London, Chatham and Dover Railway's direct line to the docks at Dover, and determined on some kind of a rail link between Hythe and Folkestone.

The part that was constructed ran down Cannongate Road and across the Canal to the sea front by the new Seabrook Hotel, which was another of Watkin's projects, and is now called the Imperial. It was built to the standard gauge, and at one time it had a small locomotive on it, which had been obtained from the Suakim to Berber railway in the African Sudan, that had originally been built to supply the British forces fighting the Mahdi's army.

However, in the event this line was mainly used to haul materials for the construction of the Folkestone, Sandgate and Hythe Tramway, which was opened in 1891, and ran from Red Lion Square in Hythe, down Stade Street, along South

Road and Prince's Parade, and under the cliff to Sandgate. Its eastern end was at Sandgate School, whence a lift took passengers up the cliff and onto the Folkestone leas.

Pairs of horses pulled single carriages along this tramway. In summer these were open "toast-racks", with passengers facing the front. But there were glass-sided coaches with longitudinal seats for winter use. The railway shed, which was the Hythe terminal and stables, has been converted into a restaurant, and can still be seen, together with a short section of the line, which was carefully left below the general level of the pavement, when that part of Rampart Road was reconstructed in 1980.

After the horses had been requisitioned for use in the First World War, mules were obtained to replace them. But the line was finally closed in 1921. Although a great attraction for summer visitors, it could no longer compete with the motor-buses.

Naturally, this tramway was a great amenity for the Seabrook Hotel, built on the site of the derelict Twiss Fort, which celebrated its centenary in 1980. This monument to Victorian

A "toast rack" tram in Red Lion Square

splendour was built at a cost of £30,000 and renamed the Imperial in 1901.

The hotel was built as part of an ambitious development called the Seabrook Estate, which fortunately was never fully realised, as it envisaged building all over the present hotel golf-course. But it was a railway hotel, in the sense of being the property of the South-Eastern Railway Company, and it was proud of having "the most recent appliances for securing that luxurious comfort, which enters so largely into modern life and manners".

Some of the features of this comfort were "well-fitted lavatories—having a constant supply of hot and cold water—and secluded closets, those at the western end being reserved for ladies, and those at the eastern end for gentlemen". The hotel prospectus also drew attention to the "small but powerful steam engine" used to heat the viands and keep the plates warm in the "hot closets", and to the soil pipes "carried up through the roof to obtain thorough ventilation".

The "well-padded spring mattresses" on the beds were mentioned, and the Axminster carpets, the silk tapestry on the couches, the grand piano, the billiard room, and so on. And all this could be had for half-a-crown a day, with an extra shilling and sixpence if one had a second person in one's room.

Indeed, a room at between half-a-crown and seven and sixpence could be cheaper than dinner at three shillings to five and sixpence for two to five courses, though you had to pay an extra one and sixpence for a hot bath. With your dinner you might have a bottle of claret for two and sixpence. But the Rothschild tipple, Chateau Lafite 1868, cost eleven and sixpence. The liquor licence for this magnificent establishment was transferred from the humble Flying Horse, which stood in the High Street just to the east of the Smugglers' Retreat.

Outside, in the grounds of the hotel, there were tennis courts and croquet lawns, and military bands came down from Shorncliffe to play "good class" music during the summer months. The tennis courts were soon to be hosting the Kent Coast Open Lawn Tennis championships. But more recently, the nine-hole golf-course, in the dried-out harbour area between the Canal and the sea wall, where seaside houses had originally been envisaged, has given the Imperial the name of a golfing hotel.

The Imperial Hotel

The great flood of 1877

Strangely enough, the handling of the "inexhaustible heaps of shingle" which were made use of as material for the large amount of fill required in the construction, nearly caused a major setback in the development of the sea front.

It was New Year's day, 1877. Workmen had been digging out shingle from the banked-up beach for the concrete-mixers. At that time there was no sea wall east of the first block of houses going along the front from Stade Street towards the hotel, and unfortunately the labourers had taken too much. With a spring high tide and a strong south-westerly wind, the sea enlarged the cut made by the builder's men, and in due course an enormous wave broke through to the landward side and made a breach.

Of course, all the land between Marine Parade and the Military Canal, reclaimed from Leland's old "large mile" of harbour water, lies below the high-water level of the sea. So on this occasion, it lost no time in rushing through to flood over the flat fields. Within three hours it had flowed over the raised banks and bridges of the canal itself.

Water was knee-deep in Stade Street, and flowed into the cellars of the High Street, which was itself awash. Some men were actually able to approach the High Street by way of Marine Walk Street in boats, and one man, a road foreman named Gravenor, was unfortunately drowned by the raging sea.

As the tide went out, the breach was blocked up and the flood waters gradually receded. But it was a salutary warning that the sea never forgives those who fail to treat it with due respect, and an earth embankment was raised from Twiss Road to the Grove to protect the town against a similar disaster, pending the extension of the sea wall.

After the disaster, a flood committee was set up to help those who had suffered loss and damage. It made a contribution to the Hythe Soup Kitchen which, according to its accounts for the financial year 1878-9, dispensed no less than 1,000 gallons of soup to 67 needy families, together with 407 loaves of bread, all bought with the £33 8s subscribed. The Soup Kitchen had, however, been founded much earlier by William Tritton, the mayor in 1821.

It was Lady Watkin who unveiled the new drinking fountain now in Red Lion Square, which the mayor, Thomas

Judge, presented to the town in 1886 and placed near the water trough for horses by the Town Hall. As the inscription says:

He opened the rock and the waters gushed out.
They ran in dry places like a river.

With the new inhabitants of Hythe came new religious groups. No longer was the vicar the sole cure of souls, sitting on the left-hand side of the mayor at public meetings of the town council. The building of new churches was vigorously pursued during the Victorian period, as the population increased.

But it was not any conversion of Hythe people to Cardinal Newman's persuasion that brought a Catholic mission to the town. It was the presence of the School of Musketry. The mission was established about 1860, and in 1865 Father Goddard was given the use of a horse so that he could celebrate mass on Sunday mornings at both the Hythe and the Shorncliffe garrisons.

The appointment by the War Office of a commissioned R.C. chaplain for Shorncliffe and Hythe temporarily obviated the need for a civilian priest. But in 1891 Hythe was placed in the cure of the Austin Friars, and with an increasing Catholic population, a church was built in 1894 for the sum of £2,587 to accommodate a congregation of up to three hundred, and a school for up to two hundred and fifty pupils. This Church of Our Lady of Good Counsel, at the bottom of Lower Blackhouse Hill, has prospered, though the proposed monastery alongside it was never built.

Soon after the establishment of the Catholic mission, the church now called the United Reform Church, embracing the Congregational and Presbyterian persuasions, was built in the High Street in 1868. This was followed by the Methodist Church, put up in Rampart Road in 1897.

St. Michael's Church, a white-painted, corrugated-iron building in Stade Street, built in 1893, was more of a mission hall, and an amenity for the poorer people living in the rapidly developing area on the seaward side of the canal. It was to be a working man's church with free pews, and also for the old and infirm of the locality and, in the words of the vicar of the day, for those who were "shy of attending their parish church".

Prior to the building of these churches, the separate religious groups had met in smaller chapels. The Congregational Church, which celebrated its 150th anniversary in 1964, had its beginnings in one man, William Marsh, a chemist, who moved from Canterbury to Hythe in 1805. He gathered around him a number of like-minded people to take part in their own style of worship, encountering a certain amount of opposition as he did so. Then, in 1814, a small chapel was opened, and the ten members of the congregation had Marsh as their pastor. In 1817 a larger building, called the Ebenezer Chapel and capable of accommodating up to three hundred people, was opened for worship. It stood near the bridge to the west of the town.

After Marsh had retired to Deal, there was a series of pastors, and it was the Rev. J. Mackinnon, a fervent evangelist, who was the incumbent when the present church was built for £2,500. He died not long afterwards, in 1870, at the young age of fifty-one. That there was no great hostility towards the established Church is shown by the fact that his grave is in St. Leonard's churchyard.

The Methodist presence in Hythe has been traced back to the same year, 1805, as that of the Congregationalists. At that time Dover was the head of the Methodist Circuit in the region, and in 1845 a small chapel was built for £60 in Rampart Road on the site of the present church, to seat 250 people.

The first Methodist preachers in Hythe came from the ranks of the soldiery at Shorncliffe, and a good proportion of the congregation consisted of military families. So, in 1864, the Folkestone Circuit was formed, and dependence on Dover ceased. The new church, or chapel, built in 1870, cost a little over £3,000, and again many of its most faithful supporters were army men.

It was the same during the First World War. In the early days, the Yorkshire and Lancashire regiment and the Queen's Regiment had men in the East and West Sandling camps up on the hills, and in the severe winter of 1915 they were billeted in the town. When they came to church, there was generally community hymn singing before the service, during which the men were encouraged to choose their own favourites. Later in the war, many Canadians of the Second Canadian

Division, occupying the same camps, were faithful to the chapel. Of those Hythe Methodists who were called up, the chapel organist, himself, was killed, and three others.

Thus, if we include the little Elim Pentecostal Church in Ormonde Road as well, we can see that, contrary to the popular idea of the Victorians being merely conventional conformists, there was a considerable upsurge of nonconformism during this period. It was also an age of good works, during which the town received two important bequests.

In 1862 an agreement was made between the Hythe Corporation, Her Majesty's Principal Secretary of State for the War Department, Joseph Horton, the miller and flour merchant, and George Shipdem, a former mayor, to set aside a large piece of land at the western end of the town "for public recreation, with no part of it to be applied for building purposes". Horton paid most of the expenses of the purchase of the meadow from the War Department, and in this way, the Green came into being, where the summer fair is held when the circus comes to town. The old wall that borders it to the north, with the plaque commemorating the agreement, can still be seen.

Then, in 1892, Mr. Alfred Bull, a draper who had previously been treasurer of the Hythe Soup Kitchen and active in other good works, founded the Hythe Institute. He donated his house on the corner of Mount Street and Prospect Road, and endowed it with the income from other properties, to be used as a club and entertainment centre for people who would not or could not join the established circles, such as the Cinque Ports Club.

The subscription was four shillings a year, and no gambling was permitted, even in the games room, nor were alcoholic drinks allowed except by special permission of the committee. No smoking was allowed, except in the games room, no dogs were allowed in the building, and no audible conversation was permitted in the reading room. Nevertheless, it was a good amenity for the town, particularly in the provision of library facilities, which visitors could enjoy as well as residents. In the 1920s the annual subscription to the library was 4s, but anybody could go into the reading room for a penny.

Occasionally, concerts were given as, for instance, on the

opening day just before Christmas, when Madame Ashworth sang "The Siren's Song" and Mr. Walter North rendered "The Bedouin Love Song". But the Institute suffered the fate of all clubs in our age in finding it more and more difficult to make ends meet, and when, in the late 1960s, the building was demolished to make room for road widening, the trustees were not sorry, in the end, to receive a sum in compensation from the Ministry of Transport, which could be converted into a trust fund with enough money to benefit worthwhile local causes.

However, the rise in nonconformity did not mean that the parish church was neglected. In 1844 St. Leonard's at last became a parish church in its own right, separated from Salt-wood in the Church hierarchy, and in the latter part of the century, at the very time when the new churches were being built, the parishioners found the sum of £10,000 for the restoration of the nave in 1875, and for the completion of the groined vaulting of the chancel in 1887. At the same time all the galleries were taken down, as the unremarkable size of the congregation had rendered them unnecessary.

Naturally, these works were done in the style of the existing structure. But a glance at the pulpit will be enough to allay the idea that only the old is beautiful. The mosaic panels of pictures, done against a background of gold leaf, were executed by Salviati of Venice in 1881, and contain over 20,000 pieces.

The development of the local schools preceded by some years the construction of the new churches and the refurbishing of the old one, and it was probably under the impetus of the demands of the new military families that the Hythe National Schools were established in 1814. There was a large Tudor, double-fronted, two-gabled house with mullioned windows in the High Street, called Captain Beane's house on the 1685 plan of Hythe, and embellished with grotesque figures bearing shields with antlered bucks on them, which represented the family crest. This became the first school house. It was leased from Lady Douglas of nearby Douglas House, and paid for by local subscription.

These schools were intended for working-class children, and were run by a committee. But they ran into trouble after the first generations of schoolchildren had passed through them, when the building became in urgent need of repair. In accordance with the terms of the lease, it had been fitted out as a school. But nothing had been said about who was to carry out the maintenance. Lady Douglas was unwilling to do so, and the school committee had no funds to restore the structure.

So the Committee received notice to quit, and was glad to accept the old workhouse in Stade Street in lieu. The schools opened in the new location in 1844. Four year later, William Vile, the schoolmaster for twenty-eight years, retired and received a clock in appreciation of his services.

Three years after that, Horton's tender of £1,272, the lowest of four, for the construction of a new school was accepted. Thus the present St. Leonard's Schools, built of ragstone quarried on the Roughs, came into being. In 1852 the children marched from the old school to the opening of the new one, with medals backed with blue ribands on their coats. The new headmaster, Edward Palmer, lived through six reigns, from George III to George V, and died in 1912, aged a hundred. In those days school may have been tougher on the children but less nerve-racking for the teacher.

In the meantime, the name of the road leading past the schools down to the sea front was changed from Hardway's End to St. Leonard's Road by order of the Commissioners of Pavement. The original school house was turned into the Walnut Tree stables and coachhouse for the horse buses plying between Hythe and Folkestone.

By this time Lady Douglas' house had been demolished, like that of Captain Beane, who was ten times mayor between 1671 and 1696. But its name has been perpetuated in Douglas Avenue. The schools continued their good work under the aegis of the Church of England. In 1920, on the occasion of a fund-raising visit from the Dean of Canterbury, there were 120 boys and 110 girls. In 1952 their centenary was celebrated.

In politics the Whig tradition continued. In 1847 there was a contest of two Liberals—Edward Brockman, the local man from Beachborough, and the Jewish outsider, Baron Mayer Amschel de Rothschild, who was narrowly defeated.

Brockman, who was Master of the East Kent Hunt for thirty-eight years, from 1832 to 1870, gave up the seat in 1857.

This was an occasion for a satirical poster from the stable of his opponent, the baron, which was aimed at the man he had put forward as his successor. Dated "Hythe, 12th March 1857", and headed "Hythe and Folkestone Election", it has been elegantly reproduced for modern readers as a printed tea-towel.

BROTHER ELECTORS
THE HUMBLE PETITION of the undersigned Electors of the above Borough MANIFESTETH that when a Man is poor, he ought to be kept so, and ought not to have any Vote or Voice about Parliamentary business.
   That Mr. E. D. Brockman, our present Member, having got a bad Cold and Cough, has declared himself unable to represent this IMPORTANT Borough in Parliament any longer, and has condescendingly announced that Sir J. W. Ramsden (a York-shireman) will be kind enough to fill his place; we hereby declare, THAT WE FOREGO OUR OWN OPINIONS, and accept the Gentlemen whom Mr. Brockman (having done with the place himself) has been so kind as to recommend to us.
   We are, Gentlemen, on behalf of you and ourselves,
       BARLEY MEAL,
       TURNIP TOPS.

One might have supposed that Rothschild was rather busy during these years, since he was building his vast palace of Mentmore Towers in Buckinghamshire, the treasures of which went under the hammer in 1980 before it became a centre for transcendental meditation. Nevertheless, in 1859 he was returned unopposed after four other candidates had with-drawn, and he retained his seat until he resigned in 1874. This was even after the Reform Act of 1867, which had been promoted by the Tory prime minister, Disraeli, had done away with the £10 householder qualification and again enlarged the electorate, so that all men who paid scot and lot were now eligible to vote.
   The Liberal landslide against James Wilde and the other candidates, who had withdrawn, was expressed in the follow-ing way by a local rhymester:

> The tocsin has sounded the signal for war,
> Though a few wild(e) notes it did sound,
> That the Campbells are coming, but soon it did prove

That the clan could not keep to their ground.
For the Liberal banner so proudly did float,
With "the ballot" inscribed on so neat,
But the sight of the flag made those candidates lag,
And they deemed it wise to retreat.
Then Folkestone and Hythe,
With other voters besides,
Proved they were unwilling to yield,
For the true Men of Kent
On Reform thus were bent,
And left Rothschild the Lord of the Field.

Mayor Rayner of Hythe welcomed the victorious baron, and the seventy-five year old Moses Montefiore, doyen of the Jewish community, who later travelled to Palestine, when he was over ninety, in the interests of his co-religionists and lived to be a hundred, addressed the crowd from a window of the White Hart.

"You have shown your sympathy with Liberal and enlightened views", he said. "You have my heartiest wishes for your prosperity".

The election had been expensive. In the run up to the poll, Rothschild had been offering a shilling a vote, but had to increase it to one and sixpence, then to two shillings until, on the eve of the election itself, half-a-crown was the going rate. As the way each person had voted was openly published, voters had to show that they had earned their cash. But no wonder the other four candidates dropped out of the race.

In 1868 the votes cast were 1,789, of which the baron had a two thirds majority. But this time he was vigorously opposed by a Tory, named Nugent. His agent produced a polite poster, which included the following words:

The direct promises which I have received are so numerous, and the public feelings so warmly displayed on my behalf, that I feel justified in expressing my surprise at the continuance of the contest by my opponents, who thereby disturb the peace and tranquillity of the Borough and take so many of the inhabitants from their business and occupations.

I shall return on Tuesday to pay my personal respects to those friends whom I have not been hitherto so fortunate as to meet with. Be assured, gentlemen, that so long as I have your support, I WILL NEVER LEAVE YOU!

Nugent fired off a much less polite poster in the heavy sarcasm that was in vogue at the time, saying:

> Wanted for tonight at Sandgate (on trial) a tub orator and party howler to assist the Leader in a "Break-down" on the platform. A permanent engagement if he rants well. No one upon the "Establishment" need apply.
> Ten guineas a day and his washing.
> Must be up to "Gag"—with a good character from his last Tub. The one already engaged, tho' "A perfect Samson", finds the pace too hard, as he has to do all the dancing, and organ-grinding as well. Also a poet to join the Caravan—The one lately engaged is too small in ideas, as in person.
> Apply at once to Baron Rothschild's Committee Rooms, or to the Old Bogie, Police News Office, High Street, Folkestone.

Rothschild's cutting riposte hit at Nugent's poverty relative to his own wealth, and at the Tory stand against the disestablishment of the Church in Ireland:

> Wanted for tonight at Sandgate, a number of Roughs and Party Howlers to assist a big Irish Tory after a Break Down on the platform. A permanent engagement for the election if they howl well. Surpliced ritualists not objected to. Threepence a night each, with lush and washing (Can't afford Liberal Salaries). Wanted also in a respectable situation, two rooms and the use of a kitchen. The bargain to be off should Mr. Nugent not be elected. The kind of accommodation required may be seen at the Lodgings, 76, South Audley Street, London.
> Apply at once to Mr. Nugent's Committee Room, or, till the Harlequin is at home, at Cheap Jack's Establishment, High Street.

However, the baron was generous to his adopted town. He bought the lifeboat and its house and other amenities. The first time he took his seat was the year after his elder brother, Lionel, who had already been returned by the City of London in 1849 and 1852, but had been unable to sit because, as a Jew, he could not take the traditional oath.

It is said that, on one occasion, when the two brothers were contesting the seats in the constituencies they had made their own, Lionel was duly returned for the City. The Hythe election was to be the following day. So he sent a fast messenger down to Hythe to tell Mayer not to bother, and, one imagines, to save his money too.

After they had been elected to parliament, neither brother ever made a speech there. It was the principle of breaking into the citadel of Christianity that had been all-important, and what happened afterwards mattered much less. Mayer, himself, was a keen man of the turf, and the first Rothschild to own a Derby winner. This prompted Disraeli to once make the remark that he was very sound, in fact "a man with a stable mind".

In 1872 Mayer was sure that he had another Derby winner in a horse named Laburnum, and told everyone in his constituency to back it. It has been said that, when the horse failed to deliver the goods, he felt he had lost too much face to stand at the next election. But, as it turned out, his health failed him, and he died in the year of his resignation.

In 1874 Hythe returned another Liberal in the person of Sir Edward Watkin, who was thus well placed to push through his projects for the development of the area between Hythe and Sandgate. In 1892, when he was returned unopposed for the fourth successive time, there were 4,219 names on the Parliamentary Register—2,648 of them in Folkestone, 882 in Hythe and 689 in Sandgate.

Sir Edward retained the seat until 1895, six years before his death at the ripe old age of eighty-two, and there could be no more fitting person with whom to end our description of nineteenth century Hythe, since his whole character epitomised the forward drive and initiative of the leaders of the golden age of the British Empire.

Watkin used to thank God that he had been born before nerves came into fashion. As a self-proclaimed imperialist, he crossed the Atlantic thirty times, and was instrumental in the formation of the Dominion of Canada. He also wrote on India.

As a promoter of great enterprises, Hythe's M.P. took the prime minister, Gladstone, up the Eiffel tower in Paris, and proposed to build one 150 feet higher at Wembley. It was never completed. Nor was his grand scheme for slicing Ireland in half with a canal and draining the bogs achieved in his lifetime.

But his grandest scheme of all was the Channel tunnel. He planned it and costed it out at 3½ million pounds. Yet, however many influential people he took to see the shaft and trial

undersea borings near Dover, he could never quite get the
project off the ground.

He reckoned that the military objections to the tunnel were
absurd, since it could easily be flooded in an emergency.
Instead, he considered that it would be a tie of friendship
between England and France, and used to say that "some old
women of both sexes would refuse to go to bed were they told
that a few French rabbits had bored a hole beneath the sea from
Cap Griz Nez to Folkestone".

Shortly after he left his parliamentary seat for Hythe, Sir
Edward received a letter from a well-wisher suggesting that he
might begin by joining England to Ireland with a tunnel. In his
reply, he pointed out that he had carefully studied the question
of the Irish tunnel, and discovered that the nature of the sea bed
between the two countries would make it a very much more
difficult proposition. He finished his letter with the following
pointed remarks:

> For at least a quarter of a century I have been boring away at this
> question, and have at last made it a living reality by showing how,
> where, and under what conditions the Channel Tunnel can be
> easily, quickly and cheaply carried out. I might therefore, regard
> my share of the work as done, were it not that it is to me a labour
> of love, not undertaken for pay or profit. If my countrymen,
> however, are such idiots as to fear a tunnel, why should I spoil my
> digestion?—Ever truly yours,
> E. Watkin.

Now, a century later, we shall see. But it would need
Hythe's own humorist, Sir Henry Lucy, to do real justice to
these Victorian politicians and company promoters, since he
was an M.P. himself, combining parliamentary duties with a
successful career as a journalist. Born in 1845, Sir Henry
became parliamentary writer for the Daily News in 1873 and
editor of that paper in 1886 and 1887.

Yet, what he is remembered for today are his contributions
to the magazine, Punch. In his humorous reports called *The
Essence of Parliament* he invented the characters of Toby M.P.
and the Member for Sark, which survived in people's
memories much longer than his *Study from Life* of Mr. Gladstone and his *Memories of Eight Parliaments.* His own memory
in Hythe, where he died in 1924, is perpetuated in Lucy's Hill,
and in the footpath which many people think is named after a
girl, since it runs parallel with Ladies' Walk down to the sea.

12

The First World War

THE Boer War came as a stern reminder that all was not entirely well in the far-flung empire of Queen Victoria, and it came to none more poignantly than to Major Thomas Hamilton's widow, who died in Hythe much later, in 1920, aged seventy-three. By then she had lost three of her sons in South Africa. One of them, who was in the Royal Irish Fusiliers, was struck by lightning at Machadodorp in 1902, aged twenty-eight. Another was in the Ceylon Contingent and died at Bloemfontein of enteric fever in 1900, aged twenty-four, and the third, who was in Bethune's Mounted Infantry, was killed in action at Sheepers Nek in the same year, aged only twenty-three.

The fourth son to die before her was in the Worcestershire Regiment, and also one of the earliest members of the Royal Flying Corps. He died on manoeuvres in 1912, two years before the greater conflict began. In the same year, as those who go to the parish church may see for themselves, Edward Colley went down with the *Titanic*.

However, the week before the outbreak of the First World War was not notable for any striking events in Hythe. The Folkestone, Hythe, Sandgate and Cheriton Herald of Saturday, August 1st 1914, reported that a runaway horse had collided with a railway van opposite the Oak Inn, turning the wagon completely over and sending a wheel flying into the air. It was also reported that the new red bus service between Folkestone and Hythe had been started, the ride costing 4d, with buses leaving every thirteen minutes.

In addition, there had been a meeting at the White Hart Hotel to form a branch of the Association of Men of Kent and Kentish Men, which was attended by the vicar, the Rev. H. D. Dale, and Hythe's Boy Scout troop had given a display on the

Town Green, which included blindfold boxing, baiting the bear, tossing the blanket and skinning the rabbit.

In the world of sport, Colour Sergeant Barton of Hythe Company of the National Reserve had come fourth in a team of eight representing the whole of Kent in shooting at Bisley, whilst Mr. Snowden had won the finals at the Hythe Bowling Club. Future events included the Saltwood Flower Show the following Monday, August Bank Holiday, and Hythe Cricket Week from August 10th to 15th, during which the Grand Venetian Fete was to be held on the Wednesday evening, August 12th.

Finally, Hythe residents had been amused to read a notice put up by the Town Council offering a £5 reward to "any person (other than the actual offender) giving such information as will lead to the conviction of any person shooting, ill-treating, or infuriating any of the swans belonging to the Council on the Royal Military Canal."

However, after the declaration of war on Tuesday, August 4th, events moved swiftly. The following evening a meeting was held in the Town Hall to take steps to deal with the situation caused by the war. Councillor Jeal complained that tradespeople had already put up their prices, and some of his own workmen thought it scandalous that this had happened as early as the previous Saturday, even before war had been declared. In mitigation the mayor said that the tradespeople did not get all the profit, as the price of maize, wheat and so on had also gone up.

The Reservists and Territorials had already left for duty, and the dependants of those who had gone to the war were asked to give in their names at the town clerk's office. The 1st Cadet Battalion of the King's Royal Rifle Corps, who had come to Hythe for their annual fortnight's training, also made a hurried departure, leaving at midnight on the Wednesday, except for a rear party detailed to strike camp on the Corporation Fields the following morning.

Meanwhile Captain Beauclerk suggested the formation of a local Vigilance Committee to watch for spies, especially at the railway station, and thought that the Boy Scouts would be useful, particularly in signalling. He considered that the quarter-staff of a Boy Scout was a serious weapon if used by three or four on one German. But one of the councillors wanted to leave matters to the local military and police, saying that a Frenchman could easily be mistaken for a German with serious consequences.

Cricket Week was cancelled, and Councillor Jeal suggested that cricketers, and others who went in for games, could give up such pastimes for the time being and go in for learning ambulance work and "other necessary things". But the Herald reported that "The situation made but little difference to the Bank Holiday and happy visitors were here, there and everywhere. It is true that some were getting anxious as the day wore on, but they did not show it much".

On Thursday evening the trams stopped running, as the tram horses were requisitioned by the army, and other horses were compulsorily purchased. But the advice of the editor of the Herald was:

> Be calm above all. Don't get alarmed if you hear any shooting. The rifle ranges will still be used for practice, and by men who want to fit themselves for active service. Do you want to take part? If you are unmarried and healthy, you should have no hesitation.

The following week the patriotic call to arms was repeated at "an enormous meeting" held in the gardens of Moyle Tower to support Lord Kitchener's call for 100,000 volunteers. It was addressed by Henry Fielding Dickens Q.C., a son of the famous novelist, Charles Dickens, who had once praised Hythe to the skies, saying that it had "such charms of sight and sound as all the galleries on earth can but poorly suggest." The meeting was reported in the journalistic style typical of the day. The assembled citizens were told that "they had a noble heritage and that they had been great on the sea as a Cinque Port. Their first sentiment should be loyalty to the Crown (Applause). Then give three cheers for the King (These were given in rousing style).

> The speaker then referred to Belgian neutrality. Give three cheers for Belgium (This suggestion was immediately acted upon). And three cheers for our friends in France (These were enthusiastically accorded). Little Belgium said 'No'. They had upset the German timetable (Laughter and applause). So far as the Navy was concerned, he believed that the spirit of Nelson remained with us.

Nelson's enemy did not lay mines scattered on open sea like the present enemy was doing (Shame). At the War Office they had got a man whom they all trusted—Lord Kitchener (Applause). Did they trust Kitchener? (Yes) Had they confidence in Kitchener? (Yes) Were they prepared to do what was asked of them? (Yes).

Men came forward in response to these calls to action, and a list of the Hythe men called up was posted in St. Leonard's Church. Bicycles were given to the Boy Scouts, who were put to work, as Captain Beauclerk had suggested, guarding sensitive places. Ambulance men drilled "almost daily" in the School of Musketry, whilst the Red Cross Voluntary Aid Detachment made its preparations to deal with casualties.

Even at this early stage of the war, which few people expected to last long, people were enjoined by the Agricultural Organiser to the Kent Education Committee to turn their gardens over to useful vegetables, such as turnips, carrots, beetroots, onions and cabbages. At the same time, the panic buying of food ceased, and with it the profiteering.

Thus it was that, at the quarterly meeting of the Town Council in the same second week of August, the Town Clerk was able to say that he was replying that "everything was all right" to the letters he was receiving daily from people wishing to come to Hythe and asking whether is was safe.

The following month, Belgian and French refugees were landed at Folkestone in large numbers—12,000 of them in three days over the first weekend of September alone. Many of the Belgians came to Hythe, and a committee was set up to organise accommodation for them. Alfred Winnifrith, a schoolmaster in Hythe for many years and author of *Men of Kent and Kentish Men* and *The Fair Maids of Kent,* particularly befriended them, together with his wife, Mary.

But since they were not without resources, it was not thought wrong to ask them to pay rent to the seaside landladies housing them. Consequently, by the end of the year a good proportion of them had moved on, having been able to find either complete hospitality or rent-free quarters elsewhere.

Shorncliffe and Hythe formed, of course, a major area of military concentration for the training and reinforcement of the British Expeditionary Force, and less than two months after the outbreak of war, Hythe residents began to have soldiers billeted on them. At the end of September there were sixty soldiers, mostly of the Yeomanry, in Hythe houses over the weekend, and numbers increased. In December the military authorities requested the Council to order the closing of all licensed premises, clubs as well as pubs, by eight o'clock every evening, and when the Council delayed action, they issued the order themselves. Many of the soldiers in the early days were coal miners, enlisted in the Yorkshire and Lancashire Regiment and in the King's Own Yorkshire Light Infantry.

By this time, the first two of Hythe's casualties had already been reported and Gunner Nichols, judging from his letters home, considered himself lucky to be voyaging to Bombay with the Foreign Service Battery of the 3rd Home Counties (Cinque Ports) Brigade of the Royal Artillery.

As the war continued, the casualty lists grew, and Gunner Nichols, son of the Borough Engineer, having learnt Hindustani and been commissioned into the Indian Army Reserve, was himself taken prisoner by the Turks at the surrender of Kut in Mesopotamia. Captain F. W. Butler, who had been twice mayor, was mentioned in despatches for his exploits whilst serving in the Northamptonshire Regiment. But Company Sergeant-Major Noaks of the 9th Royal Fusiliers was killed in action in France, and Mr. Nelson, a steward, was unlucky too, going down with the *Persia,* when she was torpedoed on her way back from India.

There were many others on the roll of honour. As anyone can see for himself on the War Memorial in the Grove, there are 154 names listed behind the model of the Cinque Ports ship, upheld by the winged angel of victory, which crowns the monument, more than double the dead of the Second World War. "These died that we might live" says the inscription.

When the "Compulsion Bill" came into operation in 1916, some people asked the tribunals for exemption. Thomas Keeler, a thirty-one year old single man, pleaded that he was the owner of fourteen donkeys which were "very necessary on the sands in the summer time" and raised a good laugh. Others said that they were the sole support of their families. Dr. Randall Davis, who was to bequeath his handsome house in

Stade Street to the Corporation in 1932, supported the application of his thirty-seven year old chauffeur, saying that his two partners had already joined the R.A.M.C. and he had a lot of extra work.

The tribunal granted a three months extension to the chauffeur. But there were many who went to the war without delay, and many who prepared themselves for it by joining the Kent Volunteer Fencibles, East Kent Regiment, Cinque Ports Battalion, F (Hythe) Company, and doing their drills on the Cricket Club field.

The mayor, William Cobay, who was five times re-elected, opened a fund for the Fencibles of the Volunteer Training Corps and collected £554 5s 10d. There was evidently no paper shortage, since every one of the two hundred odd donors was mentioned in the local press.

Those who left for service were more than replaced by men of the Canadian Expeditionary Force, many of whom were encamped near Lympne and were at the receiving end of some of the first bombs to be dropped by Zeppelins. In the words of one correspondent, who thought that they should be allowed to ride with their ladies on the banks of the Military Canal, they had "poured wealth into the town".

Indeed, the discrepancy between the pay of the Imperial and Colonial troops was marked, as it was to be again in the Second World War and in Korea. So, when the Hythe public baths had been renovated, the commanding officer of one of the British regiments had to ask the Council to reduce the fee from 3d to 1d a head, since that was all the War Office allowed, and it was his duty to see that each man had a hot bath once a week.

In January 1916, a German seaplane raided Dover and killed a man. But the blackout in Hythe had been in force for over a year by then, to such good effect that it had the reputation of being the darkest town in England. This had disastrous consequences for a Canadian soldier, who fell to his death in the basement of a house on Marine Parade. The coroner commented that the early closing of the public houses encouraged fast drinking, thus hinting that the army should rescind their order.

Kitchener died in June 1916, and his links with Hythe were

remembered—both his official visits to the School of Musketry and his private calls on his son, Colonel Kitchener, who lived in Hythe for a time. A few months later, a Red Cross fete, with accompanying pageant, raised over £1,600, an enormous sum for those days, and again all donors were listed in the paper, as were all the wedding presents, down to the last silver sugar-basin, given to Captain Sowrey of the Royal Flying Corps and Miss Adam of Cannongate Road, Hythe.

After the first battle of Ypres, the casualty lists grew longer, especially of Canadians, and some of the wounded returned. The outward mood was still one of cheerful optimism, but there were many grieving relatives and friends.

There were no air-raid sirens in the First World War. But there was a signal. When enemy planes were heard or seen, a black cone was raised to the top of the flagstaff over the Town Hall. This was seen frequently during September 1917, when German planes came across the Channel by the light of the harvest moon to bomb the seaside towns.

But it was earlier in the same year that Hythe, itself, suffered a raid. On May 25th a number of bombs were dropped, one of which fell in St. Leonard's churchyard and killed the verger, Daniel Lyth. The vicar, who was standing near him, later found a piece of shrapnel from the bomb lodged in his pocket. There was also a fatality in Ormonde Road. A Zeppelin caused many casualties and a stampede of horses in the Canadian camp at Otterpool near Lympne, but did not touch Hythe town.

At the beginning of 1918, the need for more men for the forces was acute. The President of the Hythe Tribunal received new instructions, which he described as drastic, calling on all classes "to make further sacrifices in manpower for the prosecution of the war". But the job had already been done so thoroughly that few surprises were expected. In the meantime, a councillor's son, Lieutenant Jemmett, died of wounds, aged thirty-seven.

In January 1918, the mayor inaugurated the Hythe Heroes' Fund to help the returning wounded and the families of the dead. He received a donkey and chaise to do his rounds on behalf of the fund, and set a target of £1,000 by Easter and £2,000 by June. As he pointed out, Hythe had sent a thousand

men to the war out of a total population of between six and
seven thousand. A concert to raise money for the fund was
given by the Yacka Hula Concert Party, organised by some of
the Hythe ladies, in the Mercer's Y.M.C.A. hut in Prospect
Road. With this and other encouragement, both targets were
reached.

That spring, owners of cars and drivers registered their
names in the Hythe Section of the Dover, Folkestone and
Hythe Company of the Kent Motor Volunteer Corps. In all,
forty-five people declared themselves ready to muster with
their vehicles when required, and hold themselves ready for a
possible emergency.

It was a time for the tightening of belts all round. For it is
true to say that, up till 1918, there were some people who had
been living very much as they had done before. For instance,
two ladies watching the W.A.A.C. women marching down
Cannongate Road, had been heard to comment merely on the
difficulty of getting domestic servants caused by so many girls
going into the Forces.

But now food rationing was instituted, and a Food Control
Committee was set up in Hythe. At first, only sugar was
affected. But in the spring, butter and margarine were also in
short supply. The supplies had to be delivered in bulk to a
temporary store near the Town Hall, and distributed to the
retailers by the Food Controller. Meat was likewise rationed
according to the quantity available. But this did not include
pork, and the keeping of pigs in back gardens was much
encouraged.

Likewise, rabbits could be had whenever they were offered
for sale, though at a controlled price. There was some discus-
sion about this, because the price for a rabbit was 1s 9d,
whether it was a young one, a "bolter" to use the local term for
one three-quarters grown, or a full-grown one. Sale by weight
was considered to be fairer.

Meanwhile the war was consuming both men and materials. A Hythe man, Sir William Tritton, of the same name as
the man who was seven times mayor in the eighteenth and
nineteenth centuries, invented a new secret weapon—the
assault vehicle called the tank. Another Hythe man, Mr.
Wareham-Smith, organised a nation-wide Businessmen's

Week in order to raise a million pounds to pay for tanks, ships and planes.

This Week was a great success, and the target was exceeded by forty million pounds, no doubt partly because the war bonds offered by the War Savings Association were, in the words of Hythe's mayor, "a perfectly safe investment paying an exceptional rate of interest". As for Hythe itself, the mayor's target was £15,000 to buy aeroplanes, of which £10,000 had already been pledged by the end of the first day of the appeal. The total raised by the end of the week was £28,650 7s 6d, or about £5 per head of population.

Apart from the wounded returning from hospital, there was one man, Corporal Ernest Gibbs who, in March 1918, came home from a prisoner-of-war camp. He had been wounded at Mons, serving in the first British Expeditionary Force, the "Contemptibles". He had been taken prisoner in the second month of the war and transported to Doberitz prison camp near Magdeburg in eastern Germany. After he had reached The Hague in an exchange of prisoners, organised by the Red Cross, his account of his sufferings under "the Hun" stirred people to further stiffening of the sinews to achieve the victory, which now seemed certain.

The actual Armistice celebrations in November were, of course, largely spontaneous. Effigies of the Kaiser and "Little Willie", the German Crown Prince, were burnt. Jubilant W.A.A.C. and W.R.N.S. girls went through the streets in their lorries waving British flags, and soldiers burnt the German flag on a hastily erected platform.

At nightfall, the lights went on in the premises of Cobay Bros, auctioneers, thus fulfilling the promise of William Cobay, the mayor, who had "taken the odds that the special constables would not run him in". It was the signal for the lights to go on everywhere, and many householders hung out the coloured lights that they had ready for the occasion.

The period between the Armistice and the signing of the actual peace treaty was a time for welcoming home heroes and calling for yet more money to pay the Government's bills. In March 1919, the mayor gave a tea-party for 350 returned men of all three services, including fifty who had been prisoners of war, and intimated that there would be more after the defini-

tive peace had been established, since, in all, 1,100 men had
gone from Hythe to do their duty.

It was then learned that two Hythe men, Lance Corporal
Dawkins of the London Regiment and Guardsman Page of the
Grenadier Guards, had won the Military Medal. But it was
after peace had been concluded that Lieut. Gordon Steele R.N.
won the coveted Victoria Cross—fighting the Russians, our
former allies. In a torpedo boat attack on Kronstadt harbour in
the Gulf of Finland in August of that year, he torpedoed the
battleships *Andrei Pervozanni* and *Petropavlovsk,* which had
been taken over by the Bolsheviks, at almost point-blank
range. Hythe's other V.C. was Captain J. F. Vallentin, a
grandson of Colonel John Finnis, whose memorial is in the
north transept of the parish church. He was killed in action
near Ypres in 1914, serving in the South Staffordshire Regiment.

As for money, even in the thanksgiving service, held in St.
Leonard's Church in July, the Rev. Dale urged his congregation to support War Loan Week by investing in Victory
Bonds. Further encouragement was given by Sir William
Tritton, who became President of the War Tanks Association,
and presented a tank to the town through the member of
parliament, which, unlike Ashford's, has since disappeared. In
addition, a low-flying Handley Page bomber dropped leaflets
from on high. So, as usual, the Hythe target for the Week was
exceeded, £86,550 being invested instead of the target figure of
£80,000, a sum which came to about £10 a head.

During the actual Peace Day celebrations, after the ringing
of the church bells had signalled the signing of the peace treaty,
bronze medals were given out to 1,100 children by Mayor
Cobay. They were inscribed with the dove of peace on one
side, and the words "To commemorate the victorious conclu-
sion of the Great War 1914–1919" on the other. The mayor
was able to proclaim peace through a silver megaphone,
which had been given to him for this "and other public uses"
by a Miss M. Scott in memory of her nephews, who had been
killed in the war.

This was almost the last civic act of the man who had been
mayor for all five years of the war, and had raised £236,315 for
various wartime causes. Shortly afterwards, he resigned and

presented the oak panelling to the town, which covers the east
wall of the Town Hall Council Chamber, and on which are
inscribed the names of all the bailiffs and mayors of Hythe
from 1349 to the present day. In the meantime, the tramway had been overhauled and
Cricket Week was held again. The South-Eastern and
Chatham Railway speeded up their services, so that it was
possible to get from Hythe to London in an hour and three
quarters, which is only just feasible today, using public transport. It cost 11s 2d first class, 7s second and 5s 7½d third class,
plus a war supplement. Unfortunately, shortly after this there
was a rail strike, and some people, including William Deedes
of Saltwood Castle, tried to make thinking people realise that
all was not quite as rosy in the body politic as the victorious
citizens hoped.

In fact, Deedes, himself, following Socialistic principles,
felt that it was inappropriate for him to live in an erstwhile
feudal castle and moved into an ordinary house in the town.
However, his son, also named William, returned to Conser-
vatism, being for many years Conservative M.P. for Ashford
and "Peterborough" in the Daily Telegraph before becoming
editor of that paper.

But that was after the second of the two world wars. In
Hythe, in the early part of the century, one's political persuasion made little difference. The nineteenth century Jewish
representation in Parliament under the Liberal banner was
simply replaced by a Jewish guardian of the town's liberties
from the Tory stable.

13

Between the Wars

THE member of parliament for Hythe during the First World War was Sir Philip Sassoon, a scion of the mercantile family that had gone to Bombay from Baghdad and prospered under the aegis of the Indian Empire. His father, Sir Edward Sassoon, intimate friend of Edward VII, had been Hythe's representative before him for thirteen years from 1899 to 1912.

Sir Edward was the son of Sir Albert (Abdullah) Sassoon, First Baronet of Kensington Gore, who was, himself, the eldest son of David, the Iraqi merchant who had fled the Turkish Empire and set up his business in Bombay in rivalry with Forbes and Son and other British houses. He married a daughter of Baron Gustav de Rothschild, of the French branch of the famous banking family, and it was therefore not surprising that he should continue the Jewish interest in this southeastern corner of England, which had begun with the Rothschild need for swift communication with the Continent and the smuggling activities of these bankers in the Napoleonic era.

After the great split over the Irish Home Rule question, the Rothschilds left the Liberal Party, and the Sassoons followed them into the ranks of the Unionists. Safe in the esteem of King Edward VII, Sir Edward added Shorncliffe Lodge, Sandgate to his other three residences at New Barnet in Hertfordshire, Sans Souci in Bombay and Garden Reach in Poona.

His main interest in Parliament was in the development of telegraphic communication, which fitted in very well with his needs as head of a business with many branches in India and China. He became Chairman of the House of Commons Committee on Imperial Telegraphs, and he was an early advocate of radio telegraphy, introducing a private member's bill to make wireless equipment compulsory on all ocean-going passenger ships.

Being ahead of his time, he was regarded as a crank, and the bill was defeated. He had little more success in his attempts to protect the ships of the local fishermen. He called for a gunboat to protect the Folkestone, Sandgate and Hythe fishermen from the French skippers poaching on their side of the Channel. But little was done until a young French skipper was killed in a fracas, after which the two governments decided to confer about the problem.

Sir Edward's son, Philip, was thus the member for Hythe when, a mere two months after the Armistice, Lloyd-George went to the country to obtain a mandate for the continuation of the wartime coalition government. The Folkestone voters now far exceeded those of Hythe in number, although the seat was still in Hythe. So it was natural that the largest meeting in support of the coalition should be held in the Folkestone Town Hall.

Great play was made by the chairman of this meeting with the information that the sitting member was still doing his duty "at the front". In truth, he was a staff officer at G.H.Q., British Armies in France, a fact that was not lost on his cousin, the poet, Siegfried Sassoon, who had twice fought and been wounded and decorated, and then pleaded for a negotiated peace, as a consequence of which he was classified as a mental case.

However, as A.D.C. to Lord French, and then military private secretary to the new Commander-in-Chief, Sir Douglas Haig, Philip Sassoon had managed to collect six medals—three from France, two from Belgium, and one, the Order of St. Michael and St. George, from Britain.

A canard had been put about by the Labour opposition that Sir Philip had voted against women's suffrage. So a letter from him was read out at the meeting, explaining that he would have voted for women's suffrage, not against it, if he had not been doing his duty in France at the time when the House had divided on the Bill.

This was a key point. As the arrangements for members of H.M. Forces to vote in absentia were far from perfect, the women's votes in this election were extremely important.

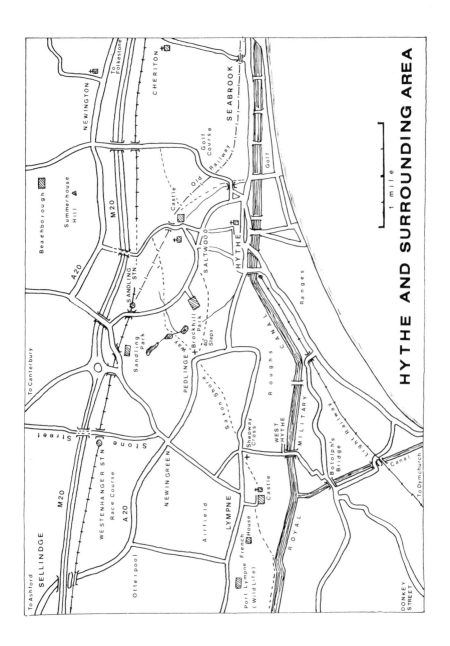

HYTHE AND SURROUNDING AREA

1 mile

Only 3,348 ballot papers had been sent out to those who were away on duty, although there were 4,279 absent voters on the Register; and of these only 1,575 were returned.

In return, the Labour candidate, Mr. Forsyth, was described in Hythe as a man who had been casting slurs on the "oldest Cinque Port" in favour of upstart Folkestone. As for Sir Philip, he did manage to get home in time to visit the polling stations on election day, accompanied by F. W. Butler, now a major with the M.C. to his name.

He was careful to woo the ladies, and it was reported that "he kindly gave his arm to an elderly lady to help her to the polling booth. Inside, she changed her mind, for she afterwards told friends she had intended to vote for Forsyth, but put her cross against Sassoon's name, and didn't think she would ever regret it".

Sassoon won by a majority of over two to one, thus continuing the Unionist tradition from the beginning of the century. After that, he represented Hythe until his death at the early age of fifty-one. Soon after the First World War ended, he had his new house completed on land sloping down from the cliff-top to the Military Canal just to the west of Lympne Castle.

Except, perhaps, for the triple arch facing the lily pond, the front of this building looks not unlike that of any traditional English country house, though it was, in fact, inspired by the Dutch colonial style. But inside it, an interior patio of Hispano-Moorish appearance, included in the designs by the architect, Sir Herbert Baker, cannot fail to remind one of the Arab world, and of the Sassoons' odyssey from Baghdad, via Bushire and Bombay, to England.

Nevertheless Sir Philip himself, played down the Jewish and recently Middle-Eastern origins of his family, even to the extent of crossing the Atlantic on a German liner well after the Nazis had begun their anti-Jewish pogroms. He called his estate Port Lympne, recalling the old Roman Portus Lemanis, which must have been nearby, and he imagined himself as a Roman, when he wrote to a friend in July, 1918 describing the site that had taken his fancy:

I am at the lip of the world, and gaze over the wide Pontine marshes that reflect the passing clouds like a mirror. The sea is just far enough off to be always smooth and blue . . .

Now the Folkestone and Hythe Division, as it was called later, became a favourite locality for weekending party leaders. The Sassoons, true to the family tradition of lavish hospitality, entertained Lloyd-George, the wartime Prime Minister, and many other political leaders.

In fact, after the construction of Port Lymne, with its noble vistas and secluded surroundings, a stream of V.I.P.s came to stay with the bachelor, Sir Philip, whilst his sister acted as hostess. Although a Unionist, Sassoon was a favourite of the Liberal, Lloyd-George, as long as the coalition lasted. And he became his Parliamentary Private Secretary. In this role he hosted several important conferences at his country house. There was an Anglo-French meeting in 1920 to discuss war reparations, and another, at which the army chiefs were also present, to consider the situation in Turkey and decide how best to carve up the Turkish Empire—a matter of particular interest to the Sassoons.

The Prince of Wales, later to reign briefly as Edward VIII, called in at Port Lympne and the Prime Minister's visits became quite frequent. They were the cause of malicious comment by some. For instance, a cartoon of the day, showing Sassoon working the strings of a puppet Lloyd George, had the following verses with it:

> Sometimes, when evening shadows fall,
>   I sit and smoke on Dymchurch wall,
> Or walk across the marsh to Lympne,
>   And muse upon the likes of him.
> I sit and smoke on Dymchurch wall
>   And cannot understand at all
> Why legislators, when at Lympne,
>   Make such an awful fuss of him!

After the coalition had ended, Sir Philip became Under-Secretary of State for Air in 1924, and retained the appointment with a brief gap of two years until 1937, when the champion of appeasement, Neville Chamberlain, shuffled him off into the Ministry of Works. The Air Ministry work was close to his heart. He had already flown on duty in the war, and was extremely air-minded, having his own private

plane at Lympne. In 1929 he flew with the R.A.F. to India on a
survey of the route for the Imperial Airways passenger planes.
In 1934 he flew to Singapore, and on the way he was able to
visit Baghdad, the city of his ancestors in Iraq.

Sassoon remained a bachelor for life, a fact that inspired the
following couplets from a satirical journalist:

> *Sir Philip Sassoon is the member for Hythe:*
> *He is opulent, swarthy and jejune and lithe.*
> *Benificent angels announced at his birth,*
> *That Sir Philip Sassoon would inherit the earth.*
> *Sir Philip was always a double event,*
> *In Baghdad a banker, a yeoman in Kent.*
> *The homes he inhabits are costly but chaste*
> *(For Sir Philip Sassoon is unerring in taste),*
> *And the daughters of Britain will wish they were dead*
> *Once Philip Sassoon has decided to wed.*

During the Second World War, the beautiful house in Port
Lympne was the officers' mess of Lympne R.A.F. station, a
key fighter airfield in the Battle of Britain and there were many
Czech pilots there. A problem then arose, because Sassoon
had willed the property to Mrs. Hannah Gubbay, plus his
motor-cars, aeroplanes and £11,000 a year. But the matter had
to go to the Chancery Court, because it was calculated that the
net value of the estate, after death duties, would be about
£600,000, and it would not produce enough capital to provide
the desired annuity. All this was very bad luck for his sister,
Lady Cholmondeley, who had been willed the residue of the
M.P.'s wealth.

Afterwards, in the 1970s, the estate was turned into a Wild
Life Sanctuary and Zoo Park, as an addition to the one near
Canterbury, under the direction of John Aspinall. It soon
proved to be the most popular attraction in the locality, with
nearly 92,000 visitors in 1980. Where once the prime minister
and his cronies strolled, the rhinoceros and bison now roam.

In the years between the wars, railways were still being built
in many more parts of the world than today, and although
Hythe was already connected with the main line at Sandling,
the directors of the Southern Railway, which had taken over
all the lines in Kent and Sussex, seriously considered extending the track, which then existed from Appledore to New

Romney, across the marsh to Hythe via Dymchurch. That
they did not do so was partly due to the fact that Sir Herbert
Walker, General Manager of the S.R., knew that a certain
Captain Jack Howey had other ideas.

As well as being a famous racing motorist, Howey was also
a miniature railway enthusiast, and he often discussed his
passion with his fellow racing driver, Count Louis
Zborowski. Together they were going to construct a 15 inch
gauge line along the new holiday coast. But the count was
killed in Italy in his last race. So Howey decided to go it alone,
with Walker obligingly leaving the field clear for him.

The "line that Jack built" is the world-renowned Romney,
Hythe and Dymchurch Light Railway, which was first built
from Hythe to New Romney and later extended to Dungeness. The first passenger was the Duke of York, King George
VI to be, who had a special interest in the area because one of
the boys' camps, which he had founded and to which he had
given his name, was located at St. Mary's Bay.

The line was opened to the general public in June 1927, and

Hythe Terminal—Romney, Hythe and Dymchurch Light Railway

the ten steam locomotives are true scaled-down replicas of main line express engines of the 1920s and 1930s, one third the size of the originals. Five of them are models of the London and North-Eastern Railway's 4.6.2. Pacific class, and two of them, the *Winston Churchill* and the *Dr. Syn,* are copied from 2.8.2. locomotives of the Canadian Pacific Railway. Still going strong after over fifty years pulling over a quarter of a million passengers a year, these engines now have the added attraction of representing the past age of steam.

The coaches are similarly to scale, and the trains run at about twenty-five miles an hour, so that the nine miles from Hythe to New Romney are covered in a little over half an hour. Sitting in one of the open coaches, with the engine puffing away up front and the smoke trailing past, is an unforgettable experience for anyone old enough to remember sticking his head out of a carriage window as a boy, against all the regulations, and getting an eyeful of smut.

The train runs close to the bank of the Military Canal at first, flanking the Hythe industrial estate of Pennypot, and then veers off amongst the back gardens of the houses in the Burmarsh Estate before striking open country and the flooded shingle quarry pits of Hythe Oaks, that are now used for small boat sailing. The only serious obstacle is the Canal Cut, running between Botolph's Bridge and the Dymchurch sluice, which it crosses on a girder bridge. But there is a great deal of steam-whistling at the approaches to the level-crossings, which adds to the authentic atmosphere of the past. Altogether, there are seven level-crossings and two under-bridges between Hythe and New Romney.

The Light Railway is a great attraction in this pleasant part of the world, and links up the settlements of caravans and seaside villas along the holiday coast. But it is not what attracted Lord Wakefield to Hythe, since it was not in existence when his first visit to the town developed into a permanent identification with it.

The year was 1912, and he was driving down the hill from Saltwood one fine afternoon, when he was so impressed by the view of the valley leading down to the sea, that he stopped to gaze in wonder. The surrounding hillsides were, as yet, undeveloped, except for two semi-detached houses, called

Highlands and Excells, overlooking the millpond on the way to the station, which were destroyed in the Second World War. He decided, on the spot, that he would build himself a house there for his weekends.

First he bought White Cottage, which is near the top of Blackhouse Hill, and when a row of rather ordinary houses was put up on Tanner's Hill opposite, on land donated to the Council by William Deedes, he planted a row of fir trees on his side of the valley to screen their bright red roofs from his eyes. He wanted seclusion. But his bid to make the track leading from Blackhouse Hill to Coldharbour Farm his own private road was thwarted in the courts, since a right of way had been created there at the beginning of the century.

Here Lord and Lady Wakefield impressed the local people with the simplicity of their lives "without their cooks, servants, butlers etc", as the Hythe Reporter put it. For Charles Cheers Wakefield was no ordinary man. Born in Liverpool in 1859, he was one of the original entrepreneurs of the oil industry. The Wakefield Oil Company, known to every motorist up to the Second World War, was the foundation and basis of his wealth.

He built his modest mansion, The Links, next to White Cottage. But he never lived in it himself, although he entertained there. In the Second World War it accommodated wounded servicemen, and subsequently renamed Bassett House, it was bought by Dr. S. A. Leader's company, Portland Plastics, for work in the development of plastics for use in medical and surgical work. Unfortunately, the house was burnt down in 1964, after which the estate was opened up for building development.

Lord Wakefield of Hythe was Lord Mayor of London in 1915 and a great advocate of air supremacy, presenting gold medals to gunners, who had been responsible for disabling a Zeppelin. In fact, he was always a friend to soldiers, and became Vice-President of the county organisation of the British Legion as well as paying for the Hythe British Legion hut.

But it was his purchase of Talbot House, the soldiers' club named in memory of Geoffrey Talbot, the youngest son of the Bishop of Winchester, who had been the regimental padre of the Buffs, the Royal East Kent Regiment, that forged a link with Hythe which is still unbroken. It was at Poperinge in Belgium, and the connection did not end with the presence of Tubby Clayton, the founder of Toc H, at his funeral in 1941. For in 1980 Hythe was twinned with Poperinge and so maintains a permanent link of friendship with the Belgian town, which was known as "Pop" to the millions of British and Commonwealth soldiers who passed through it on their way into and out of the Ypres salient.

Charles Wakefield also bought the land on the Messines Ridge, a few miles south of Ypres, which had been blown up by a colossal explosion of nineteen mines in 1917 that was even heard on the Kent coast. He had the crater turned into an ornamental lake in memory of the dead.

In caring for the church, Wakefield took over the historic role of the member of parliament, who not being at that time in the Christian tradition, could hardly be expected to be active in this respect. In 1928 three of the bells of St. Leonard's were recast and hung on ball bearings on a new frame at his expense. He also bought the town's new lifeboat and lifeboat house, and was a great contributor to Hythe's many sporting clubs. As an honorary freeman of the borough, he opened the new Prince's Parade road and promenade in 1938.

Indeed, the town continued to be fortunate in its benefactors. In 1932 Oaklands, the house of the much loved Dr. Randall Davis, was made over to the Corporation as his bequest to Hythe, provided that part of it should be used as a museum for teaching the history of Hythe and of the county of Kent. Consequently his spacious former residence was converted into offices, and thus, for the first time, the borough had adequate space in which to conduct its affairs, instead of the "rabbit warrens and little pokey holes" in which, according to the mayor, it had functioned previously.

There was also space adjoining for a museum, which was later changed into a Local History Room in order to preserve local control over it, and for a lending and reference library as well. These were opened, with due ceremony, by Sir Philip Sassoon in 1934, though the present public library, in new premises, was opened in 1963 by the then mayor, Rear-Admiral D. H. Hall-Thompson J.P.

The archives, from which much of the material for this

book has been gleaned, were again sorted out, half a century
after H. B. Mackeson and H. T. Riley had been through them
in the parvise of the church. A list of those that remained was
compiled by the retired vicar, who was also Chairman of the
Hythe Branch of the Men of Kent and Kentish Men, the Rev.
Dale, and Dr. C. Chidell, and printed shortly afterwards by
the town clerk.

Since then, there have been many more accessions to the
material thought worthy of preservation, largely because of
the keen sense of history and tradition of the people themselves. After the upheaval of the Second World War, the
Council provided a thermostatically controlled strong room
for the safe storage of these invaluable mementos of the past,
so that no more would decay or wander away from the town
to which they belong, and Mr. F. C. Elliston-Erwood, a
Fellow of the Society of Antiquaries, became Honorary
Curator and Keeper of the Archives. He was followed by Miss
Anne Roper M.B.E.

In this way it has been possible to preserve the separate
identity of the Old Borough, and to avoid its absorption into
the large complex of the Folkestone area.

At the same time, Hythe continued to cherish its long
association with the Small Arms School. The School was
always closely involved in competition shooting at Bisley, and
one year in the early twenties members of the Small Arms
School Corps won over twenty trophies at the Army Rifle
Association meeting. So the victorious marksmen were met at
the station by Hythe's horse-drawn fire tender and transported in triumph on it through the town to the School, where
the trophies were put on public display. Annual events at
which town and school mingled were the Staff Sergeants'
dinner and ball, the Chamber of Commerce banquet, the
Hythe Charity competition, and the ceremonial saluting of the
flag on Empire Day, Mayor's Sunday and Armistice Day.

But after all, what need have I to describe Hythe in the years
between the wars, when it has all been done for me by
Elizabeth Bowen, the last of the great Anglo-Irish authors? In
her novel *The House in Paris,* published in 1935, she gives
Hythe its own name:

. . . Centuries ago, the sea began to draw away from the cinque port, leaving it high and dry with a stretch of sea-flattened land between town and beach. The grey barracky houses along the sea front are isolated; if the sea went for them they would be cut off. Across fields dry with salt air, the straight shady Ladies' Walk, with lamps strung from the branches, runs down from the town to the sea: on hot days a cool way to walk and bathe. Inland, in summer, a band plays in a pavilion beside the canal, whose water is dark with weeds that catch at the oars of pleasure boats, and overshadowed by trees. On and off, there is a rattle of musketry practice from the ranges along the edge of the marsh; across the marsh martello towers in different stages of ruin follow the curve of the coast towards Dungeness, where at nights a lighthouse flashes far out. On its inland side, the town climbs a steep hill, so that the houses stand on each other's heads. The beautiful church must have crowned the town; now new houses spread in a fan above it, driving back the thickety hazel woods. Back from the brow of Hythe hill the country—cornfieldy open and creased with woody valleys, Kentish, mysterious—stretches to the chalk downs. Now and then you hear bells from Cheriton, or distant blowy bugles from Shorncliffe camp.

Many of these scenes have been preserved for us by the local artist, Arthur Baker-Clack, an Australian who rented the part of Burch's Mill facing the millpond as a studio in 1936, and kept it until his death in 1965.

Then, in 1938, Elizabeth Bowen published *The Death of the Heart,* in which Lymly Junction and Seale are recognisably Sandling Junction and Hythe in every particular:

As the train drew into Lymly, the junction for Seale, Mrs. Heccomb waved two or three times—first at the engine, as though signalling it to stop, then in order that Portia should not overlook her. This was unlikely, for hers was the only figure on the platform stretching its dead length. This unfrequented junction, far from the village, at the mouth of a cutting, exists alone among woods. Ground ivy mats its lozenge-shaped flowerbeds, and a damp woody silence haunts it—except when boat trains, momentary apparitions, go rocking roaring through . . . A porter took the luggage to another, waiting, train, very short, with only three coaches. Not for some minutes after they were settled did this train puff off down the single line through the woods. . . then the train ran clear of the woods along a high curved ridge. Salt air blew in at the carriage window . . . Seale station ran at them with no warning; the engine crawled up to the buffers: this was the terminus. The door through from the booking-hall framed sky, for this was an uphill station, built high on a ramp . . .

The taxi drove down a long curve into Seale, past white gates of villas . . . and Portia now saw only shop windows—the High Street shop windows. But what shops!—though all were very small they all looked lively, expectant, tempting, crowded, gay. She saw numbers of cake shops, antique shops, gift shops, flower shops, fancy chemists and fancy stationers.

It was during this time that the Venetian Fete, which had first been held on the Military Canal in 1860, was developed into a real pageant of the Cinque Ports. In the early years it had simply been a night out during Cricket Week. Skiffs, canoes and punts had been hired from the man who held the boating rights, and a few gondolas had been added to make its name authentic. Guitars and banjoes, instead of mandolins, provided the music, and fairy lights added to the gaiety.

But in 1935 some of the fishing-boats were brought into the canal from the shore and decorated to represent the five Cinque Ports and the two Ancient Towns, each with its appropriate mayor on board. They thus made a stately procession before the lord warden, who was then the Marquess of Reading.

The following year, the Fete Committee became a charitable society with the specific objective of donating the profits towards the provision of homes for old folk. The fete then continued to be held annually until 1954, with the exception of the five years of the Second World War.

The revival of the entertainment in 1946 presented something of a problem. But thirty-six collapsible landing pontoons were acquired from a unit disposing of surplus naval stores, which tided the Fete Committee over until floats could be made locally. As the years went on, the fete steadily increased in popularity, with a crowd of nearly thirty thousand spectators sometimes in attendance.

But in 1954, it was decided that the burden of a yearly event was too great, and it became a biennial show instead. Nowadays the local clubs and societies prepare decorated floats for the entertainment of the public, and television crews never fail to put in an appearance.

Of course, this was far from being the only amusement the

Mayors of the Cinque Ports at a Venetian Fete

town had to offer in the years between the wars, for by now the many facilities for games and sports were well established. Of these, the Bowling Club has the longest recorded history, since it dates its foundation from 1652. An entry in the old minute book of the club records that, on February 2nd 1653, "it was put to the question who should be the keeper of the Bowling Green, John Mercer or John Monds, and it was ordered by most votes that it should be John Mercer", There are even some who claim that bowls was being played at Hythe at the same time as Drake was playing on Plymouth Hoe.

In fact, Hythe people appear to have been eminently clubbable for many years. At a dinner of the Hythe Green Cricket Club, held in 1896 at the Sportsmen's Inn, an old pub that was burnt down in 1907, there were no less than eight toasts—to the Queen, the Archbishop of Canterbury and the clergy, the Navy, Army and Reserve Forces, the Mayor and Corpora-

tion, the trade of Hythe, the Hythe Club, and the Cricket
Club, itself, and its subscribers. These were interspersed with
appropriate songs, such as "The Deathless Army", "Tantivy"
(for the mayor) and "The Lost Chord" (for the club).

They were rivals of the more prestigious Hythe Cricket
Club, which had established itself between the canal and the
sea as one of the foremost on the south coast. Its earliest
recorded match was in 1855 against the School of Musketry.
The Hythe Club initiated the golf, with its club house by the
station, and the golf course was closer to the town than it is
now, as the houses in Sene Park and Cliff Road did not exist.
So there was no need for the secretary to worry about windows in Cliff Road being broken by golf balls.

Then there was croquet close to the Cricket Club and tennis
in the same area, boating on the canal, riding, except on the
Green, where they had put a stop to the exercising of
"dragoon horses and gentlemen's horses" in 1791 and, of
course, sea bathing. So no one could complain of lack of
opportunities for healthy exercise.

In addition, there was always the matchless scenery. The
death of Hythe's popular M.P., Sir Philip Sassoon, in June
1939 fittingly brought to an end the period between the two
world wars. A speech that he had made to the Folkestone
Rotary Club in 1936 was then recalled, in which he had said:

> God made my constituency the most beautiful in England.
> It remains for man to make it the most popular.

14

The Second World War

THE Second World War was less lethal than the first in terms of killed and wounded servicemen, but more disruptive of the life of the community, since enemy bombs and shells did much more damage and caused far more casualties than in the First World War. Furthermore, for over three years Hythe was in the front line again, as she had been during the Napoleonic wars.

When war did come, Hythe was not unprepared for hostilities, and no doubt many of the large number of military men, both serving and retired, in the community saw it coming earlier than the Prime Minister. So, within the first week the town was priding itself on its one hundred per cent blackout, such that "to negotiate the streets at night, even with the light of the moon and the stars, is a matter of difficulty if the greatest care is not taken".

Indeed, it proved fatal, the following month, for a young fishmonger of Bartholomew Street, who was knocked off his motorcycle and killed by an equally young nineteen-year old girl motorist in Sandgate Road.

Hythe was "prepared, cheerful and at times almost placid"—a not unnatural condition to be in when Britain and France, having declared war on Germany, failed to attack the enemy. By the end of the first month, the A.R.P. wardens and special constables had settled into their duties, gas masks had been issued, and the air-raid sirens had gone off several times, keeping the fire brigade and their auxiliaries on their toes.

A.R.P. wardens were even asking for overtime pay in a manner which incensed Alderman F. W. Butler, who had now been five times mayor. He retorted that, since they had nothing to do but smoke and play darts, they should be content with the fourteen shillings a week that a soldier was getting, plus a little extra for their keep, say one pound in all. This was at a time when the two estate agents, Butler and Chapman, were still advertising four bedroomed houses to let at anything from a guinea to three pounds a week.

In this war it was Czech refugees from the Sudetenland, which Hitler had annexed as part of the Munich agreement, who came to Hythe instead of Belgian refugees. But it was the evacuees who were more numerous. At this time, it was still the French and not the enemy coast across the Channel, and 500 London children descended on the town as soon as the war started. The W.V.S. set up their headquarters in Moyle Tower, the tall building on the sea-front that was to house Vietnam refugees in 1980, and there they accommodated twenty mothers, forty children and twelve expectant mothers as well as their own office.

Once again, the civilians who remained were pressed to economise and to lend money. Boy Scouts went around collecting waste paper, and ration cards were prepared. G. L. Mackeson was appointed local Chairman of the National Savings Committee, and reminded the people of their great efforts in the First World War. Men took their places in the National Defence Company, which came to be known as the Home Guard, and work was put in hand for the construction of air-raid shelters big enough to accommodate a total of three hundred people.

Thus the year 1939 ended. So far the enemy had been seen on two occasions—once dead, according to the Folkestone and Hythe Herald, and once alive. In November, the body of a German sailor was washed up on the beach. It was one of five that came ashore between Folkestone and Dungeness, thought to be from a sunken U boat. The drowned sailors were buried with military honours at Shorncliffe, a swastika flag being found for the occasion—or so the paper said, though the story has never been corroborated. The live enemy was a pilot flying high over South-East Kent at midday. Onlookers had a good view of bursting anti-aircraft shells, but no air-raid warning was given and no bombs were dropped.

During this phoney war period, before the Germans attacked and over-ran Holland, Belgium and France, men were, of course, joining the colours, and there was considerable activity in coastal defence. Concrete block-houses for machine-guns were built at the very same points beside the Military Canal, which had been made for guns during the Napoleonic war.

Yet the atmosphere was still rather unreal. News was received that Petty Officer H. Pitt had recived the D.S.M. for service in the gunboat *Sandpiper*. But it was for being bombed the previous year by the Japanese on the River Yangtse in China, and not for fighting the Germans.

Meanwhile, the Hythe Bowling Club decided to carry on in spite of wartime difficulties, and in May 1940, the mayor, Captain G. Few, bowled the first wood of the season. It was the Golf Club that decided to close, and it was another one, the Sene Valley Golf Club, that eventually opened in its place.

In fact, at this time Hythe was being told to prepare itself for an influx of more evacuees from the metropolitan area—900 children from Gravesend—and the news of battle was still from distant places. There was an appeal for help for Finland, which had suffered from the Russians and accepted peace under duress on March 13th. One of the clergy referred to "the horrors and cruelties inflicted upon this brave people by the monstrous people of the U.S.S.R.", a sentiment that was to be completely reversed when Russia became an ally.

Then, in May, Seaman George Blackman appeared on his mother's doorstep in Cinque Ports Avenue wearing a soldier's trousers and cap, and a Norwegian parka and ski boots, having lost all, including fifty-eight shillings in cash, whilst escaping from Norway on a trawler.

At the same time, the church was provided with new altar rails in memory of Henry Mackeson, the Hythe Druids planted an oak tree in the grounds of Oaklands, and the Hythe and Romney Branch of the Association of Men of Kent and Kentish Men made Lord Wakefield their President.

At the end of the month and in early June, the British Expeditionary Force was evacuated from Dunkirk. The Hythe lifeboat, the *Viscountess Wakefield,* was summoned, along with others, to Dover, and the coxswain, H. "Buller" Griggs, was told to go over to the French beaches and take off as many men as he could. Unfortunately, he declined to risk his craft, although he, himself, had served in the Royal Navy in the First World War and in 1929 had received the R.N.L.I. silver medal for an outstanding feat of life-saving at sea. Consequently, it was taken over by naval ratings.

The lifeboat, which had cost Lord Wakefield £6,000 in 1936, was never seen in Hythe again, and was the cause of much controversy. Griggs, who was dismissed from the lifeboat service, maintained that the boat would inevitably have been lost, since he had been ordered to "run it up on the beach". But the fact remains that eighteen other lifeboats returned safely after bringing thousands of men off the beaches, interpreting their orders in a practical manner. Stories that the lifeboat had been seen afloat on the other side circulated for years after the war.

However, the opportunity arose for the fifty-three year old Griggs to redeem his reputation when he and his fellow fishermen were able, in August, to rescue two British airmen, who were floating in their Mae West life-jackets off Dymchurch. A third was saved from the sea by a lady in a ten-foot canoe, named Miss Prince.

In two months the picture of the war had changed radically. The evacuation of children was put into reverse. 450 of Hythe's own children went, with 50 teachers, to various places in Pembrokeshire in the furthest south-west corner of Wales, whilst some of the older ones, who attended Harvey Grammar School, went to Merthyr Tydfil. At the same time many Hythe families made their own arrangements for departure.

After the fall of France, families were told to get out or be ordered out. But the separation of children from their parents was never compulsory, and by the end of the year makeshift arrangements were being made for the education of children who had stayed on in the town. They were the offspring of the remaining population, who were busy with local defence work or, like the hoteliers and publicans, helping to make the lives of the troops more bearable. The local brewery was still advertising that "Quality-maintained Mackeson's Milk Stout does you double good", and the Hythe Brewery Concert Party was spreading good cheer.

It was possible to get into Hythe if one had a valid resident's pass. But the area south of the canal was strictly out of bounds except to the select few. Many of the bridges were rendered useless, and those that remained were well guarded. The Stade Street bridge was blocked by a steamroller, and the Ladies' Walk bridge was destroyed.

From July onwards the people left in the town were able to see the Battle of Britain unfolding in the air above them. For instance, on July 13th a large force of bombers tried to cross the coastline, escorted by Messerschmitt fighters. Spitfires and Hurricanes did battle with them, and for over an hour the sky appeared to be full of planes.

The picture repeated itself many times, and by August it was quite clear to the Hythe folk that Hitler intended to succeed where Napoleon had failed. It was only necessary to look through a telescope on a clear day from any vantage point to see unusual shipping activity around Boulogne, just as there had been a hundred and forty years before. Afterwards, there was no doubt in their minds that the Royal Air Force had saved them from destruction.

Meanwhile, even the old Martello towers were brought back into use. Squads under instruction at the Small Arms School, commanded by instructors, manned them on guard duty. But all this front line activity so disrupted the training programme of the School that, at the end of 1940, it moved to Bisley.

One of the trains on the Light Railway was armoured and equipped with a Lewis gun and a Boys anti-tank rifle, as the little railway was pressed into service for supplying the watchers on the coast. At the same time, the 9.2 inch railway guns of the 4th Super Heavy Battery arrived on the big railway behind the town, and their fields of fire were planned. There were also Bofors anti-aircraft guns at West Hythe for the protection of Lympne airfield.

The latter suffered badly. On Monday, August 12th Junkers bombers, attacking the radar installations as well as the airfield, dropped 141 bombs on Lympne, causing considerable damage. Fortunately for Fighter Command, since June the airfield had been for use only in emergencies. On August 15th it was dive-bombed. The sick quarters suffered a direct hit and most of the buildings were damaged, putting the place out of action for two days, though some British fighters did manage to land there during that time.

On August 30th Lympne airfield was again attacked. Four bombs were dropped there in the afternoon, killing five civilians. This was followed by another raid on September 1st, in which a member of the ground crew was killed and another seriously injured, and in the morning of September 4th the airfield suffered more bombing and strafing with gunfire. On September 24th Hythe suffered its first casualty, when bombs fell on the station and elsewhere and a man was killed.

On September 3rd, there had been an attempt by the enemy to reconnoitre the coastline that he intended to invade, albeit a very ill-managed one. Early in the morning two spies were put into the water by a U boat and paddled ashore in a dinghy to land near the Dymchurch redoubt. They were Dutchmen, who had been convicted of currency smuggling and told that their offences would be overlooked if they carried out the mission. They were equipped with a wireless transmitter to send back information about troop dispositions and defences. But they spoke little English, and one of them, whose mother hailed from the Far East, did not even look European.

On landing, the two men separated, but both were captured soon after dawn by watchful sentries of the Somerset Light Infantry. Another pair was seized at Lydd, and the four were taken to Seabrook police-station for preliminary interrogation. Eventually three of them were sentenced to death at a secret trial at the Old Bailey, the fourth being found not guilty, as his defence that he had been forced to become a spy and intended to give himself up as soon as he landed, was accepted.

Hythe suffered a worse disaster in the following month, on October 4th, when a bomb fell on the arcade on the north side of the High Street, smashing it to pieces and killing three women. It was the second time the site had suffered, since the arcade had been built where the burnt-out Sportsman pub once stood.

In the same air-raid the stained-glass windows in the east wall of the parish church, behind the altar, were shattered by a bomb, which fell where the church car-park now lies. They were eventually replaced by new ones, designed by a local man, Wallace Wood, whose theme was defence, ancient and modern—on the left a Cinque Ports ship with the church, itself, in the background, and on the right an anti-aircraft gun. The names of Lionel Lukin, the inventor of the lifeboat, and of Thomas Quested Finnis, the member of the well-known British-Indian family, who had been Lord Mayor of London, were preserved in the lights, as these two men had been commemorated in the windows that had been destroyed. The new windows were unveiled in 1951 by Major Max Teichman-Derville, Bailiff of the Romney Marshes and a Deputy Lieutenant of Kent. It was a fitting tribute from a man whose family was partly of German origin.

A few days after this destructive raid another woman was killed, this time in Prospect Road. Then, on October 22nd, a single raider dropped a bomb in Napier Gardens, and a Folkestone man, delivering coal, was killed. Two days after this, a bomb designed to spread flaming petrol was dropped without causing any casualties, as well as two high explosive bombs in Twiss road and on the ranges. On October 26th hit-and-run raiders dropped two bombs. One fell harmlessly on the ranges, but the other demolished the A.R.P. messenger hut close to the Light Railway terminus. Fortunately the bomb fell before the air-raid sirens sounded, and the messenger boys had not yet gone to their duties there.

On November 5th a bomb struck Nelson's bridge, carrying Stade Street over the canal, and the houses in Rampart Road were spattered with mud and dead fish. The bridge was not permanently rebuilt until 1956. There was also some low-level strafing, which resulted in Mr. Appleton getting a bullet in the leg in the Quarry nurseries on October 30th.

The following year, 1941, started with two bombs falling harmlessly on the golf links on January 7th. But on February 24th mines exploded on the beach on the edge of the ranges near where the gasworks used to be. A group of newly arrived soldiers had walked into one of our own minefields and ten of them were killed and four injured. Then, on the 26th, three soldiers were killed and six injured by a bomb dropped on the ranges by a lone raider.

On March 24th Hythe was deliberately raided by eight planes, coming in from the west into the dawn. They dropped sixteen bombs between Tanner's Hill Gardens and Fairlight Road. The fatal casualties were on Tanner's Hill, where the

whole Wonfor family—father, mother and daughter—were
killed. Next door, however, where their son had been taking a
cup of tea up to his wife in bed, both emerged unscathed. Half
a mile away, in Fairlight Road, Mr. and Mrs. J. Green were
also in bed when their house was destroyed around them. But
they recovered in hospital from their injuries.

In May another single raider only succeeded in wrecking the
Cricket Club's treasured pitch. But on May 10th 1942, the
bombers did more irreparable damage. One bomb fell on the
canal bank near Red Lion Square, and wrecked Mr. W. Trice's
refreshment rooms, killing his daughter and a young man,
who were inside at the time. Another three bombs fell in the
Frampton Road area, injuring twelve people. Afterwards, the
Germans announced on the radio that they had attacked a
factory near Hythe, little realising that it was simply a brewery.

August 21st was another black day for Hythe. In Ormonde
Road a bomb demolished several houses without inflicting
serious injury. But at the other end of the town, a bomb
exploded in the air above the Grove cinema in Prospect Road,
damaged the Cinque Ports Club and demolished the Conservative Club. Lt-Col. Charles Crauford-Stuart, Commanding
Officer of the 8th Battalion of the Kent Home Guard, was
killed in the former, and Dr. Mandy was badly injured. Outside, Mr. Martin, who was painting one of the walls of the
Nelson's Head pub, was killed, and so was a young taxi-
driver.

Houses in Prospect Road were damaged beyond repair by
the same bomb, and even in the High Street, the Borough
Coroner, Mr. J. E. Chapple, was seriously injured. This
devastating air explosion also inflicted serious injuries on eight
more people and lighter wounds on twenty-eight others.

On September 24th, on the last of the damaging raids, a
bomb hit Philbeach, the holiday home for the families of
London Transport workers and seemingly bounced off the
building to explode two hundred yards away in Mill Road,
where a number of houses were badly damaged, together with
some in Seabrook Road, and eight people were slightly
injured.

Altogether, the count was seventy-nine high explosive

bombs and one petrol bomb, as well as the occasional machine-gunning of the streets. According to the Civil Defence War Diary, held in the County Archives at Maidstone, the total number of casualties, excluding the soldiers on the ranges but including one killed and two injured on March 20th, 1941 by machine-gun fire, was fifteen deaths, nineteen seriously injured and sixty-five slightly injured.

There had been nineteen actual air-raids on Hythe, although, in the whole duration of the war, the air-raid sirens went off no less than 2,865 times, the raids being more frequent on neighbouring Folkestone and the two front-line airfields of Lympne and Hawkinge.

The fact that they petered out in the autumn of 1942 was an indication that the tide was turning. The watchers on the coast at "hellfire corner" now saw the R.A.F. getting its own back on the would-be invaders. That summer they were able to see the Blenheim bombers go over the Channel with their escorts of Hurricanes and Spitfires, and hear the bombs exploding on Calais and Boulogne.

There was, no doubt, a grim satisfaction in knowing that, at the beginning of 1941, together with Folkestone, they had reached their target of £5,000 to buy their own Spitfire. Seven months later, in August, they learned that it was operational. Named the *Folkestone and Hythe,* it had the latest Merlin 1,350 h.p. engine and was capable of 370 m.p.h. Then, in War Weapons Week in April, they had been asked to lend £40,000 in National Savings for two bombers, and had actually produced £63,000 in the purchase of Defence Bonds and War Savings Certificates.

When Hythe's young M.P., Lieutenant Brabner R.N., got back to his constituency on leave that August, he was able to echo Winston Churchill's sober confidence in the war's eventual outcome. He had been very critical of the Ministry of Supply and their muddles over petrol and coal, and he expected the Prime Minister to appoint a supremo Minister of Production, which he did. Brabner said that a vast superiority in aircraft over the enemy was what was required, and he spoke as an officer of the Fleet Air Arm, who had seen the German superiority over Greece and Crete.

The Member of Parliament addressed his constituents in the

grounds of Oaklands after entertaining the Mayor and Corporation to lunch at the British Restaurant, which had been
opened in Red Lion Square at the end of June. It could not have
cost him much, since the restaurant was staffed by members of
the W.V.S., with the exception of the paid cook and kitchen
assistant, and the price of meat and two veg. was sixpence,
with an extra penny for soup, twopence for a sweet and a
penny for a cup of tea. Even at these low prices, it showed a
profit, unlike the two similar institutions in Folkestone.

This was a tribute to the personnel of the Women's Voluntary Service, who were also busy with other activities. In their
stocktaking at the end of September, they announced that they
had already made 5,000 lbs of jam with the surplus fruit,
which was a good contribution to the total of sixty-nine tons
made by the women of East Kent as a whole. They also had
fifty-six home knitters, and a number of sock-darners, who
received soldiers' socks for treatment daily at the Y.M.C.A.
canteen. In addition, they were running the local library service and making over 25,000 book loans a year.

This was an indication that, for every hour of fighting in this
war, there were many more training, waiting and simply
being prepared. Rather belatedly, 500 Anderson air-raid shelters were provided, and the fire-watching service was strengthened.

In the meantime, news was coming back to Hythe of her
men in action. Marine V. Swatton won the D.S.M. for land
operations in Norway, carried out from H.M.S. *Nelson*. Later
in the year, Sergeant E. Rosam, son of a former regimental
sergeant-major at the School of Musketry, got the D.F.M. for
his part in raids on Berlin and elsewhere, but he did not live to
see final victory. Soon after that, there was news of the son of a
former commandant of the school, Major V. Street M.C.,
who had escaped from Greece on a 170 ton schooner, and
reached Alexandria after a voyage of seventeen days.

The big new factor in the war was now the German attack
on Russia, which started in June. Early in 1942 people were
being urged to contribute to the Anglo-Soviet Medical Aid
Fund. Whilst the "red" Dean of Canterbury, Dr. Hewlett
Johnson, urged on the good people of Folkestone and Hythe
with his belief in a Russian victory, Mr. A. T. D'Eye, the

Secretary of the Fund, visited Hythe and told people assembled in the Institute about the Russians' planned society, in which "The people work for society and for themselves, and it comes back in higher wages and conditions" and in which "You do not have to have an old school tie to become a Commander in the Army".

The Mayor of Canterbury even went so far as to tell the citizens assembled in the Town Hall that "when we read stories of what the Russians are doing, and what they have done, we should be ashamed of ourselves". This was in order to urge people to support Warship Week, which started on March 14th. In fact, the £40,000 worth of savings required to name a new minesweeper *Hythe* was exceeded by £23,146. Now it was not only the Germans but also the Japanese, who had to be beaten—albeit with some help from the Americans.

The ringside view of the war obtainable in this corner of England enabled people to have a good view of the naval and air battle that took place when, in February, three German battleships successfully managed to slip through the Straits of Dover into the North Sea. And in the spring, there were more raids on Boulogne to watch.

Apart from these local spectacles, there was often the roar of R.A.F. planes going overhead on their way to the Continent, and of German planes sneaking in to make their nuisance attacks. In August, the thunder of the guns in the Dieppe raid could be heard, and the sky was again filled with planes.

In spite of the large number of soldiers in the vicinity, Hythe was considered to be a sober town at this time, the drinking being dispersed over the twenty-two fully licensed houses, which had been thought fitting for a population of about 8,600 before the wartime evacuations. Nevertheless, life was not all peace and quiet for the publicans. In September, three young soldiers lifted three bottles of whisky, valued at £1 3s each, from Ben Strawson, proprietor of the White Hart. They were given "a straight talk" in the police court and fined £2 each.

Also, by the end of the year, the spiv was appearing on the scene. In December, a thirty-two year old gunner was charged with acquiring twenty-four pairs of silk stockings from a trader "in circumstances that prohibited the latter from supplying them". The mayor, sitting on the bench, showed leniency to a serviceman and let him off with a fine of £1.

This was the year in which the borough member, now Lieut-Commander Brabner, was awarded the D.S.C. for his actions whilst serving on the aircraft-carrier *Eagle,* convoying British ships to Malta. It was also the year in which John Fisher of London Road appeared on the radio programme *In Town Tonight* to describe his experiences after his ship had been torpedoed and sunk by gunfire from a submarine in the South Atlantic. With fourteen other seamen in one of four lifeboats, he had lived for six and half days on two biscuits and two and a half ounces of water a day until they were picked up by a Dutch ship and taken to New York.

In this year, too, Stoker Jarvis of Victoria Avenue died when his ship, the destroyer *Veteran,* went down in the North Atlantic on convoy duty, after he had done nearly two years in the navy. In the army, Major Peter Blundell died of wounds, aged twenty-nine, whilst serving with the King's Royal Rifle Corps in the battle of El Alamein and received a posthumous D.S.O., whilst thirty-four year old Lance-Bombardier B. H. Bull of Stade Street, a local scout-group leader, died in India.

As the attacks by the U boats continued, the following year, 1943, also took its toll of naval casualties. Leading Seaman Friend of St. Nicholas Road, only nineteen years of age, was now presumed dead, having been posted missing when the destroyer *Blean* went down in December, and Charles Coe, a thirty-three year old man of Prince's Terrace, who had enlisted in the navy as a boy, was lost with the destroyer *Achates.*

In the army, Captain J. Worts, who had joined the Supplementary Reserve on the eve of war, had done three years in Palestine and Egypt, and received the M.C. for his gallant service with the Buffs in their action in the Western Desert. As the commander of an anti-tank platoon, he had fought in the battle of Point 204 near Gazala, been taken prisoner to Derna and then got away again.

In the Royal Air Force, Flight Lieutenant R. M. Hackney, well-known in Hythe as the chief instructor of the Cinque Ports Flying Club at Lympne, which had closed down in 1940, was now flying night sorties. Squadron Leader E. W. Anderson, a schoolmaster, received the D.F.C. for attacks on

Lubeck and Rostock at extreme range, and Sergeant Pilot "Dickie" Dray of Martello Cottages returned home after getting his wings in Canada. He was aged twenty and had already been a despatch-rider at Civil Defence headquarters for two years before going into the R.A.F.

The danger of invasion was now past, and few doubted that the war would be won in the end, although at the cost of much blood, sweat and tears. In March the Hythe Prisoners-of-War Club was formed, and the mayoress, Mrs. Whittle, who was the mayor's daughter, was one of its first members, since her husband had been captured in the Middle East and was a prisoner of the Italians.

News now slowly filtered through of prisoners who had been captured by the Japanese when they swept into South-East Asia. Lance-Bombardier E. Rolfe of Frampton Road had been captured in Java. For thirteen months there had been no news of Sergeant F. C. Shipton, a regular in the East Surrey Regiment, who had joined the army as a boy, when notification was received that he was a P.O.W. The same applied to Private Burgess R.A.O.C., who had been caught in Malaya. In August the mother of "Clarrie" Burgess of St. Leonard's Road, who was a well-known footballer, received a badly burnt postcard, that was just decipherable, saying that her son was a prisoner in Sarawak. This was after a year and a half of silence.

But some prisoners-of-war were actually repatriated from the European theatre. At the end of October, Guardsman H. McLaughlin of the Scots Guards, formerly a Hythe police constable, disembarked at Liverpool. He had been wounded in Norway, and spent three and half years as a prisoner in Poland.

Nevertheless, the mayor's message for the year 1943, given at the annual dinner of the British Legion, was to be happy and communicate happiness. At the same time the Legion premises continued to be open to all servicemen.

Nuisance raids now took the place of concerted attacks, and an air-raid shelter was opened at Oaklands, to which children in the area could run if necessary. But the mastery of the air space over the Channel was now definitely in Allied hands, and it was possible to see American Flying Fortresses as well as the British planes crossing the coast in formation to attack occupied Europe. Another big effort in the Wings for Victory Week in May produced over £68,000 in war savings, the target having been £50,000 for five Spitfires.

The borough member was able to fly in from "somewhere in the Atlantic" to launch the Week, and delivered a rousing speech, full of hatred. "I dislike the Germans, and I always shall," he said. "I wish you could have heard them scream in Crete when they were killed in their thousands by the Maoris. When they squeal, as all bullies do when you are hurting them, don't go to your M.P.s and say, 'Stop hurting these chaps' because I shall want to say, 'I want to hurt the swine'."

His own bravery excused his bloodthirsty remarks. The following month he was selected to move the address in reply to the King's Speech at the opening of Parliament. "The people of the Borough of Hythe," he said, "have borne with me patiently in my almost continuous absence—which perhaps indeed has a certain charm for them—up to this time". He praised his stalwart constituency in South-East Kent, and hoped for generous treatment for it after the war.

Indeed, thoughts were now increasingly turning to "after the war". Hythe was going to build fifty new council houses and try to get the population up to 10,000. At the end of the year, a Reconstruction Committee was formed to consider these matters. The member of parliament, now Commander Brabner, even indulged in some post-war party politics when addressing the Hythe Women's Conservative and Unionist Association. He told them that they should ask the returning ex-servicemen what kind of an England they wanted instead of the Socialist planners at home. Only then should they take part in the "enormous, vapid and rather stupid argument about the Beveridge Report". Ironically enough, in the event it was the servicemen who opted for Socialism.

Although the invasion scare was over, the rules for guarding the restricted coastal area were tightened up because of the plans to invade in the reverse direction. So Hythe's Police Constable Humphrey, seeing John Oram of Holloway cycling down the High Street in the wrong direction, deduced that "he did not know the town well" and arrested him. Oram pleaded that he was on a cycling tour, and was fined one pound for entering a restricted area and ten shillings for cycling the wrong way down a one-way street.

Hythe's P.C. also found Ronald Albon of Ilford and Peter Hadley of Plaistow on a tandem in Red Lion Square, and could "see from their dress that they were not local people". They also said that they were on a cycling tour, and asked the way to Sandgate and Canterbury, the signposts being, of course, obliterated. They too were fined one pound each.

There was also Ruby Stiles of Berkeley Street, London, who pleaded that she had gone to Hythe because she suffered from colds, and sent a doctor's certificate saying that the sea air would do her good. And in December, Freda Clarke, a clerk of Walsall, was caught out of bounds in Hythe, visiting her "young man".

Anything considered to be looting was, however, much more severely dealt with. Thus, a Hythe man of the Kent County Civil Defence Mobile Reserve was sentenced to five years as being the man in charge of a party of nine, who had taken seven pairs of boots, eleven pairs of shoes, four suits, one pair of trousers and a waistcoat from a wrecked shop. The offence was considered to be the more heinous because he had once served in the Kent County Police.

Whilst the troops were massing in England, waiting for the signal to go, news still kept coming in from the fighting fronts. Of the three sons of Mrs. Uden of Stade Street, Sergeant John Uden of the Buffs had been wounded in the Trigno River battle in Italy and was recovering in hospital in Algiers; David was at a rest camp in Eritrea, recovering from wounds sustained whilst serving on the light cruiser *Sirius;* and Peter, in the Royal Marines, had sadly gone down with H.M.S. *Barham* in the Mediterranean in the third year of the war.

Flying Officer Leonard Crampton of Palmarsh Cresent had also lost his life on operations. But Flight Lieutenant Gordon Hatherly, born in Hythe in 1919, had survived nine attacks on U boats and gained the D.F.C.

Lieut-Commander Edward Blundell, formerly of Hillcrest Road, whose brother had been killed at El Alamein, got the O.B.E. for his part in the Salerno landings. But Private Arthur Moore, a butcher of St. George's Place, lost his life, dying of wounds incurred in Italy whilst fighting for the Buffs.

H.M.S. *Hythe,* the ship for which the town had collected money in 1942, was also lost. But not all the casualties were from enemy action. In February, a U.S. Army Air Force bomber crashed at Dymchurch, after the crew had baled out, and wrecked a bungalow, killing a soldier who was chopping wood outside it. And in April, eight U.S. airmen from a Liberator bomber were picked up in the Channel a few miles offshore from Hythe by Folkestone fishermen after being in two rubber dinghies for two days.

When the whole coastal strip up to ten miles inland was out out of bounds to non-residents, it was clear that D day would not be long delayed. In the preparations for the landings in Normandy, Hythe played its part in the deception that was intended to lead the Germans to think that the attack would come across the narrow seas instead of from the Southampton area to the beaches further to the south.

A veneer of concreted netting was laid on the beach at the end of Stade Street to deceive observers in high-flying reconnaisance planes into the belief that tanks would run down it into waiting landing-craft. The criticism of the local fishermen, who pointed out that such fragile material would soon be undermined by the sea, had to be patiently borne by the contractors. In addition, dummy tanks were moved into conspicuous positions on the hills round Aldington to make the picture even more convincing, and there were camps at Sandling and Sandgate.

The actual D day invasion fleet, which sailed in June 1944, was not visible from Hythe. But almost at the same time a new menace appeared. It was the flying-bombs, called doodlebugs, which started coming over in the middle of the month and were bravely attacked by the R.A.F. pilots. These V 1 revenge weapons, the original missiles, continued to come over until the Allied Forces were able to reach their launching sites on the French coast at the end of September.

Altogether, eleven of them fell on Hythe, killing six people, seriously injuring six and slightly injuring thirty-five. The most notable of them fell in August and September, shortly before the nuisance was destroyed for good. On August 10th, one wrecked Tudor House in Cannongate Avenue and killed

Mrs. Galway in it. In 1941 a Lancaster bomber had crash-landed in the grounds of the same house. On August 15th, another one demolished the whole of the west end of Earlsfield Road, killing five people. Houses in Seabrook Road, that had been damaged by the previous flying-bomb, were again damaged, and so were houses in Twiss Road, East Street, Prospect Road and the eastern end of the High Street.

This was after Field-Marshal Montgomery and the American Ambassador, Joseph G. Winant, had visited Hythe and stayed overnight at the White Hart in order to get a first-hand impression of the situation. It resulted in the decision to move all available anti-aircraft guns to the coastline between Dover and Dymchurch, covering the corridor through which the flying-bombs would have to pass on their way to London.

The British and American batteries were placed alternately along the coast, and a keen spirit of competition was generated. This, together with the new American radar system, based on the original British radar, resulted in an eighty per cent success rate, thus enabling the metropolis to avoid massive destruction in the period before the French coast was cleared of the enemy. No less than 266 of the flying-bombs were destroyed off the coast of Hythe.

The large concrete dishes, looking like gigantic ears, which were put up in the 1930s and still stand on the Ministry of Defence land in the Roughs between Hythe and West Hythe, show that Hythe had been for some time no stranger to microwave technology. And now the later fruits of that field research were being put into use in deadly earnest in the same locality.

Apart from the high-explosive bombs and the flying bombs, there were shells from the long-range coastal batteries, located in the cliffs of Cap Griz Nez in such a way that they were almost impervious to aerial bombardment. Hythe had warning of shelling forty-seven times, and was itself shelled twice, with four shells doing serious damage. There was one fatality and one serious injury, and eight people were slightly injured. The fatal casualty was on September 15th, when a shell demolished Highlands in Station Road, killing its elderly lady occupant. The day before that, a shell fell near Elm Passage and another on the ranges.

An early radar dish on the Roughs

A few days after this, Hythe heard the thunder of the battle
for Boulogne, and at the end of the month the guns were
silenced. The casualties had been caused by the gunners getting rid of their ammunition in a cause that they already knew
to be lost.

In October 1944, the Home Guard was stood down, and in
1945 it was no longer a question of how the war would end but
when. In the meantime, there were more casualties and more
awards, with the country waiting till May for V.E. day and till
August for V.J. day. It would take a longer book than this to
enumerate all of them.

For instance, John Blackman's widow, living in Stade
Street, had no less than six sons serving in the forces, four of
them in the Royal Navy and two in the army. A seventh had
been invalided out of the navy, and one of her two sons-in-law
was in the army, the other in the R.A.F.

Amongst naval personnel, Lieut-Commander Argles, whose parents had lived at Apple Tree Cottage, received the D.S.C. for his role in an action off the Andaman Islands in the Indian Ocean, whilst Able Seaman John Wright, a twenty-two year old baker from Cinque Ports Avenue, got the D.S.M. after the operations leading up to the landing at Anzio in Italy.

Corporal Watkins, of Eversley Road, was also at Anzio. He was the son of a sergeant of the Buffs in the First World War, and he received the M.M. for the part he played with the same regiment. But Private R. F. Simmons of Cinque Ports Avenue, also the Buffs, had now to be presumed dead, as H.M.S. *Eclipse,* the ship he had been travelling in, had been blown up off the island of Cos in the Aegean Sea.

In the Royal Air Force, Flying Officer F. J. Goulding of Spring House, who had trained in South Africa, got the D.F.C. after going on forty-five bombing operations, whilst Warrant Officer C. W. Newman received the D.F.C. after sixty-five operational flights over Germany.

The Mayor, Captain Few, had this to say to the V.E. day crowd outside the Town Hall:

> This is the Day. Victory is ours. We knew the miracle of 1940 when we really waited for the invasion of the barbarians. That should make us thankful for this great victory. There is still another war to finish, so when you celebrate, remember your relatives, your friends and all those who are fighting the other enemy in the Far East.

The total number of Hythe's citizens, who were killed in the war, was sixty, according to the War Memorial. But perhaps the most ironical and widely lamented casualty was one that does not appear on it. Commander Brabner, the member of parliament, after battling with the enemy so many times and surviving, was given the appointment of Under-Secretary of State for Air, thus following in Sassoon's footsteps, and seemed to have a brilliant career in politics ahead of him. But in March, he was flying to Canada with a number of senior Air Ministry officials, when his plane, a Liberator of R.A.F. Transport Command, went missing off the Azores. It was never seen again.

The ensuing election was part of the general khaki election, which was held immediately after V.E. day. For the first time the Tories had to face a serious challenge from Labour instead of from the Liberal candidate. They held the line, however, with Lt-Col. H. R. Mackeson, who won with a majority of just under two thousand, though half of the sixteen seats in traditionally Conservative Kent went to Labour.

As the men gradually came home, Hythe's M.P. complained that the demobilisation rate was too slow, and that there was too much manpower wasted in the forces on fatigues and paper work. However, the town was glad to welcome her men one by one, as they returned. Some thought, no doubt, of the text from the ninety-first psalm, that was to be written into the new stained-glass windows of the church:

> Whoso dwelleth under the Defence of the Most High shall abide
>   under the shadow of the Almighty.
> Thou shalt not be afraid for any terror by night
>   nor for the arrow that flieth by day.

15

The Town Today

After the Second World War, the Hythe Wing of the Small Arms School, which became the Small Arms Wing of the School of Infantry in 1949, returned to Hythe, thus continuing the military presence there. Extra accommodation for the non-commissioned officers and administrative offices was available at Turnpike Camp to the west of the old school, though Fort Sutherland, which had accommodated some of the officer students right up to the end of the nineteenth century was no longer available.

However, there was nothing to replace the colourful appearance of the pre-war army. The church parade, in particular, which W. S. Miller has described in his book *The School of Musketry at Hythe,* was never resuscitated. "It presents a brilliant spectacle," he wrote. "Life Guards, Blues, Dragoons, Lancers, Hussars, Guardsmen, Highlanders, Riflemen, Fusiliers, Royal Marines, Militia men and Volunteers, with a sprinkling from the West India Regiments and Lagos Constabulary, combine to form a picture which, for variety of uniform and brilliancy of colouring, is quite unique."

There was a brief return to this colourful past from the drab khaki of the present when the School celebrated its centenary in 1953. On this occasion all available members of the Small Arms School Corps marched from the School to the Town Hall behind the band of the Royal Marines to form a guard of honour for the ceremony in which the Commandant, Col. G. V. Britten C.B.E., received the freedom of the borough from the Mayor, Alderman Mrs. Farmer, and the School presented an 1853 pattern Enfield rifle to the U.S. Military Attaché to be displayed in the entrance to the main hall at Fort Benning. A permanent reminder of the occasion was the suitably inscribed mayoral chain, which the School presented to the town to commemorate their long association together.

It was a fitting sequel to the ceremony two years before, at which the aged General Sir Ian Hamilton had become a Freeman of Hythe by virtue of having been Commandant between 1898 and 1900. He was the last survivor of the Afghan War of 1878 to 1880, and one of the last commanders of the First World War to be still in the land of the living.

In 1965 Elizabeth Bowen came to live in Hythe, where she remained in residence until her death in 1973. It was not for the first time. As a child she had been brought to the town by her mother from Bowen's Court, the family home in County Cork, during the period of her father's insanity. She had actually preferred the Victorian and Edwardian seaside "villas" in which they rented accommodation, to the mansion her ancestors had built in Ireland not long after being planted there by Cromwell.

By now an elderly woman, aged 65, she was returning to roost and to recall childhood days. Southstone—in reality Folkestone—figures prominently in *The Little Girls,* published in 1964. Before her permanent move, she had often been a visitor to Hythe, and had actually spent Christmas there in 1950. A few years later, she was writing to her husband:

> It is a nice little town—reassuring and right-and-tight and sound. One of the few places that make me love England and Englishness. But I think that apart from Englishness there's a peculiar quality of Kentishness that I like. The Hythe people are flamboyant and hardy and unmawkish. The town has got the sort of density—in its life, I mean—that I associate with small towns in France . . . Also I suppose I like Hythe out of a back-to-the-wombishness, having been there as a child in the most amusing years of one's childhood—8 to 13. But I can't see what's wrong with the womb if one's happy there, or comparatively happy there.

The house that was Elizabeth Bowen's is a modern red brick building on Church Hill, which she bought for £4,700 and renamed Carbery after the ancestral home of her mother's family, the Colleys of Castle Carbery in County Kildare. It overlooks the churchyard to the east and the marsh to the west, and the steep-stepped footpath, which leads to it, and

was appropriately called Clyme Street in the past, does not
seem to have worried the elderly novelist any more than it did
the young girl, who plied up it eating sweets.

Her favourite hostelry for putting up and entertaining her
guests was the White Hart. There she paid their bills and left
shillings in their rooms for the gas meters. On the other hand,
the night of love in Hythe, which is the centre piece of *The
House in Paris,* takes place in the Swan, which she calls the
Ram's Head.

She was able to visit Hythe again after France had been
liberated, but before Victory in Europe day, and reported to a
friend:

> Small shops gradually reopening, residents creeping back to the
> rather pleasant villas clustered in gardens all the way up the hill.
> The sea front is 'open' again; the miles of coils of rusty barbed
> wire snipped away and flung back. Soldiers about still, but not so
> many. I like the narrow, steep-roofed High Street, so quiet now
> that one hears nothing but rooks in the early morning . . .

After Elizabeth Bowen had returned to Hythe, she attended
St. Leonard's Church. But she was so disturbed by the change
from the traditional ritual to the Alternative Service in the late
1960s that she went no more. In a letter to a fellow-author, a
copy of which she dropped into the letter-box of the, as she
put it, "excellent but deluded vicar", she said she was appalled
"by the defeatism of many of my fellow communicants here in
Hythe, on whom the Alternative Service has been imposed. I
have taken my own course—left our parish church for a
neighbouring village one where the 1662 service still goes on".

But we have to turn to some of her later writings, which
were published posthumously, to find her describing, in
detail, aspects of Hythe in change. She writes of the "hinter-
land" with "hollows, creases and dips, which, sunk between
open-airy pastures and cornfields, are not to be guessed at till
you stumble upon them: then, they are enticing, breathless
and lush, with their wandering dogpaths and choked thick-
ets". Then she goes on to describe Cliff Road, the road that I,
myself, lived in for six years:

> Slanting upwards from Seabrook, it zigzags across the face of a
> steep slope, finally to emerge from a tunnel of greenery, and

terminate, at a high-up point where once stood Hythe's railway station. The ascent is continuous, but gentle.

On your left, as you mount from Seabrook, is the sea—ever farther below, out there beyond the Military Canal. Also below you, but mostly tree-hidden, runs the trafficky main thoroughfare, A 259. On your right you are accompanied by the derelict cutting of what was once a single-track railway line—first above you, then on the same level, then, as the road rises, risen above. Where it used to deepen, the cutting has silted up and become a jungle, overhung by vertical woods, invaded by saplings. Here and there, buttresses of South-Eastern and Chatham brickwork, darkened by moss and time, remind you that this primitive-looking landscape is in origin structural and was manmade. The road shows signs of being of the same epoch as the vanished railway, and of surviving only because *it* was impossible to remove. Each side it is encroached upon by its grassy verges; remnants of some attempt to "surface" it adhere, in macerated tar-dark patches, to what elsewhere is gutted as though by tropical torrents, fins of rock bespeaking unthinkable cruelty to motor-cars. Accordingly, contrary to my fears, there has been not more than half-hearted residential development. Late-coming villas and bungalows peter out still not far from Seabrook; on the Channel side, for a little way farther up, costlier homes in the Spanish manner (patios, ironwork) cliffhang on slithery pine-clad slopes, but there are few of them.

Now, nearly ten years later, there are more. It is St. Saviour's Hospital that is often said to give a Spanish appearance to the scene. But in reality, the style of the hospital and chapel, which were built in 1964, when the Sisters of the Community of the Presentation had to move St. Saviour's from the Euston Road, London, stems from the rococo of Bavaria, and is particularly noticeable in the onion-shaped steeple, typical of Southern Germany and Austria, which was lowered onto the chapel from a helicopter and is now threatened with destruction by the present owners. Before the hospital passed into private hands, and the chapel was deconsecrated, it was embellished with precious baroque wood carvings from that region of Central Europe, which were returned in 1980 to Buxheim, whence they had originally come.

The Hythe end of Cliff Road has been surfaced again, but the Seabrook end and the narrow bridge are just as they used to be:

The baroque Buxheim carvings in St. Saviour's Chapel

The bridge's command of the line it was built to span enabled us—once, long ago, as children—to watch the train coming romping out of the distance, loudened by the acoustics of the gulley . . . What had been the perspective was now blocked by the falling across it of a huge tree, whose deadness accentuated the hush. Weeds sprouting up between its torn-up roots, brambles matting its shattered branches, the tree stayed wedged there: nobody's business . . .

There was, or was held to be, only one train. Indefatigably (if that were so) in motion, it shuttled to-fro over the short track between Sandling Junction and the terminal, Sandgate, its purpose being in some part military, for on top of the bluff over Sandgate station (which was in Seabrook) is Shorncliffe Camp. A poor day when soldiers were not aboard! Soon after passing under the bridge, on its way to Sandling, the train underwent a personality transformation: woods began, giving it, as it tailed away into them to at last vanish, the flickering secretiveness of a reptile . . . The road, once over the bridge, said goodbye to the railway and struck off on a course of its own.

As long as the military remained, Hythe was very well provided with public houses, serving not only the permanent staff of the Small Arms School, but also the thirsty soldiers, who came on courses. But when the brewery ceased operating and the army left, many closed, amongst them the appropriately named Ordnance Arms, the Cinque Ports Arms, the Oak and the Nelson's Head, all at one time Whitbread's houses. Another casualty was the Rose and Crown.

However, most people would agree that there are plenty left, ranging from the smallest of them all, the Three Mariners, to the large Red Lion, formerly also called the Three Mariners. Of the two hotels described by Elizabeth Bowen, the White Hart is the one that has been most intimately connected with the government of the town.

The earliest reference to this hotel is in the record of an Assembly held in January 1625, at which the Duke of Buckingham's letter recommending the chancellor of the exchequer for Hythe's parliamentary election, was read out. The mayor, jurats and commons stuck to the two men they had already elected, drafted a letter to the duke in reply, and then "went down to the White Hart".

But since the White Hart was the emblem of Richard II, the inn could well have had its origins in the late fourteenth century. Although the exterior looks as if it belongs to the seventeenth century, parts of the interior are older. The fact that it has no cellars suggests that, at one time, it was not far from the waterfront.

In 1648 a man named Henry Hart of Sellindge made a feoffment of the property to Ferdinando Bassoch or Bassocke for £241, and also sold him the wine licence belonging to the inn. On the St. John's Hospital map the hotel appears as the "White Heart".

That Bassoch was the Ferdinando Bassett, who was mayor in 1649 and again in 1654 is clear from an indenture, dated 1665, in which his son, John, buys out his other son, Richard, who is a sailor. The inn prospered, and in 1670 John Bassett was issuing his own token coins as small change. Indeed, Bassetts were twelve times mayor between 1649 and 1728.

In 1733 the White Hart passed out of the hands of the Bassetts, and later in the century it belonged to Julius Deedes.

When the new Town Hall was built next door to it, a communicating doorway was made between the upper floor of the hotel and the lobby of the council chamber. Thus the mayor was able to use one of the rooms as a robing chamber before going in to meetings, for which the hotel charged a small fee. At the beginning of the nineteenth century, the White Hart was known as a commercial and posting inn, "having the luxury of both hip bath and shower". It was taken over by Mackesons at the same time as the brewery.

When the nearby Lympne Airport became a favoured take-off point for the record-breaking international flights of the 1930s, the hotel became known as a good hostelry for the pilots. Thus Jim Mollison and Tommy Rose, who cut the time to Cape Town, stayed there, and so did Charles Scott, who blazed the trail to Australia, and Jean Batten, who flew even further to New Zealand. The White Hart remained open throughout the Second World War, entertaining many servicemen at a time when few civilians were permitted inside the restricted area.

As for the Swan, we first hear of it in 1506, when William Knight made the inn over to his wife, Margaret, in his will. In the eighteenth century it was the recognised posting inn, when the milestone let into its front wall would tell passengers how far they had to go—12 miles to Ashford and 71 miles to London, the route being via Charing, Lenham and Maidstone.

Another interesting point about this inn is the metal plaque of the Sun Insurance Company higher up the wall, which would survive as proof of insurance even if the building were burnt to the ground. But the fact that it accommodated the office of the Inland Revenue in the mid-nineteenth century could not have endeared it to everybody.

The age of the Swan is not known for certain. Nor is that of the King's Head, for which we have a reference in 1583, when it was called the George. One day in 1653, £3 14s 6d were spent there by the Council on wine and beer on the proclamation of the Lord Protector, and a further 2s 6d for beating the drum. In 1714 it changed its name to the Sun, which is still the name of the lane opposite. In 1750 it changed yet again to the present name.

However, old as these three houses are, the Bell, which is

probably the ancient harbour pub, is likely to be older than any of them. Yet it has no recorded history, only smugglers' tales.

As far as the beer is concerned, the long history of home brewing in Hythe goes back, at least, to the fifteenth century. But it was in 1669 that a proper brewery was set up by one, James Pashley, who was a man of some substance. The previous year he had witnessed the sealing of the last of the royal charters, which was issued to the Cinque Ports by Charles II, and seventeen years later he was one of the barons appointed to carry the canopy at the coronation of James II.

Thus brewers were already considered important when the Mackeson family bought the brewery in 1801. In due course the stout from this brewery at the west end of the town next to the barracks became well-known throughout the country, and was also brewed under licence in the West Indies, Singapore and Nigeria.

The excellence of the beer was attributed to the purity of the spring water that gushed out of the Hythe beds and went into Hythe ales. The Table magazine of November 17th, 1888 remarked that: "Pure water is the primary essential in good beer, and much of the long continued popularity of the Hythe Ales is due to the purity of the natural streams which flow direct into the brewing coppers of the firm, and account in great measure for the invigorating freshness characteristic of the Hythe brewings".

At this time draught bitter was 1s a gallon, and Imperial pint bottles of Light Pale Ale and Pale Ale cost 2s 6d and 3s a dozen respectively. But the last brew there was in 1968, and then the whole area was flattened for redevelopment with the exception of the brewery offices, which were taken over by Portex and renovated in 1977, and the old malthouse, which became a centre for the sale of antique bric-a-brac.

During their century and a half of brewing, the Mackesons had played an important part in the town. H. B. Mackeson was nine times mayor from 1872 to 1880, and George L. Mackeson, who died in 1950, made it possible, with Mr. E. Osborne, for the church to have a new organ in 1936. Brigadier Sir Harry Mackeson was M.P. up to 1959. But after that, the family moved away.

The final ceremony marking the departure of the military

The Swan Hotel

The Bell Inn

was held in the Town Hall in November of the same year, 1968. The Commandant of the Small Arms Wing, Colonel J. Sale C.B.E., received a carved cigar box, with golden replicas of Hythe's two maces on it, from the Mayor, Councillor Mrs. Fisher, and presented a deputy mayor's badge to the Council in return.

That industry should be encouraged in Hythe as well as holiday-making, was scarcely surprising, when it became known that the army was definitely going to leave the town. And so the Rotary Club of Hythe has been more than willing to promote light manufacture as well as commerce.

The small factories are mostly concentrated on the Penny-pot estate between the canal and the Dymchurch Road at the western end of the town. Hythe Printers Ltd. and Mill-brooke Printers are the successors to the presses which, in the past, produced the Hythe Reporter, the training manuals and pamphlets for the School of Musketry, guide-books, and all kinds of miscellaneous posters, programmes and printed stationery. Tiffen, the printer of the gallant lady's poems about the Napoleonic wars, ceased business in the 1880s. His premises, standing on the corner of the High Street and Mount Street, were pulled down in 1885 and rebuilt the following year as a wine merchant's establishment, only to be converted, later, into a restaurant, called Upstairs and Downstairs after the book by John Hawksworth, which became a popular T.V. serial.

The stationers, who have now come to Hythe, are Andrew Brownsword's, who specialise in greetings cards of all descriptions. In addition, there are several small engineering companies on the Estate, including Alton Wire Products, Dore Precision Engineering, Hythe (Kent) Engineering, and R.S.R. (Forgings) Ltd. The largest company, Portex, mainly located at Reachfields on the seaward side of the Dymchurch Road, received the Queen's Award three times in the 1970s for its record in exporting medical and surgical materials.

By this time, the founder of this company was no more. In 1957 Dr. Leader returned to his native Switzerland, where he died. But the fact that he was bombed out of Great Portland Street in London, and so decided to move to the Kent coast as Portland Plastics, and then, absorbed into Smith's Industries, to Hythe, proved to be a great gain for the town. It was the reason for the twinning of Hythe with Berck-sur-Mer in France in 1980, as well as with Poperinge, since the company has another factory by the French seaside town.

Together with all this innovation, many of the old-established businesses continue, adapting themselves to modern times. Kipps bookshop, occupying one of the Wealden houses "on the left hand side of the High Street coming from Folkestone", to quote the words of H. G. Wells in his well-known novel, lasted until 1981, when it was turned into a café, but part of it remains as a general stationer's.

Hythe Crafts Ltd., in Windmill Street have switched from saddlery and harnesses in their leatherwork to briefcases, satchels, belts and straps, and the Forge in Chapel Street has abandoned horseshoes for decorative ironwork and sheet metalwork. The latter company has received the shield, presented by Christopher Capon, the last mayor of the Old Borough, to the group that, in the opinion of the Committee of the Hythe Civic Society, has made the best contribution, during the year, to the improvement of the quality of life in the town.

It was in 1974 that the reorganisation of local government took place, which still fortunately left Hythe with a Mayor and Town Council, though with more limited powers. After that, it was no longer possible to talk about the borough member, since Sir Albert Costain, who was first elected in 1959, was now the Member for Folkestone and Hythe. During his uninterrupted occupancy of the seat in the subsequent years, he maintained the Tory tradition, which had lasted since the early years of the century. The announcement in 1981 of his intention to retire at the next General Election then gave the local Conservative Association the task of nominating a new candidate for the first time in twenty-two years.

Even after 1974 it was still possible to be a hereditary freeman by virtue of being either the son or son-in-law of a freeman. But, in fact, there is only one family, the Clarkes, who have continued to claim this ancient privilege, three of them being alive today, and the fourth freeman being married to a Clarke. The only honorary freeman left is Mr. James Nowell, the former town clerk, who received the freedom in

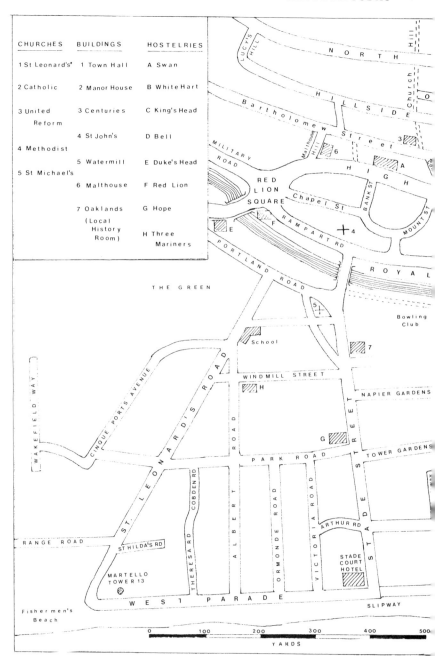

CHURCHES	BUILDINGS	HOSTELRIES
1 St Leonard's'	1 Town Hall	A Swan
2 Catholic	2 Manor House	B White Hart
3 United Reform	3 Centuries	C King's Head
	4 St John's	D Bell
4 Methodist	5 Watermill	E Duke's Head
5 St Michael's	6 Malthouse	F Red Lion
	7 Oaklands (Local History Room)	G Hope
		H Three Mariners

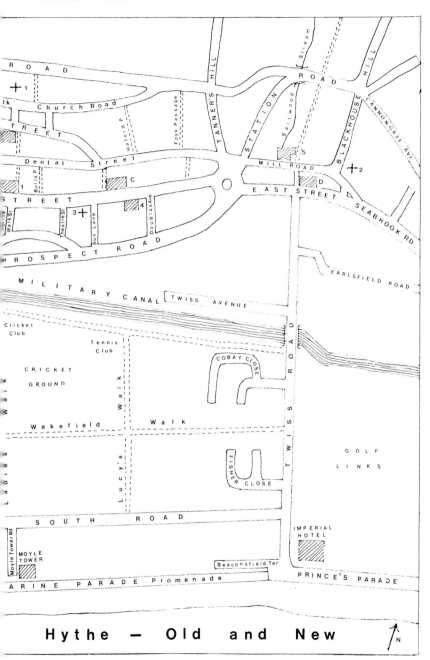

Hythe — Old and New

1974. So these are the only folk alive today, who have sworn
the ancient oath:

> I do swear that I will faith and truth bear to our Sovereign Lady
> the Queen's Majesty, her Heirs and Successors, and to the Mayor,
> Aldermen and Burgesses of this Town of Hythe; I will well and
> truly use, support, maintain and keep all the Liberties, Privileges,
> Franchises, and Customs of the Five Ports, Two Ancient Towns
> and their Members, but especially of this Town and Port of
> Hythe; to the common profits of this Town I will have regard; I
> will truly pay all Scots and Lots which shall be due or which shall
> happen to be lawfully assessed or granted to be levied within this
> Town; I will be obedient to all Mayors of this Town in all causes
> lawful, and will observe and keep all lawful Acts and Decrees,
> Laws and Statutes made by the Mayor, Aldermen, and Burgesses
> for the good profit and benefit of this Corporation, and all other
> things which do appertain and belong to a Freeman, I will truly
> and duly do and execute to my power. So help me God.

In recent years a signal occasion for remembering the old
traditions and privileges was Wakefield Day, celebrated in
1957 to honour Hythe's principal benefactor in modern times,
when Charles Sandford was mayor. The day was one of pomp
and ceremony, attended by the Lord Mayor of London as well
as the mayors of the other Cinque Ports.

Amidst all the processions and speechifying, Lord
Wakefield's record was remembered, as founder of the still
flourishing Wakefield and Co. Ltd., backer of many of the
record-breaking flights from Lympne and of the breakers of
speed records on land and water, and initiator of many
benefactions. Lady Wakefield's bequest of £10,000 for the
benefit of the poor of Hythe was also recalled.

There appears, at that time, to have been some idea of
making the festive day an annual event. This did not take
place. But such is the respect still held in Hythe for this
impressive man, that every year at the making of the new
mayor, a wreath is hung beneath his life-sized portrait in the
Town Hall. The tangible memorial to the actual Wakefield
Day is the town sign at the Seabrook end of Prince's Parade,
which was unveiled by the Lord Mayor of London.

Political changes have been matched by changes in the
landscape. "Kipps took Anne for a row on the Hythe Canal,"
wrote H. G. Wells. "The sun set in a mighty blaze and left a

world warm and very still. The twilight came and there was
the water, shining bright, and the sky a deepening blue, and
the great trees that dipped their boughs towards the water . . ."

But, like nearly all the other elm trees in the country, the
great, spreading wych elms from Huntingdonshire, which
had been planted on both sides of the canal to retain the banks
and to provide timber for making muskets, succumbed to the
deadly Dutch elm disease in the late 1970s. It was a sad sight to
see them attacked by power saws and come crashing down,
and to see the bonfires of good timber, that it was too costly to
cart away.

Yet Hythe was ever resilient, and never at a loss for an
occasion. Already, in 1976, the Hythe Civic Society was plant-
ing five Australian ash trees in Ladies Walk, which had been
similarly denuded. On Ash Wednesday of the same year the
Rotary Club of Hythe planted 25 more to celebrate the 25th
anniversary of the granting of its charter. Then, in 1978, the
Kent Branch of the Men of Trees planted seven maple trees
near the Stade Street bridge to commemorate the 700th
anniversary of the granting of the Great Charter to the Cinque
Ports by Edward I.

These efforts were followed by a regular replanting campaign, ably promoted by Ron Collins, who was then Chairman of the Civic Society, and involving the schoolchildren in
the educational aspects of the project. In the first two winters,
1980 to 1982, the target of replanting 400 trees a year was
reached. And so it goes on.

An even greater change in the landscape was brought about
by the Charlier group of builders, another enterprise that owes
its origin to foreign expertise. E. Charlier, a Belgian, started
his business in Lyminge in 1922, moved it to Saltwood in
1924, and by 1929 had built several hundred houses in the
locality. After the war, the business grew steadily in Hythe
and was responsible for the flat-roofed bungalows in Sene
Park on part of the old golf course, as well as the more
attractive Dene and the monstrous blocks of flats on the sea
front.

As for the two castles at Lympne and Saltwood, they had
been sadly neglected in the midst of all the thrusting moder-
nity of the nineteenth century. They were both ruinously run

down, and it was the task of their twentieth century owners to restore them to the handsome buildings that we see today. Lympne Castle was the first to be recovered. In 1905, when H. G. Wells wrote *Kipps,* it was a farmhouse, with the great hall converted into two storeys and partitioned into a number of separate rooms. Thus:

> The Castle became a farm-house, and the farm-house itself now ripe and venerable, wears the walls of the castle as a little man wears a big man's coat. The kindliest of farm ladies entertains a perpetual stream of visitors, and shows you her vast mangle and her big kitchen, and takes you out upon the sunniest little terrace-garden in all the world.

But that year the castle was bought by a Mr. Tennant, who engaged the architect, Sir Robert Lorimer, to restore it, and also to build a new wing for living accommodation. In this way it became possible for Mr. and Mrs. Margary to live there and open the historic parts of the fortified house to summer visitors with the minimum of inconvenience. Unfortunately, the ancient foundations discovered during this rebuilding programme were not recorded. But the work was well done and saved it from total ruin. It certainly became popular enough for 20,000 people to visit it in 1980.

Saltwood Castle was in equally poor shape, as one can see from old engravings. Some basic repairs were carried out at the end of the nineteenth century, when Sir William Deedes lived there. But it had to wait until the 1930s for a major restoration. Lady Conway acquired the property, and employed the restorer architect, Sir Philip Tilden, to bring it up to its present-day condition, the work being done over more than a decade.

This work included making the massive gatehouse habitable, and constructing a new residential wing in neo-Gothic style to blend in with the existing Tudor wing. This was where "Civilisation" Clark who bought the castle on the death of Lady Conway, housed his library, wrote his books on art, and thought out his major television programmes for the B.B.C.

In 1970 Lord Clark made way for his son, Alan, a member of parliament, though not for Hythe. His castle has remained a favourite goal for summer visitors, who enjoy feeding the peacocks with crumbs from the tea tables and studying the vintage cars, as well as making the historic circuit. Nearly 7,000 people were received in this way in 1980. Sandling Park, which was visited by 10,000 people in 1980, has no old buildings at all on show. After Bonomi's late eighteenth century mansion had been damaged by a bomb in the Second World War, Major Hardy had a new red-brick one built in its place, leaving only the stone balustrade and gateway as reminder of the older building. But the park has one of the finest old gardens in the country. Hidden from road and railway, it lies at the top end of the deep vale in the hills, down which the Slaybrook runs on its way to Hythe, after passing the old Tudor house called Slaybrook Hall.

The lakes in this park are artificial. But the deep, soft and peaty soil in the nearby American gardens at Saltwood, which were laid out years ago by Archdeacon Croft, has been attributed to the action of beavers, damming up the waters and creating a morass of fallen tree-trunks and branches. It is so soft that one can push a stick down into it for fifteen feet, and draw it out again like a needle out of a pin-cushion. And out of this soil grow magnificent azaleas, magnolias and rhododendrons, and towering trees.

Thus the new blooms appear every year without fail, rooted in the ancient soil. And thus Hythe, itself, continues, supported by traditions that are ancient in comparison with those of most English towns, but always developing new sides to its life.

Once a port in the formative years of the navy, and then an important centre for the army, the new Hythe, no longer host to either, has become more and more a place of retirement for people who appreciate as a good a climate as England can offer, pleasant surroundings of town and countryside, and immediate access to the Continent.

TABLE OF EARLY RECORDS
AND OF SIGNIFICANT EVENTS

2nd C Ptolemy's *Geography* mentions Lympne

4th C *Notitia Dignitatum,* Civil and Military List of the Roman Empire, mentions Lympne

488 Aesc, son of King Hengist, builds a fortress at Saltwood

732 Ethelbert, King of Kent, makes a grant of land at Sandtun, near Lympne

833 Egbert, King of Kent, makes a similar grant at Sandtun

833 Saltwood mentioned in a document of King Egbert

1026 Halfden makes Saltwood over to the Church

1086 Domesday Book details Saltwood, Hythe and Sandtun

1155 Charter of Henry II to Hythe as one of the Cinque Ports

1170 Knights go from Saltwood to murder the Archbishop of Canterbury

1229 Henry III's ordinance to the Cinque Ports

1278 Charter of Edward I to the Cinque Ports. Hythe has the only original copy

1278 Grant of Edward I to *Hethe* to hold two annual fairs

1287 Great Storm

1293 French raid Hythe

1298 Second Charter of Edward I to the Cinque Ports

1313 Charter of Privileges granted by Edward II to his *men of Heia*

1328 Charter of Edward III for Hythe to provide ships for the King's use

1380 "Earthquake" at Saltwood Castle

1392 Articles of Agreement, in Norman French, made at a Brodhull Court

1399-1449 Papers of the Hundred Court, briefed by H. T. Riley

1400 Great Fire and Shipwreck

1403 Charter of Henry IV to the Cinque Ports

1412-13 and 1419 Jurats' Accounts, translated by the Rev. T. S. Frampton

1414	Opening of the new harbour
1437	Charter of Pardon granted by Henry IV to Hythe
1480	Churchwardens' Accounts, briefed by H. T. Riley
1555	First recorded Innings
1566	Survey of Shipping, including Hythe
1575	Charter of Elizabeth I, granting the right to elect a Mayor
1580	Second "Earthquake"
1582	Thomas Torney presents the Moot Horn to Hythe
1588	Cess on the inhabitants to provide a 50 ton ship to face the Armada
1596	Hythe agrees with Dover to provide a 160 ton ship to face the expected second Armada
1624	Attempt begins to cut out the harbour again
1636	Charles I calls for Ship Money for the second time
1648	Kent Petition and the storming of Maidstone
1652	Hythe Bowling Club founded
1658	Manor House built
1670	Charles II's proclamation about pirates
1689	Act of Parliament nullifying Lord Warden's patronage of M.P.s
1739	Church tower falls down
1744	Maces for the Mayor's Sergeant and the Town Sergeant donated by Thomas Hales
1750	New Tower and South Transept built for the Church
1785	Lionel Lukin patents his lifeboat
1794	New Town Hall built
1803	Peace of Amiens broken
1805-8	Martello Towers built
1805-9	Military Canal dug
1805	Royal Staff Corps moves to Hythe
1805	Royal Waggon Train in Hythe
1810	Ladies' Walk laid out
1832	First Reform Act
1833	Royal Waggon Train disbanded
1836	Municipal Act
1838	Royal Staff Corps disbanded
1839	S.S. *Archimedes* equipped with Pettit-Smith's propeller
1843	London to Folkestone railway completed

1853   School of Musketry opens in Hythe
1860   First Venetian Fete
1862   The Green obtained for the town by Joseph Horton
1867   Second Reform Act
1868   Congregational Church built
1874   Branch railway line to Hythe opened
1877   Hythe Innings flooded
1880   Seabrook (Imperial) Hotel opened
1891   Folkestone, Sandgate and Hythe Tramway opened
1892   Hythe Institute founded
1894   Catholic Church built
1897   Methodist Church built
1917   First air-raid on Hythe
1921   Port Lympne built
1927   Romney, Hythe and Dymchurch Light Railway opened
1938   Prince's Parade opened
1940-2 Hythe bombed by enemy planes
1944   Hythe suffers from shelling and flying-bombs
1951   Hythe Railway Station closed
1951   Replacement unveiled for the East Window of St. Leonard's Church, destroyed by a bomb
1957   Wakefield Day celebrated in Hythe
1964   Portex Factory opens in Hythe
1968   Small Arms Wing, School of Infantry, leaves Hythe
1968   Mackeson's Brewery closed
1973   Court of Brotherhood and Guestling meets in Hythe
1974   Old Borough of Hythe included in the new Shepway District
1980   Queen Mother visits Hythe as Lord Warden of the Cinque Ports
1980   Hythe twinned with Poperinge in Belgium and Berck-sur-Mer in France

HISTORIC BIBLIOGRAPHY

16th C   *Itinerary in England and Wales in the years 1535 to 1543* by John Leland

1570   *Perambulation of Kent* by W. Lambarde

1586   *Britannia (Cantium)* by W. Camden

1799   *History of the County of Kent* (Vol. VIII) by E. Hasted

1803   *Hythe and Sandgate Guide* by W. Lee

1816   *Hythe Guide* by W. Tiffen, ill. J. Jeakes

1823   *Guide to Sandgate, Hythe and Folkestone* by W. Tiffen

1830   *Rural Rides* by W. Cobbett

1850   *The Antiquities of Richborough, Reculver and Lympne* by C. Roach Smith

1860   *Handbook for Hythe* by Hans Busk

1874   *Fourth Report of the Royal Commission on Historical Manuscripts* (Hythe Section) by H. T. Riley

1888   *The Cinque Ports* by M. Burrows

1892   *The Barons of the Cinque Ports* by G. Wilks

1895   *Hamo of Hythe* by R. O'Gorman

HISTORIC MAPS AND PLANS

1570   *Card of the Beacons in Kent*, pub. in Lambarde's *Perambulation*

1596   *Map of Kent* by Symonson

1611   *Map of Kent* by Speed

1617   *Map of Romney Marsh* by Matthew Parker

1684   *St. John's Hospital Plan of Hythe* by Thomas Hill

1685   *St. Bartholomew's and St. John's Plan of Hythe* by Hill

1805   *Map of Kent* by Stockdale

Early 19th C *Survey of Hythe* by R. K. Dawson R.E.

MODERN BIBLIOGRAPHY

Collyer, D. G., *Battle of Britain Diary*, Deal: 1980

Dale, H. D., *The Ancient Town of Hythe and St. Leonard's Church*, Hythe: Kipps, 1931

Davies, W. J. K., *The Romney, Hythe and Dymchurch Railway*, Newton Abbot: David and Charles, 1975

Glendinning, Victoria, *Elizabeth Bowen*, London: Weidenfield and Nicholson, 1977

Guy, John, *Kent Castles*, Rainham: Meresborough, 1980

Igglesden, Sir C., *A Saunter through Kent*, (Vol. XXIV), Ashford: Kentish Express, 1930

Jackson, Stanley, *The Sassoons*, London: Heinemann, 1968

Jessup, R. and F., *The Cinque Ports*, London: Batsford, 1952

Mothersole, Jessie, *The Saxon Shore*, London: John Lane, 1924

Murray, K. M. E., *The Constitutional History of the Cinque Ports*, Manchester: University Press, 1935

Rootes, Andrew, *Front Line County*, London: Hale, 1980

Sutcliffe, Shiela, *Martello Towers*, Newton Abbot: David and Charles, 1972

Roth, Cecil, *The Magnificent Rothschilds*, London: Hale, 1939

Vine, P. A. L., *The Royal Military Canal*, Newton Abbot: David and Charles, 1972

SELECT INDEX